D1020095

Birds of a Feather

The Press and the Politicians

Allan Fotheringham

KEY PORTER·BOOKS

Copyright © 1989 by Allan Fotheringham

All rights reserved. No part of this work covered by the copyrights hereon may be reproduced or used in any form or by any means–graphic, electronic or mechanical, including photocopying, recording, taping or information storage and retrieval systems–without the prior written permission of the publisher.

Canadian Cataloguing in Publication Data

Fotheringham, Allan
  Birds of a feather: the press and the politicians

ISBN 1-55013-166-4

1. Press and politics–Canada.   2. Press and politics–United States.   3. Press and politics–Great Britain.   I. Title.

PN4751.F68 1989   070.4′4932   C89-094079-7

Design: Marie Bartholomew
Typesetting: Southam Business Information
and Communications Group Inc.
Printed and bound in Canada by
T.H. Best Printing Co. Ltd.

Key Porter Books Limited
70 The Esplanade
Toronto, Ontario
Canada M5E 1R2

89 90 91 92 93 5 4 3 2 1

Contents

for Kip Scott Fotheringham

This project has been possible only because of the perseverance and belief and assistance of my editor, Phyllis Bruce, whose patience under fire is equalled only by her determination. Her sense of humor, though tried, has kept both of us sane. Margaret Allen has been most valuable with advice and a sharp eye. The mistakes, in judgment as elsewhere, are my own. Beverly Rockett, K.T. Oslin and the Benny Goodman Quartet know the contributions they have made.

Preface

The writer's only responsibility is to his art. He
will be completely ruthless if he is a good one.
He has a dream. It anguishes him so much he
must get rid of it. He has no peace until then.
Everything goes by the board: honor, pride,
decency, security, happiness, all, to get the
book written. – *William Faulkner*

One Thursday morning in August of 1973, a thirty-two-year-old
thief and safe-cracker by the name of Jan-Erik Olsson walked
into one of Stockholm's largest banks, the Sveriges Kreditbank,
carrying under a folded jacket a loaded submachine gun and, in a
large canvas suitcase, reserve ammunition, plastic explosives,
blasting caps, safety fuses, lengths of rope, a knife, wool socks,
sunglasses, two walkie-talkies and a transistor radio.

In what eventually fascinated the world, not to mention stolid
and stable Sweden, as the first major hostage-taking drama–a
phenomenon now a staple of our unstable society–Olsson held
four captives in a vault for six days, defying all the wiles and the
force of police authorities. (All this was happening while the
country was in the middle of a national election campaign and
ninety-year-old King Gustaf Adolf VI lay dying.) As part of the
negotiations, the escaped convict talked on the phone with
Prime Minister Olof Palme, himself murdered 13 years later on a
street not far away. It was intriguing James Bond stuff.

More interesting to students of human behavior, however, was
what came out of the drama. When it ended–without any
deaths–the world learned of the apparent intimate relationship
during the ordeal between one of the female bank employees and

the criminal. Two psychiatrists who treated the hostages for ten days after their rescue, Dr. Lennart Ljungberg and Dr. Waltraut Bergman, observed that what went on within the bank was similar to what happens in a lifeboat at sea. "As it happened," explained Dr. Ljungberg, "each of them very much wanted to go on living. The same may be true of the robber."

Another psychiatrist, Dr. Anna Freud, calls the reaction "identification with the aggressor." It has occurred among prisoners of war in Korea and Indo-China and at Auschwitz. One of the female hostages even visited Olsson later in the penitentiary (while her husband and children waited outside in the car). Dr. Nils Bejerot, the police psychiatrist at the time, said, "It is to be expected that after a point a bond of friendship springs up between the victims and their captors."

It is commonly referred to (in the repeated circumstances where it now occurs) as the "Stockholm Syndrome": the phenomenon wherein captives form a bond of affection with their captors. That is the relationship, in essence, between the politicians and the press we are about to examine in the following pages.

This scribe, eking out a meager living that provides thin gruel and the occasional weak sherry, has been observing this strange nexus for some thirty-five years spent in the black art of journalism. The trail has led from Vancouver to Fleet Street, through China and the Soviet Union and Africa and fifty-odd countries in toto, into Ottawa and more recently Washington–with Canada, Britain and the United States as the three most familiar working locations for this professional observer of the press. The peculiar relationship detected by the Swedish shrinks does not change from country to country, continent to continent.

In Britain, a special breed of parliamentary correspondents acts as mouthpieces for the government by never divulging the sources of their information. In Washington, formal White House dinners in honor of foreign dignitaries are never complete without a clutch of the top anchormen and heavyweight columnists present. In Ottawa, reporters–not politicians–fight to keep their annual incestuous soirée, the Parliamentary Press Gallery dinner, off the record.

The two "enemies" are in unconscious cahoots, more in-trigued with the game itself than with the whole picture. They have a wary respect one for the other. They are fascinated, one with the other, even while they express mutual contempt one for the other. It is love-hate, with all the usual ramifications known to those who are in a marriage.

In fact, in truth, the press and politicians are in bed together. In the *ménage à trois* of the political spectrum, the one element left outside the sheets is the public.

The standard screed on the press and the politicians is usually one in which the former examines the latter. Journalists are considered the contemporary experts on politicians. Academics are unreadable and historians are too slow. So it is left to the reporters who are close to their subjects to provide the inside information on politicians, which everyone likes to read.

Peter Newman, with his brilliant *Renegade in Power* dissection of Diefenbaker, as readable now as it was in 1963, set the tone in this country, following Bruce Hutchison's *The Incredible Canadian*, an examination of that kinky little cutey William Lyon Mackenzie King. George Radwanski and Richard Gwyn have examined Pierre Trudeau, and Jean Chrétien has examined himself, the fingers on the computer terminal being those of Ron Graham. Claire Hoy has taken a run at Brian Mulroney and there is the suspicion he does not like him. Geoffrey Stevens described his idol, Robert Stanfield, and Larry Zolf, the probing proboscis of Canadian journalism, took on both Trudeau and the Senate, one of which is funnier than the other.

Susan Riley has examined the important political wives, and Margaret Trudeau, you may recall, examined her own ex-mate. (Margaret came out the winner.) We do not expect an equivalent tome from Mila Mulroney. Greg Weston aimed at John Turn-er–and shot himself in his own credibility. Conrad Black, who is now in journalism in the sense that he employs a lot of journalists, wrote a terribly fat book on Duplessis that one always takes away to the beach planning to read, as one does with *War and Peace*. It is the dream of every journalist to follow the success of a Newman or Hutchison by writing a really important book about a really important politician.

What few have done is write about the journalists who write about the politicians. It is an interesting relationship between the two species, always has been, and it is becoming increasingly important since the media filter so much of the information of politics to a wondering public, now that the days of church basements and school gym pulpits are practically gone.

Journalists themselves don't like to be examined–mainly because they are so seldom examined. The universities have been bashed about, and the church and the medical profession and the legal profession (badly needed), but there has been surprisingly little X-raying of the press, which is usually on the lethal end of the stethoscope. The politicians, in fact, always complain that they have no way of answering back, which brings guffaws from the scribes, since they claim to know just how adroitly they are being manipulated in the first place.

Publishers (and owners) shape policy and tune their newspapers just as columnists rule their tiny roosts. (This particular columnist is always amused by those who claim a particular columnist in a newspaper or magazine has tremendous "power." He has no power at all. He may, if he is lucky and talented and has the right platform, have some "influence." The person with the power is the employer who can fire the scribe tomorrow if the whim strikes. It–surprise, surprise–happens.)

Newspapermen, generally, tend to underestimate what sway they have on the public. Politicians, who know the often devastating results, are perhaps better judges. It's interesting, therefore, to note the linkage between the two segments of the information industry–the one side generating the news, the other side interpreting it. It's a constant struggle as to which side's view is the most convincing to the public.

Some of my colleagues in "the black art"–as Kipling called journalism–will not like my assessments of them or the proprietors of their newspapers. Them's the breaks. The over-balance here–more journalists than politicians–is because the former have been too much ignored. Someone has to do it.

The myth that must be dispelled is that there is an all-out war being conducted here. That is the public perception–that two implacable foes are in a constant state of hatred, the one side barely speaking to the other.

Whatever the surface animosities, however, the links between the press and the politicians become apparent in times of trouble. When *Globe and Mail* Ottawa columnist Geoffrey Stevens, no fan of Pierre Trudeau or the Liberals, suffered the tragedy of the death of a teen-age son, Trudeau wrote him a most moving letter. When *Ottawa Citizen* columnist Marjorie Nichols, who had savaged John Turner in her usual objective style, contracted lung cancer, Turner unannounced came to her hospital room. When Global TV Ottawa bureau chief Doug Small checked into a Toronto clinic for alcohol problems, he received a personal call from Prime Minister Brian Mulroney, who quit drinking, cold turkey, painful years ago.

The press and the politicians have a mutual, subliminal, understanding that they are in an esoteric game together. The phenomenal growth of the media in Ottawa, Washington and London has come about because of the growth of government. The technology of television and radio and computer-run newspapers has become so swift and efficient that it has made every political event an instant event–and transformed politicians, the previous inhabitants of church basements, into instant celebrities.

They are not unaware of this. They realize, while never admitting it, that they are captives to the grubby and young and arrogant practitioners of the art who can decide whether they get on the tube that night in prime time. There is contempt on both sides–the politicians realizing they are slaves to the whim of a thirty-two-year-old field producer, the media types rolling their eyes as they try to decide how many of the palpable lies they will air this night.

Timothy Crouse, in his classic *The Boys on the Bus* dissection of journalists on the campaign trail, came to the conclusion (accurate) that most reporters are "shy egomaniacs." It is one side of the equation that forms the partnership, the uneasy alliance between those who report and those they report on.

Journalists, on the whole, feel morally superior to those they cover—believing that they themselves are without ulterior motives, with no axe to grind, fearless in the pursuit of the real truth and scornful of the compromises they are sure all politicians must make to ensure their upward path to power.

Politicians, on the other hand, have barely disguised contempt for those they must meet every day bearing notebook or tape-recorder or camera. They feel that most all are subject to the vagaries of their medium, their editors, faceless directors and, no doubt, ideological enemies back in Toronto or New York or London who will twist and distort whatever they say in front of the cameras or the notebook. (In the age of Sony, I am the last remaining scribe in the land who still uses a notebook; Val Sears admits he makes it all up.)

Each is convinced that the other is a fraudulent, supercilious, fakeur opponent. Both acknowledge—with a cynical, accepting shrug—that the other side *cheats*. It surprises neither side. The other guys are intellectual crooks. That having been accepted, let's go have a drink.

Sometimes it's hard to tell which is the prisoner and which the jailor, since in different ways both parties are also imprisoned by the roles they have chosen. As George E. Reedy has pointed out in *The Twilight of the Presidency*, politicians are prisoners of a system that allows them very little intellectual, or personal, freedom. As an example at the top, the fear of assassination in the White House ensures that the president must live in a virtual cocoon, kept as much as possible throughout his term from actual contact with the people who elected him.

Of the six presidents who preceded George Bush, Kennedy was assassinated and both Gerald Ford and Ronald Reagan narrowly survived assassination attempts. Reagan, in his own country, had to open the Los Angeles Olympics from a bullet-proof glass cage, unable even to breathe the famous smog-filled California air (which might have been more dangerous to him than any bullet) in the Coliseum where O.J. Simpson, the new wife-beater, and Crazy Legs Hirsch and Hugh McIlhenny once danced.

For fear of air attacks from terrorists, George Bush, to deliver his own inaugural address on his own street, Pennsylvania Avenue, in front of his own abode, the White House, had to speak behind a bullet-proof shield under a concrete-and-steel canopy that took three weeks to erect, and was so sturdy that it took two weeks to tear down the structure that was used for only forty-five minutes.

As Reedy also points out, most every politician – the further up the ladder the more convinced – feels a prisoner of the deadly bureaucracy that is so hard to move and has its own internal momentum – and often its own agenda. Especially in Britain, almost as much in Canada, and less so in Washington, where new administrations bring their new bureaucrats with them, senior bureaucrats regard elected politicians as transitory figures who do not know the ropes and must be guided like errant children.

Politicians, particularly since the post-Watergate concern for personal behavior, feel prisoners of the press. The people who have changed forever the way Canadian and American politics is conducted in fact live in Tokyo. The days when reporters (lacking the shorthand of their British compatriots) scribbled in notebooks – and politicians could always claim "misquote" – have been replaced by hand-held cigarette-package-size tape-recorders that make obsolete political lies and obfuscations.

As a result, politicians become more circumspect, more cautious, less spontaneous, less interesting, fearing the deadly fallout from Sony. "Every politician is just one quote away from disaster," former Trudeau cabinet minister Ron Basford used to say – and John Crosbie is our living example of that.

Politicians are quickly made aware by press veterans just how ephemeral their momentary importance may be. Charles Lynch, the dean of the Ottawa Press Gallery, has been around for eight prime ministers but has never bothered asking any of them for an interview; he was betting on his tenure and not theirs. James Reston, when he was the most powerful journalist in Washington as boss of *The New York Times* bureau, did not like anyone in government to push his men around. In the early Kennedy years when the administration was at the height of its arrogance, Reston perceived that the brainy Jack Kennedy insider Ted Sorenson had been bullying Tom Wicker, the new *Times* man at the White House. Reston picked up the phone and called Sorenson and suggested, quietly, that it wouldn't be a good idea to push Wicker around. "We were here before you got here, Ted," said Reston, "and we will be here after you're gone."

Politicians–the smart ones–inherently know that and it frustrates them.

Political leaders are also prisoners of the verdict of history, constantly worrying about how they will be viewed in the long run, often to the neglect of current problems. The public mood on Richard Nixon finally shifted when it was revealed that he had been secretly taping all his phone calls. As it turned out (other presidents had done the same) his real intent was to have a perfect record for his memoirs so he could make a lot of money. Brian Mulroney (as Sinc Stevens goes down the tube, as Michael Wilson gets in the glue) too often seems so intent on cutting an image in China or Africa that he misses the feel for the domestic mood.

Finally, the politician these days feels a prisoner of the higher standard of behavior expected of politicians than is expected of private individuals (or, increasingly, the press itself). Gary Hart just asked for it, daring reporters to follow him.

The press, by contrast, see themselves as the resident prisoners of governments whose vast resources and powers of manipulation give them control of information. Reporters watch, with some bemusement, colleagues who sit at the next desk to them disappear one day into the faceless void of government, seduced away for much more money (taxpayers' money that the reporter, being a taxpayer, pays) so as to become propagandists whose job is to conceal rather than reveal. Members of *The Globe and Mail*'s Ottawa bureau still speak fondly of the occasion when Wayne Cheveldayoff, a respected economics reporter, suddenly left to accept an "information officer" position with the Bank of Canada and, within a week, was telling *Globe* reporters who bugged him for information to go and do the sexually impossible to themselves. Those who go over the wall–as in religion, drinking or smoking–tend to become obstreperous in their retroactive guilt.

The media, quite willingly, will acknowledge that they are the prisoners of deadlines, the cruelest mistress of all. There is never enough time, never enough hours, to collect all the details before the presses roll, the five-minute radio newscasts call, the evening TV news beckons. Reporters now have to come in at 4:00 a.m., as the afternoon papers all switch to morning papers, on shifts when no one else is awake, and executives are more than shirty and unhelpful at being wakened by 6:00 a.m. calls from kids on the rewrite desk they have never heard of. In essence, on breaking stories and new controversies, a daily paper may have three hours of actual tracking-down time (*i.e.*, telephoning) on a story.

Journalism is the first rough draft of history but there is never enough time to sift the rumors and the facts. The consumers on the other end–not to mention the editors–don't want it writ in stone; they want it now.

When I was in high school, in downtown Chilliwack, British Columbia, the teen-age years were a cornucopia of delights. There were the mates on the track team, as we travelled off to meets in Vancouver and elsewhere, who were friends but never really social companions. The colleagues on the soccer squad were somewhat the same, basically sane. My basketball comrades, however, were the wild ones, party types who cut a swath through school and many a Friday night used-car lot where the smooching went on, a couple to a car.

My dear mother, as all mothers, worried about the speed of the fast-lane gang and the temptations being dangled in front of innocent son. When I would assure her that all was well, my vows of abstinence were intact and that I simply carried the hootch for those who consumed it, she would always shake her head sadly. "Birds of a feather," she would warn, "flock together." Tis true.

1

Not Worth a Goddam Cent

Deep in the desk of every hard-bitten,
wisecracking, deadline-haunted reporter,
alongside the bourbon and the Maalox, is an
unfinished novel. Typically, the manuscript is
not about great events but about what is truly
important to the journalistic fraternity: sex,
office politics, money, fame and lunch.
–*Time* magazine

The pattern of a newspaperman's life is like the
plot of *Black Beauty*. Sometimes he finds a
kind master who gives him a dry stall and an
occasional bran mash in the form of a
Christmas bonus; sometimes he falls into the
hands of a mean owner who drives him in
spite of spavine and expects him to live on
potato peelings.–*A.J. Liebling*

One spring afternoon in 1954 my journalistic career seemed over in my eyes–before it had really begun. I was in the press box of Thunderbird Stadium at the University of British Columbia covering the annual World Cup (founded by the old *Vancouver World* newspaper) rugby series between the University of California and our valiant UBC boys who used swift rugby guile to thwart the Berkeley lads who enlisted massive tonnages of All-American flesh from their football squad.

Up the long stadium steps toward my perch of no retreat strode Erwin Swangard, the most fearsome temper in Vancouver newspapering. It meant, as I was foolish not to expect, that he had seen the term-ending "goon" issue of *The Ubyssey*, the campus paper of which I was editor.

For this annual tradition of university goofishness, we had done a wild satire of the three downtown Vancouver newspapers–complete with stealing typefaces from their composing rooms so as to make our front-page mastheads authentic. It included a vicious satire on one "Squirming S. Vanguard," then *The Vancouver Sun* sports editor, celebrated for his chauvinism and home-town favoritism and his predilection for featuring the feats of his own son in Little League baseball. He also happened to be the unconscious patron who had partially subsidized my way through university via nightly stints on space rates detailing the brilliant exploits of our campus athletes in the *Sun* sports pages.

"Okay, kit," said Erwin, who had never really mastered his second language after arriving in Saskatoon at age twenty-nine from Germany, "I'm suing you, *The Ubyssey*, the Alma Mater Society and the university." It was the entire low point of a life that by then had stretched to twenty-one years.

I was in the middle of graduating year exams. This meant that there was no prospect of a job. I was three years in debt through university loans and borrowings from a sister. Only desperation and death awaited.

Several days later, a letter arrived, on creamy thick stock, couched in intimidating legalese. It was from Donald C. Cromie, publisher and owner with his brother (described in the satire edition as the "Crummy brothers") of *The Vancouver Sun*.

Dated April 5, 1954, the letter from the "Office of the Publisher" read as follows:

Editor
Ubyssey
University of British Columbia
Vancouver, B.C.

Dear Sir:
It has been drawn to my attention that a purported newspaper titled *The Vancouver Son*, imitating the type and hed style and satirizing some of *The Sun*'s general styles and manners, has been

published, allegedly by *The Ubyssey*. This satirical publication libels, ridicules and in general damages *The Sun* to a grievous degree, with malice aforethought. It also applies a lesser amount of its pages to similar malicious mimicry of two other local newspapers.

After legal advice, it would be appreciated if the writer could be informed of the identity of the author and editor of this work, and advised also whether said Perpetrator might be interested in a Salaried Position at *The Sun*. (see footnote)

It was signed: Don Cromie.

The footnote read: "We might refuse to break our editorial rule of starting newcomers above $1,000 a month, but despite our editorial condition of already being well staffed by highly skilled 'position foot-workers,' a person of the skill and ruthless-ness of the above mentioned Perpetrator should have no misgivings about advancement once installed, as offered above, within knife's reach of the morocco-covered swivel chairs."

Still not sure whether this was a joke or a hoax, I went to see Cromie, who spent most of the interview obsessed with his well-known penchant for attempting to flip, from his chair, paper clips into the base of the overhead light of his sumptuous office. He thought the whole thing a hoot and sent me to his legendary managing editor, Hal Straight, who used to calm my nerves in subsequent years during varying crises by remarking, "Fother-ingham, I can't understand what you're worried about. If you're right, you're right. If you're wrong, you're fired."

On this occasion, on my first employment interview, drained by exam ordeal and the threat of a ruinous libel case I had no way of (and no funds for) defending, I vowed to demand two things on entering Straight's office: a salary of at least fifty dollars a week and a sufficient spell at my parents' home to recover my nerves and health before plunging into the maelstrom of full-time employment.

Straight, a huge 300-pound bear of a man then in his drinking days—he quit later, though it was concluded that he still had a high lifetime average—was greatly amused by my punch-up with

Swangard, a man he did not hold in high regard, and sent me to work for him, a circumstance that resulted in Swangard's not speaking to me, his neophyte employee, for six months.

"How much money do you want?" enquired Straight, imperiously playing the part of a William Randolph Hearst, peering over his desk at a nervous kid who was rather proud of being the first *Ubyssey* editor in ten years actually going to graduate.

"Am I worth"-dumb mistake-I heard myself saying, "fifty bucks a week?"

"At the moment," replied Straight, "you aren't worth a goddam cent. Forty-five bucks. Seven o'clock Monday morning. Goodbye." It was two days after the final exam, 1954.

It was a good introduction, in retrospect one supposes, to the "black art." Every day at 3:00 p.m. as the shift ended, we repaired across Pender Street from the Sun Tower, then a Vancouver landmark, to the old Lotus Hotel beer parlor on the fringe of Chinatown. A downy-cheeked twit, I would sit in silence as I listened to the seasoned and cynical veterans-Barry Broadfoot, Tom Ardies, Jack Cahill-explain the real truth behind the hot poop they hadn't handed in to the city editor.

It puzzled me then, and somewhat puzzles me still. Why not hand in what you really know-and make the editor (not the reporter) make the decision about what is going to be held back and what is going to be kept in? My minor success, to this day, I attribute to what I determined in the Lotus; print what the other guys talk about in the beer parlor. It is a simple task, not requiring much courage.

I still retain the two best pieces of newspapering advice I ever received (the best advice I give my daughter and any other incipient journalist) . Straight, on that first meeting, told me that on questioning any politician as to his statement, just say "Why?" When he replies with the usual obfuscation, ask again, "Why?" If you ask them "Why?" long enough and persistently enough, he advised, they might become so flustered they tell you the truth.

The second piece of advice came from Himie Koshevoy.

Koshevoy was a gnome, Straight's alter ego, who weighed in at 120 pounds when drenched with puns, an editor who dubbed the women's department the Ovary Tower. When awakened by a night city editor with the news that Father Divine, a Chicago-based religious charlatan who had a devoted following of nut cases, had run off with a rich blonde Vancouver heiress, Himie deadpanned: "Here's the headline. Local Girl Makes God."

(Father Divine, among other things, was famous for a celebrated riposte. Charged with maintaining a public nuisance–that is, harassing his unhappy white neighbors in Sayville, Long Island–he was appearing in court proceedings when Judge Lewis J. Smith suddenly dropped dead with a heart attack. Father Divine's immediate response: "I *hated* to do it." I digress.)

And so Himie instructed me one day, after a horrendous goof I made when I "assumed" that what the interviewees were saying was true: "*Never* assume anything." If your mother tells you her age–check it out.

After the more than three decades since Hal and Himie, I have done Fleet Street, done Ottawa, done Washington and the White House. I have chased Khrushchev in Berlin and Chou En-Lai in Beijing and Bobby Kennedy the week before he died and a lot of people who came in between.

What I have observed in my thirty-five years as an ill-paid journalist is that as the power of the media has increased, the governments in all the countries I have covered have simply increased the funds they spend to counteract and thwart and parry the press and its offshoots in its new power. It's an equivalent of the arms race. It's the propaganda race: deadly serious, since the most vital element of all–truth–is the matter at stake.

Everyone has his own version of truth, of course, and it would be an arrogant scribbler indeed who claimed there were no influences, no idols sitting out there in the void to emulate.

George Orwell once wrote about his favorite London pub, The Moon Under Water. It was only two minutes from a bus stop, but on a side street, so that drunks and rowdies never found their way there, even on Saturday nights. The "regulars" occupied the same chairs each evening and went there for conversation as much as for the beer.

The whole atmosphere was uncompromisingly Victorian. There were no glass-topped tables, no sham ceiling beams or plastic panels masquerading as oak. The ornamental mirrors behind the bar, the florid ceiling stained dark yellow by tobacco smoke, the stuffed bull's head over the mantelpiece—everything had, to Orwell's great satisfaction, the solid comfortable ugliness of the nineteenth century.

There was a good fire in at least two of the bars, the joint had neither a radio nor a piano, the barmaids—all middle-aged women with hair dyed in quite surprising shades—knew practically all the customers by name. You could buy both aspirins and stamps and could use the telephone. You could get a soft, creamy draught stout, liver sausage sandwiches, mussels, cheese and pickles, and out back was a lovely little garden where on summer evenings you could sit having beer or draught cider to the tune of the squeals of delighted children going down a chute that was placed under the trees.

The Moon Under Water, in short, was perfect and, as Orwell went on to explain, of course didn't exist: it was an amalgam of everything he wanted to find in one pub but never could.

A columnist, asked to name his favorite columnist, has the same fantasy as Orwell with his favorite pub. A little bit of this, a little bit of that, a dash of this and a smidgen of that and—bingo!—there is one's favorite columnist. This paragon not of virtue but of virtuosity would possess the wit of Shaw, the breadth of Lippmann, the anger of Cassandra and the disdain of Mencken. Probably could have got a job.

One of my heroes has always been Stanley Woodward, a legendary sports editor on the New York *Herald Tribune* who, as a colleague once described him, "was unfailingly kind to his inferiors, barely tolerated his equals and was openly contemptuous of his superiors." I always liked Dennis Braithwaite when he wrote the television column for *The Globe and Mail*, mainly because the column almost never dealt with television. He would mention a show he had seen the previous night and then launch into a screed on what it reminded him of in life, love, politics, sport, food and dogs. Creating great acerbic themes out of sit-coms. His columns generally were better than whatever he was supposed to be reviewing. Robert Fulford does the same. That's good column writing.

Probably the most famous-and powerful-columnist Britain has ever produced was "Cassandra," compulsory Fleet Street reading in the London *Daily Mirror* for all his admirers, who could never match his language or his cold fury when aroused. The *Mirror* was heavily pro-Labour Party in his day, and Cassandra was credited with being the chief influence in convincing British voters to defeat, at war's end, the man who had done more than any other to win the war, Prime Minister Winston Churchill-an electoral result that astonished the rest of the world. Winnie was great in a crisis but, as Cassandra persuaded millions and millions of voters, the country post-1945 had to get on to a kinder, gentler society.

Cassandra in real life was William Connor, and his power came in large part (aside from his obvious talent and common touch) from that anonymous byline. In ideal circumstances, it is the most effective way to label a column: the absence of a name of a real person forces readers to concentrate solely on the argument contained therein, the logic of it and the passion with which it is delivered-without mixing it up with the personality or the face or the personal life of the writer. *Deus ex machina.*

Probably the best reporter I have ever met is David Halberstam, in Saigon, in that October of 1962 when the rest of the world was consumed and terrified with the Cuban Missile Crisis. In Vietnam there were other concerns. Halberstam, who won a Pulitzer Prize for his despatches to *The New York Times*, was the leader of the young gang of correspondents that included Malcolm Browne and Neil Sheehan, who spent nine years writing the 1989 best-seller *A Bright Shining Lie*-all of them trying to tell their editors in New York that General Westmoreland and his staff were lying and that the war was being lost even then. The press used to sit at night in the rooftop bar of the Caravelle Hotel in the center of Saigon and watch the flashes of the gunfire in the jungle across the river. It was the safest way to cover a war.

Heroes? Role models? I seldom read Art Buchwald any more, finding him stale and formulaic. When he first started his satire column in the Paris *Herald Tribune* when I lived in Europe in the late fifties he was superbly funny, whereas now he is predictable. When I was very young I secretly wanted to be Eric Nicol. This terribly shy man was so idolized by the swollen post-war veterans' enrolment at the University of British Columbia that they raised the money to erect a commemorative tablet, still there, to "Jabez," the pen name that adorned his wickedly witty column. No one on the campus knew who Jabez was–nor did most of the staff of *The Ubyssey*, finding only in the assignments' basket the celebrated column that was furtively slipped in after the staff had gone home (*i.e.*, Pierre Berton's apartment for beer). His anonymity added to his allure, as did Cassandra's. It has always been my real desire. A bland pseudonym would enable a columnist to roam his city unfettered and gather material without being recognized and bothered–and shunned.

The sermon for the day is that one can write a better column when one is hardly known than when one is widely known.

When I lived in London in the late fifties the best and most literate journalist on Fleet Street was Kenneth Tynan, drama critic of the *Observer* who had these instructions pinned above his desk: "Rouse tempers, goad and lacerate, raise whirlwinds." He was already a legend when he left Oxford, with his leopard-skin trousers and exotic parties and he landed in London to a career as the "first postwar British myth." His second wife was the beautiful Kathleen Halton, daughter of the celebrated CBC war correspondent Matthew Halton, from Pincher Creek, Alberta–and sister of the CBC broadcaster David Halton.

Tynan was considered the finest drama critic since George Bernard Shaw and delighted in being a flamboyant provocateur of the Establishment on both sides of the Atlantic. Like Orwell, like Brecht, he believed everything was political. He raged against the state of the English theater, noting that in the 1953-54 London season, twenty-two of the twenty-six straight plays were concerned with life in the upper or upper-middle classes, and the other four were broad farces. The breakthrough came in 1956 with John Osborne's *Look Back in Anger*. Good taste and middle-class understatement were replaced with the voice of "a sophisticated, articulate lower class."

Tynan became the greatest champion of the "kitchen sink" drama, and his review on opening night stated flatly: "I doubt if I could love anyone who did not wish to see *Look Back in Anger*." He also once pronounced that he could never have anyone who was a Conservative in his own home.

He chased the bulls with Hemingway and drank with Tennessee Williams, was friends with Orson Welles, John Lennon and Marlene Dietrich. He founded Britain's National Theatre with Sir Laurence Olivier and, for his jollies, enjoyed that peculiar British vice of spanking young girls. A heavy smoker, he died of emphysema in California in 1980 at the age of fifty-three.

One would go to the grave content if able to write as well as a model critic, A.J. Liebling of *The New Yorker*, who could write equally well about boxing and restaurants, liking the "sweet science" as much as he did his stomach. It is hard to imagine a better craftsman than Jack Scott of *The Vancouver Sun*, who was worshipped by his readers in the forties and fifties. Scott's father, an old-time newspaperman, used to take his young son down to the Hotel Vancouver on Saturday afternoon to sit in the cavernous lobby and watch the passing parade. "Look at everybody who crosses this lobby," the father instructed the son. "In every one of them there is a story."

Every time Erwin Swangard, as managing editor, wished to punish me for some long-forgotten sin of insubordination or mopery, he would assign me to the dogwork of "the desk"—meaning the sedentary duties of the dead-drunk or dead-lazy ex-reporters whose flat feet and livers had given out and who were resigned to await their retirement by inserting commas and spelling corrections in the illiterate reporters' copy that passed their eyes on the way to the composing room.

As particular punishment for some imagined crime against humanity, at one time I was forced into one clear black hole of literacy–editing the "Island page," a first-edition wonder that could catch the ferry to Vancouver Island and detail to faithful *Sun* readers the meandering wisdom emitting from the craniums of aldermen in Nanaimo, plus the adjacent bank robberies and gripping new bylaws affecting real estate development.

The only plus in this mind-glazing shift that started at 7:00 a.m. was that Jack Scott had just moved to Saltspring Island, out in the Gulfstream between Vancouver and Victoria, and I got to be the first person in the world to read his column as I ripped open his mailed-in envelopes.

The move to the isolated island retreat, Scott explained in his column to his rapt readers, was because he was thinking of them first. By moving out of the hustle and the bustle of the city, he would have more time to read, to do research, to reflect, and by writing just three days a week rather than five, he would ensure that the columns the *Sun* readers received would be more insightful, more thoughtful, more worthwhile.

After some six months of clam-digging and delving into the wisdom of the ages and thinking himself to death, Scott offered–in one envelope that I opened–a confessional. His mail told him one thing: his readers didn't want him to be good every day. They just wanted him there every day. Newspaper readers are creatures of habit. As Marshall McLuhan explained, readers don't so much read a daily paper as "they get into it, somewhat like a warm bath."

Scott confessed that his mail had revealed to him that his readers didn't mind an off day. ("Oh God, he was on a toot last night, he'll produce better tomorrow.") They just wanted him there in the same spot, a familiar friend whose ups and downs could be related, in a way, to their own good days and bad days. Scott concluded the column by announcing that, as of then, he was returning to five a week.

As someone who wrote five a week for eight years and now has done three a week for the past thirteen, I am an authority on the subject. The readers would prefer you there five days a week. They want you there five days a week. It would be desirable, granted, for you to be there five days a week. The only thing they don't know is that the bod and the shoe leather give out after a while.

Scott was the greatest stylist seen in Vancouver, save perhaps Bob Bouchette, a revered newspaper figure in the 1930s who was so worshipped and tortured that one day, burdened down with his fame, he loaded his pockets with large rocks and, in dignified fashion, fully clothed, walked out from the sloping beach of English Bay in Vancouver's waterbound bosom in the direction of Japan and was never seen again.

The reason Pierre Berton was the talk of the town when he wrote his daily *Toronto Star* column–after being sacked from *Maclean's* for stating that he hoped his teen-age daughters would be introduced to sex in the comfort of a bed rather than in the groping backseat of a car–horrors!–was that you never knew what he was going to write about on any specific day and therefore couldn't afford to miss him in case you'd be left out of a cocktail party conversation.

One day he came into the office, opened the paper to peruse its regular page five upper right-hand slot and found his column missing. He stormed into the editor's office in a rage, only to be told that his column that day was so good, so sensational, that they had splashed it on the front page.

Berton smiled sweetly, as he is wont to do, and suggested that the editor look at his contract. Put it back on page five, he instructed. By the home edition it was back where the readers always expected it to be. McLuhan knew of what he spoke. Readers like to get into the warm bath. They don't like surprises.

Berton had a fantastic readership at the *Star* because he is a superb journalist and also because he is an instinctive show-man–knowing that mixing up the columns between exposés of used-car sleazebags with satires and funny-names columns kept the readers delighted and off guard.

His successor, Ron Haggart, one of the best journalists this country has ever seen, had a comparatively low rating in the readership surveys for one simple reason. Every one of the five weekly columns was well-researched, serious, on the issue, read by every other journalist in town–and of equal value every day. There was no variation–as Jack Scott had learned was so necessary–no sense that the guy had been fighting with his wife or into the sauce the night before.

The problem of a journalist in 1989 is not in producing material. The main problem, the major part of the time, is taken up with ingesting material. There's simply too much of it. It comes too fast and it comes relentlessly, from all directions. It never stops. You can never get on top of it.

A typical day? There is, on awakening, the relentlessly earnest, attempting-to-be-casual CBC radio, ever the sucker for the right cause, mainly just a way to pass the time until the authoritative 8:00 a.m. world news to determine if World War III has broken out. (If so, there's no point in going to work.)

A glance, perhaps, at "Canada AM" to see how new co-host Deborah McGregor is making out. Her clothes a little zippier. Just out of early morning boredom, a peek at the ABC news show, because I like Kathleen Sullivan's graying bangs. And the NBC equivalent, to check whether Bryant Gumbel is as unbearably arrogant as always. Confirmed. Willard Scott, the oaf of a weatherman, at least gained some brownie points when he told an audience that the reason he was limping was because he had tried to lift Gumbel's ego. "Bryant has applied to be a state," he explained, "and if he's accepted he will be the fifth largest."

On the drive to the office, catch a bit of Peter Gzowski's "Morningside," the most intelligent thing on radio anywhere. Pick up *The Globe and Mail*, to see if Jeffrey Simpson is writing about the cod stocks in Newfoundland. Bill French's book column and Trent Frayne on the sports pages–a relaxed observer, as opposed to the purse-lipped new breed of young sports writers who seem to have graduated with degrees in

Freud. Plus the hilarious columns in the Report on Business by Terry Corcoran, who seems to feel that capitalism would be better served if the children went back into the mines.

Pick up *The New York Times,* because of William Safire and the fact that it *is* the *Times.* Pick up *The Toronto Sun,* for The Sunshine Girl, Doug Fisher, Donato, McKenzie Porter on his wild days, the replies to the letters to the editor, and always take a look at the contributions of the humor columnist, Barbara Amiel. Pick up *The Toronto Star,* mainly for Doonesbury, but look at Carol Goar on her better days, Richard Gwyn, and Milt Dunnell on the sports pages. Otherwise, there's not really much. Pick up *The Financial Post.*

Go through the mail first since the bad news (the insults) makes the good news-the newspapers' recitation of terror, famine, disaster, murder, recession and rape-seem so much more palatable.

Several hours deep in the papers. Phone calls from liars, tipsters, self-interest groups wanting help so they can make money, students wanting immediate assistance on an essay on Herbert Hoover that was due yesterday, and several friends. In *The Financial Post/Toronto Sun* office in Washington, the CNN channel would be on constantly in the background noise along with the Teletypes, the computer printer and the fax machine. "This isn't a newspaper office," said a visitor one day, "this is a Toshiba warehouse." Column deadline, three times a week, is 11:00 a.m. The column is always handed in faithfully at 12:00.

Catch, on the way to lunch, the CBC noon news, in case World War III has broken out. (If so, no reason to go to lunch.) Lunch is with some amusing liar or entertaining gossip-monger-or a politician, who usually turns out to be both.

Jurgen Gothe, droll, droll, on CBC FM in the afternoon. At 6:00, there is the reliable Corporation back with a solid thirty minutes. At 6:30 try to listen to "As It Happens" a bit while watching Peter Jennings on ABC, but the handsome Ottawa high-school dropout, the best of the three New York-based anchors, almost always wins out. At 7:00, there is, for amusement, "Entertainment Tonight," mainly because of Mary Hart. You can turn off the sound. Mary, the Betty Boop of the 1990s, with gams that surpass her brains, is sufficient.

There is not a single thing on television worth watching (back to the magazines) until the bald pate of Peter Mansbridge appears at 10:00 p.m. with "The National." Sometimes we can make it to "The Journal," to see if Barbara has a new hairstyle, but Ted Koppel is too late for geriatric journalists. And so to sleep, sweet prince.

On Monday morning arrives *Maclean's*, plus *Time* and *Newsweek* (the latter being more readable and innovative than *Time* these days). The *New Republic* from Washington. A glance at *The Economist*. The weekly *Financial Times*, to see what the opposition is doing. *Vanity Fair*, the hottest thing around these days. *Saturday Night*, with John Fraser trying to keep owner Conrad Black at arm's length. *Esquire*, although we don't read as much of it as previously. *Sports Illustrated* - but where do you find the time? Enough.

It was the evil Senator Joe McCarthy who stumbled on a fact he made so apparent - now - to all of us. It is that typical citizens are so "steeped" in the news that they lose all sense of continuity and find their memories of even very recent events either blotted out or distorted.

McCarthy's wild charges of Communist infiltration of the U.S. State Department could never be refuted, or checked into, or parried in time for the daily deadline of newspapers because the next day he would be on to the next case, and then the next - all the while giving the impression that he had information that no one - not the president, not the press, not even the mighty FBI - possessed.

The denial, the counter-evidence, never seemed to catch up with original, sensational, front-page accusations. Journalists and editors to this day still discuss with guilt how they were suckered by McCarthy, a politician eventually brought down by his own excesses when the televised Congressional hearings revealed his venality and that of his young aides, David Schine and Roy

Cohn-the celebrated New York lawyer who died in 1986 of AIDS. (Lillian Hellman described them at the height of their fame as "Bonnie, Bonnie and Clyde.") McCarthy knew that journalists, obsessed with the new, wanted a headline more than they wanted time for analysis. He "taught" newspaper editors a lesson they ponder to this day.

Nancy Reagan had a bigger personal staff in the White House than Franklin Delano Roosevelt did at the height of the New Deal. It's all part of the Information Explosion. Mrs. Reagan needed more press officers to polish her image than Roosevelt did to run his whole office as he lifted his nation out of the Depression.

In Washington, in 1961, there were 1,522 reporters accredited to the Congressional press galleries. There are now more than 5,000. And another 10,000 journalists from around the world and independent organizations operate in the city, mainly on the phone, without direct physical access to the White House and Capitol Hill. If all the reporters with White House credentials showed up on the same day, the presidential home on Pennsylvania Avenue would have to shut down. Since 1961, the number of officially registered lobbyists has increased from 365 to 23,011, meaning there are now some five lobbyists for every single member of Congress. The corridor outside the House of Representatives where they lurk to muscle and press congressmen as relevant legislation comes to a vote is known as Gucci Gulch. Understandably, the bodies in the government information bureau have increased in proportion to deal with the proliferation of scribes and slick-suited lobbyists.

On a summer weekend in 1984, the media sent 14,000 people to San Francisco for the Democratic convention, a mob that outnumbered the delegates by a factor of three to one. The total of their travel and entertainment costs over the four days, as Harper's editor Lewis Lapham pointed out, would have paid Louis XIV's costs for the construction of Versailles.

The inundation of information never stops. The difference is that a more discriminating audience now gets it from more sources. In Canada, by example, there were 127 daily newspapers in 1979, which dropped to 120 by 1981 and 110 by 1989. But the number of periodicals in the country rose from 1,395 in 1979 to 1,423 in 1981 and by 1989 had hit 2,069. Daily papers were shrinking, but community papers went from 1,027 in 1981 to 1,439 in 1989. People are reading more, but from different angles, different perspectives. One suspects that as the media biggies are becoming more monolithic, the suspicious subjects in the land are becoming more wary of getting their information from a few sources and are becoming more discriminating. It doesn't prove there is any improvement in quality, but in 1978 there were 102 television stations in Canada; by 1989 there were 138. The trend, naturally, is the same in the United States. There were 152 public television stations in 1968. Nearly two decades later there were 303.

(The last time I looked, *Playboy* sold 3,732,948 copies of each issue in the United States, whereas the more raunchy and explicit *Penthouse* sold 2,251,491 copies. For some reason that someone should examine, the figures are reversed in Canada, *Penthouse* outselling *Playboy*. I digress.)

The problem is that there is a large surplus in the world today. The surplus is not of wheat or oil or talk about AIDS or of too many football teams in too many leagues. The human brain can absorb only so much. Modern journalism and modern communications think they are doing a grand job of transmitting into our living rooms and our newspapers and our car radios the up-to-the-second crisis of the moment.

Instead, they induce ennui in the viewer/listener/reader. We become unshockable. Did you know there was a military coup in Uganda the other day? Or an abortive one in Thailand? Do you care anymore? I'm afraid not.

It is called media overkill. (Some media guys were killed in a coup attempt the other day. Quick–tell me which one.) Do you remember Lebanon? Surely you must. That was the crisis before Namibia. Where, exactly, is Namibia? Do you recall the Air India crash? You're allowed a moment to think. That was the one before the Japan Air Lines crash, which preceded the blaze of a jet at Manchester airport, and then there was Lockerbie. How many were killed in each? Gotcha.

One of the reasons why you can't remember is that those of us in the information/communication/titillation trade now treat air crashes as we treat Hank Aaron's home run record up against Babe Ruth's. Each crash sets a new record for something: the "largest death toll in a single-aircraft crash"–as opposed of course to the death toll in a two-plane crash. Meaning those two 747s that collided on the runway on that little island where we used to holiday. Quick now–the Spanish Canary Islands, right? Or was it Bermuda? The Bahamas? The Bermuda Triangle? Atlantis? I forget.

You get the picture. You faintly remember Patty Hearst? Was she the one who married her prison guard or was that Lyndon Johnson's daughter who married her bodyguard? Or was it Gerald Ford's girl? Does it matter? They're all daughters of famous men. It figures. Who was Squeaky Fromme? Was she the one who tried to kill Ford? Or George Wallace? Do you confuse the demented young man who shot Ronald Reagan outside the Washington Hilton with the demented young man who killed John Lennon? What are their names again? Welcome to the club.

We get too much news. Just as we get too many calories, too much gossip and too much information about AIDS, more than we really need to know. It has long been the contention of this writer that newspapers were better before the invention of the telephone; those being the days when reporters actually had to leave the office and meet, face to face, the people they were writing about.

They had a cup of coffee or a beer or a martini with the objects of their later derision. It both informs and aids the derision. Long lunches are good for journalism (and therefore readers).

It's a more appealing style of journalism, but it has its own risks. Having contacts–getting access–is what this style of journalism is all about. The risk is that sometimes writing what you learn can alienate the contact and end the access.

The columnist walks a constant tightrope, wanting to keep contacts intact and on fairly friendly terms in the belief that a feel for leaders and top officials can be best gained with one foot inside the tent. There might have been a point in printing the stories about Margaret Trudeau's late-night solo visits to the National Press Club bar in Ottawa, but Margaret was somewhat of a friend then and the occasional drink or chat with her was deemed more valuable in acquiring a feeling for what was going on at 24 Sussex Drive and in the prime minister's entourage. Would I have changed my *modus operandi* regarding her in the light of subsequent events? No, I don't think so. We still get along, somewhat warily today, no doubt partially because of my sympathetic review of her first sensational book, which, as I wrote, revealed more about Pierre Trudeau than it did about Margaret. Should the beat reporters in Ottawa have reported what they knew about her behavior? I think so.

On the celebrated night of The Slap in the ambassadorial residence on leafy Rock Creek Drive in Washington, I knew nothing about it. Like the several hundred other guests, I was inside, seated on a shaky false floor built over the swimming pool under a huge party tent, waiting impatiently for the tardy star guest, George Bush, to arrive. No one inside, including Brian Mulroney and Mila and the cream of Georgetown, knew what was going on at the front steps.

That's where Sondra Gotlieb—in front of spotlights, TV cameras, the Secret Service, the RCMP, aides, flunkies and a clutch of Canadian reporters not invited to the party who were doing their bored coverage from across the street—chose to slap her social secretary, Connie Connor. She couldn't have picked a more public spot in Washington, except possibly the White House lawn on Pennsylvania Avenue.

In discussing the theme of this book, a friend asked an interesting question: if I had witnessed the slap in private, would I have reported it? After some contemplation, I don't think so. I was a friend of both Sondra and Allan Gotlieb, had been a guest many times at their home, lunched privately with each of them during the years in Washington and was rather treated by them as the pet of the Canadian press ghetto in that city. If Sondra, whose eccentricities were enjoyed by the Georgetown matrons until she went one step too far, had slapped Connie with only this reporter present, that would have been regarded as a private matter in a private house. By doing it where she did it, she turned a slap into The Slap.

It's a constant tightrope. The way anyone survives in the strange art of column-writing–and this is my twenty-first year in the dodge–is to know occasionally what to leave out. You allow your contacts to live for another day–when you eventually may have to do them in for the greater good of a story that is too good to resist.

Janet Malcolm, a *New Yorker* writer who has never been a journalist, caused a great stir in American journalistic circles–her charges apply to journalism anywhere–in 1989 with an examination of the relationship between author Joe McGinniss and Jeffrey MacDonald, the young U.S. Army doctor charged with the brutal murder of his wife and two small children.

MacDonald, insisting he was innocent and needing funds for his defense, invited McGinniss to write a book on him, promising complete cooperation in return for one-third of the royalties. McGinniss was allowed to move into a dormitory with MacDonald and his defense team during the trial, and he slowly came to the realization through the evidence he was hearing that his new friend was a psychotic liar and indeed was guilty of killing his own family and blaming it on mysterious intruders.

For several years McGinniss kept in close contact with MacDonald, now in prison, never revealing that his 1983 best-seller, *Fatal Vision*, would depict the brilliant young doctor as a monster. MacDonald, alleging fraud, sued for $15 million and eventually received $325,000 in an out-of-court settlement.

McGinniss maintains that MacDonald, by lying endlessly to him, negated any contract between them. Malcolm takes all this to mean that, in all journalism, hidden in the relationship between reporter and subject is a "deliberately induced delusion" that, after publication, becomes "a moment of shattering revelation." This is a bit much, somewhat similar to Joan

Didion's observation in *Slouching Towards Bethlehem* that "a reporter is always selling someone out."

Bob Woodward is regarded as the finest investigative reporter around. His boss, *Washington Post* executive editor Ben Bradlee, says flatly that he is the finest reporter he has ever seen. Woodward, despite such accolades, came under serious criticism from some of his colleagues on publication of *Veil*, his examination of the Reagan era conspiracy to hide from Congress the illegal funding of the contras in Nicaragua. In *Veil* it was revealed that Woodward had been having unreported meetings over the years with CIA chief William Casey-dead by the time the book appeared.

If he had been receiving all this information from the secretive Casey, journalists wondered, why wasn't he spreading it out on the front page of his employer, *The Washington Post?* Woodward's answer was that he couldn't have obtained the full story if he had blown any part of it beforehand. He refuses to explain how he got into the hospital room of the dying Casey for-the climax of the book-the death-bed confession. Just as he has always maintained that he will never reveal the identity of the shadowy Deep Throat in the Watergate drama until the man is dead. You use the contact until the point when the contact is not as valuable as the story. Casey died just in time for Woodward's best-seller.

If access is the Scylla of the columnist's life, deadlines are surely the Charybdis. For years I felt tuggings of Protestant guilt at approaching a typewriter or computer deadline with absolutely no idea of what that day's column might be about. Until, one day, I was saved by one of the more literate figures of the age, the elegant Alistair Cooke, the familiar host of "Masterpiece Theatre" who has been beaming to the BBC for some thirty years his celebrated "Letter from America."

In an introduction to a collection of his radio letters, he explained that he most always sat down at his typewriter two hours before his broadcast with little idea of what he was going to say. He said he saw nothing wrong with this, pointing out that when one is on the way to a dinner party, one does not practice beforehand the *bon mots* and insights that emerge over the food and the wine. I have felt considerably better ever since.

In all, in a life spent in journalism, blessed with several fine publishers and some tolerant editors, I have found it far easier getting what passes for the truth into print than I have extracting it from the politicians who think they have an exclusive on it.

2

Kissing the Chains

To borrow a line from Mark Twain, "First get
your facts, and then you can distort them as
much as you please." As for the headlines,
which, after all, are the only journalistic things
that matter, they are, of course, outside your
control–or, so far as I can gather, anyone
else's.–*Lester B. Pearson to newspapermen*

Governments employ different ways of doing it, but whatever
the country and whoever is in power, there is one thread: they
would like to control the information available to the public.

In the game of the Stockholm Syndrome, the government
sometimes takes the initiative. In 1980, the police were finally
closing in on thrill-killer Clifford Olson, the despicable animal
who got his jollies from, among other things, driving a spike
through the head of his teen-age victims, male and female, as he
sexually assaulted them. The attorney-general of British Columbia, Allan Williams, came calling on the publishers of *The
Vancouver Sun* and the Vancouver *Province* and powerful
broadcaster Jack Webster, since the media was rife with rumors,
asking for their cooperation.

Olson was involved in a diabolical scheme. A long-time police
informer, he was offering the RCMP information as to the
location of the graves of the missing youngsters in return for
money–which in the end amounted to the $100,000 paid to his
wife. The longer he bargained, and the more kids he killed, the
more his information was worth. The attorney-general of the
province told the publishers that it was vital that nothing be
printed until enough evidence could be gathered to arrest Olson.
The publishers of the *Sun* and the *Province* and Webster agreed

to his pleas-his preemptive strike to keep from the public the information that was common gossip among the "insiders" in society-the journalists, the lawyers, the politicians.

Not common, however, among the parents of the children who were subsequently murdered. Since every other body he unearthed would mean more money for him, it was to Olson's advantage to kill more before he was finally taken in. It was not one of the great moments in British Columbia justice-or journalism.

In the three countries in which I have worked regularly as a journalist-Canada, Britain and the United States-the most manipulated press has been that in Mother England, what is thought of as the font of parliamentary democracy. Naturally, all governments attempt to control information-whether democratic or blatantly autocratic-but Britain does it best in what we think of as open societies.

Of the three, the American press is the most aggressive, with the Canadian variety-as in most everything else-coming somewhere in between the two.

In Britain, the government's technique of managing the news is far more sophisticated than in, say, the Soviet Union. The techniques have reached a new level of polish under Margaret Thatcher, but she has been solidly in the tradition of her predecessors at 10 Downing Street.

James Margach, the former political correspondent for the London *Sunday Times* who has covered twelve prime ministers from David Lloyd George to James Callaghan, has written: "With obsessional ruthlessness and even ferocity they almost all sought to dominate the press, radio and television as the vital precondition to their domination of Parliament, parties and public opinion. They desired to enrol and exploit the media as an arm of government. Two objectives possessed them. First to establish and fortify their personal power; and second to reinforce the conspiracy of secrecy, to preserve the sanctity of government behind the walls of Whitehall's forbidden city."

One of the best studies of the "surprising" reality behind the

British myth (still believed in by those foreigners who exult about the Mother of Parliaments) has been done by Michael Cockerell, Peter Hennessey and David Walker in their *Sources Close to the Prime Minister: Inside the Hidden World of the News Manipulators*. They concede that the British people live in one of the most stable and sophisticated parliamentary democracies in the world, "yet in a vital sense that democracy is a sham. It is a sham because the British are governed by a system which does all it can to deny them the facts." Parliament, the people and the press not only tolerate this British obsession with secrecy, "they allow it to act as a formal and intimidating apparatus within which governments may practice an anti-democratic technique to their hearts' content. The technique is news management."

Margaret Thatcher's chief boast as prime minister is that she is passionately against big government, a champion of the individual against the state, an opponent of the faceless bureaucracy. Yet, as the three authors document, since 1979 she has been a dedicated supporter of the very secrecy that shelters the civil servants she so scorns.

In her bald hypocrisy she emulated the leader she was so close to, Ronald Reagan. The Great Communicator, elected to Washington on an anti-Washington ticket, swore to slash the numbers of useless bureaucrats on the government rolls. When he left the capital after eight years, there were more people working for the government than when he arrived.

More crucial, the Reagan who railed against government was revealed, just as he left, as using government secrecy and compliant un-elected factotums named Bud McFarlane and John Poindexter and the basement cowboy Ollie North to carry out secret and illegal missions against the laws of the U.S. Congress. Like Thatcher, Reagan loved the mask of secrecy that his "despised" government provided for him. The two of them are most undemocratic democrats.

The most remarkable tools of news management are the Westminster Lobby correspondents. These are the reporters at the Palace of Westminster who cover government, but not through the House of Commons debates. They write about the cabinet and the prime minister and the major issues under such labels as "political editor," "political correspondent," or "our man at Westminster."

They are organized into their own group, with its own rules. Much of what they do is secret, the details kept from other reporters and often even from their own editors. Journalism is supposed to provide the public with an accurate first draft of history. In Britain, the first draft comes through a Lobby correspondent–with the words themselves often provided by the government. Lobby journalists rely on off-the-record briefings from government officials. They operate in a world of make-believe–because the briefings supposedly never take place and the government spokesmen do not officially exist.

It was 1884 when the Sergeant-at-Arms of the Commons first starting keeping his little list of privileged journalists who had permission to mingle with members of Parliament in the Lobby outside the debating chamber. Over the past century the Lobby's "journalistic freemasonry," as it has been called, has grown in power.

There are now about 150 Lobby correspondents from the provincial newspapers, the national papers based in London, the weekly press and the broadcast organizations. They are briefed every day by the prime minister's press secretary, and what he discloses, of course, is what the prime minister wants the press, radio and television to report. Yet these journalists never name the source of their information–to do so is against Lobby rules.

Parliament was first opened to reporting in 1828. When Lord Macaulay in 1835 pointed to the reporters' gallery and called the press the Fourth Estate, there was already an organization of reporters with its own rules. In democratic theory, private citizens were supposed to be allowed to approach freely their members of Parliament once they emerged from the Commons chamber. But London in 1884 was under attack by Irish terrorists who twice planted dynamite at Westminster. Because of the threat, the area known as the Members' Lobby had to be sealed off from the public, and admission was restricted to MPs themselves and to certain journalists whose names were kept on a list by the Sergeant-at-Arms. Thus was the Lobby born.

There's a curious coincidence between the birth of the Lobby and the beginning of the first legal moves to limit how much the public knew about government and its doings. The first Official Secrets Act was introduced in 1889, five years after the Lobby started. Even as Britain was moving toward becoming a democracy–by extending the vote to men of all classes (women had to wait forty more years)–the mechanisms were being created to control, channel and even manufacture the political news.

From the start, those journalists admitted to the Lobby tried to emulate the MPs. They took up the parliamentary dress code of frock coat and top hat. In return for their loyalty, they became almost honorary MPs, even having their own quarters. The suite of rooms given to them after World War I included a bath. Today they even have their own bar–Annie's–for use solely by Lobby correspondents and MPs.

It is physical access to parts of the building where other reporters are not allowed that is so valuable to this information cartel. Members of the Lobby mingle and gossip with MPs and ministers in the antechamber outside the Commons. They can wander the Ways and Means corridor and go to the Vote Office to pick up papers.

Such privileged access lends an air of authority, however spurious. One of the great Lobby stories recounted by Cockerell, Hennessey and Walker concerns one of its members, a provincial journalist, sitting on the stairs one evening desperately wondering what to write on a night of so little news. Prime Minister Gladstone, coming down the narrow stairs, absent-mindedly asked the reporter to let him get past. The correspondent jumped up and stood aside and the prime minister thanked him. Readers of his paper next morning were undoubtedly impressed to read an article that started, "Meeting Mr. Gladstone this evening in the Lobby I had a brief but interesting conversation with him." There followed a long rehash of some of the prime minister's recent speeches, all cloaked in the air of an exclusive.

There are thirteen different drinking places in the Mother of Parliaments, and lubrication between press and politician naturally fuels the exchange of information. The rules are that the Lobby journalist must never use a notebook and must "not see" anything in the Members' Lobby or any of the private rooms or corridors.

"If anything happens in the Members' Lobby," stated Christopher Moncrieff, chief Lobby correspondent of the Press Association, "like a punch-up between MPs, which once did happen, you are blind. You do not see it." *Sources Close to the Prime Minister* also quotes reporter James Fenton, who on his first day as Lobby correspondent was introduced to an MP in Annie's Bar. "The MP was so drunk that as he reached forward to shake my hand he fell off the barstool and slumped onto the floor. But of course under the rules I never saw this."

The Lobby correspondents have their own cryptic code on their notice-boards to foil ordinary reporters. In the Lobby cupboard they are given White Papers and other government documents—hours before publication—on the condition that nothing is released in advance. The documents are labelled "Confidential," but both reporters and government pretend they don't exist. In this way, in the make-believe world, the constitutional fiction can be maintained that Parliament is always informed first.

The Lobby system is completely astounding to Canadian or American reporters when they first see it in operation. The day-in and day-out manipulation stuns veterans of even such leak-happy newspapers as *The New York Times*.

Each weekday morning, a group of Lobby correspondents go to 10 Downing Street for a briefing from the prime minister's press secretary. Just before 11:00 a.m. the herd can be seen from Parliament Street headed for No. 10 and their daily feeding. (In Ottawa, the press gallery regulars refer to the ritual daily emanations from the Prime Minister's Office as "Gainesburgers.")

As Anthony Sampson, one of the finest journalists in Britain, points out in *The New Anatomy of Britain*, "These briefings find their way into the newspapers with phrases like 'it is understood that,' or 'it is believed that'–whereas a truthful report would say 'the prime minister's press secretary told me that.' The distortion conceals the fact that the news is being managed, and also implies that the newspapers' perspective is the same as the prime minister's. . . ."

At four o'clock every afternoon at Westminster, the Lobby boys gather at the House of Commons to mount their own private spiral staircase. (In Washington, Lesley Stahl and a dozen equivalents cover the White House. In Ottawa, Marjorie Nichols and Pam Wallin and Carol Goar and many other female journalists blanket Parliament Hill. In London, there still is no prominent female byline on major political coverage.)

At the top of the private staircase is the boys' own secret hideout, a room in a turret–rather like the tree-house that pubescent lads build in the backyard to hide their secrets and copies of *Playboy*. Here they are given (never for attribution) what Mrs. Thatcher wants them to hear, delivered once again by her press secretary, Bernard Ingham. In the papers next day, of course, he is never Bernard Ingham, but "sources close to the Prime Minister" or "government circles."

Political writers such as Michael Cockerell acknowledge that Ingham is the Deep Throat of Westminster. Woodward and Bernstein at least had the grace to state that the real identity of Watergate's Deep Throat would never be revealed while the man was still alive. Everyone in British journalism knows that Ingham is their own Deep Throat, but that fact is never transmitted to the readers.

There is plenty of evidence that the press lords of Fleet Street were in bed with Neville Chamberlain and his appeasement policy in the late 1930s. The politicians of the time have been condemned by the historians for their naive and quavering approach to Hitler, but the English newspapers and their proprietors were just as bad.

A major example always cited is *The Times* of London, where editor Geoffrey Dawson wrote a "memorable" editorial in

September of 1938 urging the Czechoslovak government to make itself a more "homogeneous state" by seceding the Sudeten population to Germany. But it was just one example of the remarkable failure of Britain's national newspapers to tell their readers the truth about Hitler's Germany. It was more than failure–it was refusal.

The papers, through their Berlin correspondents, in fact learned the truth but most of them wouldn't print it. Mainly because they were birds of a feather. Newspaper owners and editors were leaned on by ministers of Chamberlain's government to mute anything–both in editorials and the news columns–that might offend Hitler.

All this has been documented by Richard Cockett in *Twilight of Truth: Chamberlain, Appeasement and the Manipulation of the Press*, a work that began as a Ph.D. thesis. Prime Minister Chamberlain, the man who went down in history carrying an umbrella, was determined to establish complete control over news in Whitehall. He was particularly concerned about killing off any contradictory information coming out of sources in the Foreign Office that might upset his strategy toward Hitler, and he used powerful cabinet ministers, such as Lord Halifax and Sam Hoare, in his wooing of Fleet Street. Two of the mightiest press barons, Lord Beaverbrook and Lord Rothermere, were quite willing to cooperate. As Cockett writes: "Rothermere exercised a rigorous control over his own papers, and the *Daily Mail* was trumpeting Chamberlain and refusing to publish any condemnation of the Fascist powers even as its circulation started to fall sharply. Beaverbrook was particularly eager to act as a guardian of the Government's political interests and was quick to act if there was anything in the *Daily Express* that might offend the sensibilities of any foreign governments that Halifax and Chamberlain were eager to please."

At *The Times*, editor Dawson had a difficult time because some of his staff disagreed with the appeasement policy, but he won out–he loved being a sounding-board for Chamberlain and Halifax. One of his editorial writers, Colin Coote, wanted to quit but was persuaded by Churchill to stay put since Winston, the chief foe of appeasement, preferred "a friend in the enemy's camp."

Even the Fleet Street press on the left gave in. Lord Southwood, who controlled the *Daily Herald*, was a willing visitor to Lord Halifax's offices at the Foreign Office. He agreed to appeasement chiefly for commercial reasons. At the *News Chronicle*, Sir Walter Layton was compromised by Sam Hoare, much to the contempt of his senior editors. The brilliant cartoonist David Low of the *Evening Standard*, who was passionately anti-Fascist, bothered the appeasers. The editor of the *Yorkshire Post*, Arthur Mann, vigorously attacked Chamberlain and appeasement and so displeased the paper's owners that he left.

The Daily Telegraph, because of Lord Camrose's close friendship with Churchill, was the only major paper with Conservative loyalties that treated Chamberlain and appeasement with some caution. When its Berlin correspondent, Victor Gordon-Lennox, wrote two stark pieces in 1937 about Germany's colonial claims, Lord Halifax sympathized with the British ambassador to Germany and told him that he had written to Anthony Eden to urge him to "come as near as possible to wringing Gordon-Lennox's neck."

Gordon-Lennox and other disillusioned journalists left their compromised employers and started their own newsletters in London in an attempt to get the truth out. And, after war was declared in 1939, the newspaper owners and editors fulminated loudly against the censorship set up by the government. But at no time was the official censorship of news laid down by the government as blanketing–or as despicable–as what the proprietors inflicted in those crucial years on their own newspapers.

Just after World War II, under Clement Attlee's Labour government, one Lobby correspondent, Paul Einzig of the *Financial Times*, began to write a series of stories–all accurate–about the government's plans for nationalization of the steel industry. The Attlee regime moved quickly. Documents that slipped through those officials whose job it was to suppress embarrassing material showed that Einzig's phone was tapped by MI5-the British secret service.

Sir Norman Brook, the secretary of the cabinet, sent a memorandum to Prime Minister Attlee, saying that MI5 should use "special facilities" to put Einzig under surveillance since, Brook noted, this reporter had been responsible in the past for embarrassing disclosures. Einzig, as was apparent, was writing about a domestic situation that in no way was connected with national security. Yet his phone was being tapped because he was acquiring information that the official government news machine did not want released.

This was some thirty years before it was discovered that Henry Kissinger, as U.S. secretary of state, had tapped the phones not only of some of his own staff he suspected of leaking but also of prominent Washington journalists who criticized the Nixon administration.

Margaret Thatcher now represents the culmination of a hundred years of political news management. Not a single one of her predecessors at No. 10 has been so conscious of image, so willing to bring in advertising experts and public relations executives (usually looked down upon by the British as vulgar Americans).

This wasn't, of course, the same Margaret Thatcher who was elected in 1960 as a young and eager Member of Parliament. Cockerell tells us that at that time, she introduced-much against the wishes of the front bench of her own Conservative party-a private member's bill the aim of which was to cut back on secrecy in government.

Enthusiastically, she pronounced that publicity was the greatest and most effective check against any arbitrary action. This was in her speech on her bill urging that municipal committee meetings be completely opened up rather than held behind closed doors with press and public shut out.

When she became leader of the opposition after being elected Conservative leader, she was still on the same kick. She gave out a complete list of home telephone numbers of herself and all her senior party colleagues to television, radio and newspaper editors. She even asked to be tipped off if any of her senior colleagues declined invitations from the media mob.

When she became prime minister, her attitude changed considerably. In 1977, at the Washington home of Ambassador Peter Jay, she met with British correspondents who were stationed in the United States and who had become admirers of the much more open American system of government. She was asked if there were some aspects of the greater openness of the American system that might be introduced into Britain. Mrs. Thatcher's reply: "Nothing at all. Our system in much more open than the American one."

Well, one reporter persisted, was anything going to be done about the restrictions of the British Official Secrets Act? "It should be reformed," she replied, "but only to make some of its provisions against the unauthorized disclosure of official information stronger, not weaker." So much for the rookie MP who wanted to reduce secrecy in government.

The British government has always been clever at controlling the news. The real story of Churchill's illness and stroke while prime minister in 1953 was never told because of the reluctance of the Lobby to look beyond the bland briefings they were given. Documents available since 1984 show that Churchill's intimates were censoring medical bulletins about his condition. Among the intimates were three prominent newspaper proprietors.

Books discussing press freedom frequently quote the famous phrase, "In wartime the truth is so precious, she must always be attended by a bodyguard of lies." (This bon mot is attributed to Churchill talking to Stalin in Teheran in 1943.) In the Falklands, where what passed for wartime was actually a Tory re-election campaign, that convenient nostrum became a guiding principle. In an eye-opening chapter of their book, authors Cockerell, Hennessey and Walker reveal that nowhere was news management more blatant–or more successful–than in the farcical little war with Argentina over the Falkland Islands in 1982. (A South

American poet said the conflict reminded him of two bald men fighting over a comb.)

When it became clear that the Argentinians were going to invade the Falklands (for political reasons at home), it also became quite clear to the prime minister and most everyone else that her survival as prime minister and the survival of her government were on the line. It was the lowest point in her political life. For the next ten weeks, until victory was won, the press, radio and television were used in every way to strengthen her position as well as to win back the Falklands.

At first the British Navy didn't want to take any reporters with the task force that was sailing to the Falklands. The media protested vigorously. "You can't have a war without *The Times* being there," its editor Charles Douglas-Home told Mrs. Thatcher personally. She saw the point. She insisted there be first ten, then twenty-nine press bodies on board, but made it clear she expected a "good news war."

When the Ministry of Defence spokesman announced he would give war details only on the record and would suspend the usual unattributable Lobby briefings, he was beaten down by No. 10, which could see its control over information disappearing. When two British helicopters crashed at the very start of the operation with a possible loss of life of seventeen, the event was officially admitted a month later–after the news came out accidentally through a letter sent home by an eighteen-year-old sailor.

The task force commander, Admiral Sandy Woodward–not skilled in the lies of Whitehall–told reporters aboard his ship quite flatly that he planned to use the press as part of his attempt to confuse the enemy. He talked, in the jargon of Montgomery of Alamein, of how "the big match" should be "a walk-over." When Downing Street told Lobby correspondents their papers should be writing about the risks the valiant British lads were taking, he reversed his approach.

It was learned later that there was in fact a major split in Thatcher's inner cabinet as the task force approached its destination, since soundings of British public opinion unearthed a feeling that the islands should be retaken, but without any loss of life. It was a familiar British xenophobic sentiment—a whiff of grapeshot across the bow should frighten the lesser breeds or, as the Fleet Street tabloids called them, the "Argies."

Thatcher was furious about the story on the split and, Cockerell tells us, through the Lobby spread reports that unnamed colleagues were "vilifying" Foreign Secretary Francis Pym, the principal foe of her head-down tactics. When the BBC broadcast an interview from the United Nations with the Argentinian spokesman José Herera Vegas, Mrs. Thatcher, having failed to declare war on Argentina, declared war on the BBC instead. Its chairman was hauled before a Conservative media committee for what one former minister described as "the ugliest meeting I have ever attended in my years as an MP."

Unlike other modern wars, the Falklands clash was fought without the usual instantly available TV pictures. Downing Street feared the "Vietnam syndrome"—the public revulsion at seeing the carnage over the evening meal that caused American viewers eventually to side with their college children to stop the war. Since the government controlled the transmission by satellite from its ships and military bases, it controlled British television.

In the five weeks after the task force sailed, the key point of South Georgia was recaptured, Argentina's cruiser *General Belgrano* was sunk with a loss of 250 lives (immortalized by the Murdoch London *Sun* headline "GOTCHA!"), HMS *Sheffield* was destroyed by an Exocet missile, there were bombing raids on Port Stanley airport, Britain's largest battle fleet since World War II was hot for battle—and not a photo or piece of film had appeared in London. (Meanwhile, the Football Association Cup Final—highlight of the English soccer season—was shown to troops on the task-force's ship within twenty-four hours.)

In Buenos Aires, hundreds of American and Canadian reporters and TV crews covered the war, getting out more information than the press travelling with the British were allowed to report.

London papers were fed official photographs of British soldiers drinking tea with happy islanders, but a *Daily Express* shot of the sinking of the HMS *Antelope* was held up for a month until the fighting was over. The government wanted "a very deodorized sort of conflict," said the editor of *The Guardian*. By the time television film was released, it was like receiving "the Dead Sea scrolls," said one TV editor. Many despatches never reached London at all.

Cockerell *et al* found that military censors killed a television interview with a young British pilot who was asked how he felt when first in action and who replied, "Well, for about two seconds it scared me fartless." Censors killed a scene that showed a body, but no injuries, from the *Sheffield*. The best film of the fighting reached TV sets twenty-three days after it had happened, after the Argentinians had already surrendered–which was three days longer than it took in 1854 for *The Times'* correspondent in the Crimea to get into print his report on the charge of the Light Brigade.

But though some members of the press complained, for the most part they played along. As the chief of the defence staff, Admiral Sir Terence Lewin, boasted, "The press were most helpful with our deception plans."

The Commons Defence Committee, in an examination of all the misinformation that had been handed out, found that in fact some of the non-attributable briefings about one particular piece of lying had been tape-recorded at the Ministry of Defence. The committee asked for the tapes to be handed over, but came up against a peculiar objection. The ministry wrote back complaining that the request for the tapes raised questions of principle: "unattributable briefings are in a sense recognized by well-understood conventions as 'meetings that never took place.'" But, most interesting of all, the reporters attached to the defense ministry themselves voted nine to seven against having the tapes handed over, apparently because they wanted the traditions and the secrecy of the Lobby to be retained. "They are," Cockerell quotes one reporter as saying, "like prisoners kissing the chains that bind them." Who's the jailor and who's the jailee?

The Falklands exercise in press censorship and manipulation showed that the British government had indeed learned from the American disaster in Vietnam that information is power and that whoever controls the information can control the public perception, especially of a short war. American politicians–Kennedy before he was gone, Johnson and Nixon–couldn't control the information coming out of Vietnam, and they lost to public opinion. Thatcher successfully limited and managed the information coming out of the isolated Falklands–and she won.

The Lobby system allows any British government to be much more successful than a Canadian or American government in doctoring the presentation of news through briefings, leaks and disclosures given to the selected scribes who are pledged not to reveal their sources.

The current ringmaster of the system, Maggie Thatcher's press secretary Bernard Ingham, is a burly Yorkshireman with the craggy face of a safecracker. (It was Ingham, when asked by Canadian reporters at the Commonwealth conference in Vancouver in 1987 what Mrs. Thatcher actually thought of Brian Mulroney, who said point-blank, "She thinks him an empty windbag." All off the record, of course.)

The most telling illustration of Ingham's use of the Lobby system–the Stockholm Syndrome of print–came in 1986 when Michael Heseltine, a devilishly handsome minister of defence who lusted after the prime minister's job, was seen to be in need of discipline. Ingham leaked to his Lobby friends a Heseltine letter dealing with his proposals for saving a British helicopter company from bankruptcy. Heseltine was forced to resign and hasn't been heard of since. When Sir Leon Brittan, another former high government figure who was involved, fessed all in a television program in early 1989, the subterfuge revealed led to calls in Parliament for Mrs. Thatcher's resignation. Some hope.

In the same spring, Tory Transport Minister Paul Channon got into one of those famous press and politicians lunches, this one at the top-drawer Garrick Club, where the oysters and the

champers never end. There were four journalists present, operating under the arcane Lobby rules. The four filed differing
despatches to their papers, saying that investigators had either
arrested, or soon would arrest, or had identified the terrorists
who blew up the Pan-American jet over Lockerbie, Scotland, in
December 1988.

The British government officials who were in charge of the
long investigation absolutely denied any such thing the next day
and, further, said such stories undermined their attempts to
complete their work. Mr. Channon, who apparently had partak-
en of more champers than oysters, then claimed he hadn't said
any of the things in the four differing accounts, prompting the
tabloid Daily Mirror to shout in headlines, "YOU ARE A LIAR,
MR. CHANNON." Mr. Channon has been rather low-profile
ever since.

Another Lobby correspondent, explaining the advantages of
the system, pointed out the elasticity of what passes for the truth.
"The nice thing about it is that you aren't bound by the exact
words the minister said," he noted. "You can give it a bit of an
interpretive twist." Pity the poor reader.

On July 12, 1987, the London *Sunday Times* published excerpts
from a new book called *Spycatcher*. It was being issued simultaneously in the United States and contained very serious allegations about misconduct by the British security service, MI5.
Author Peter Wright, a former MI5 officer, charged that Sir
Roger Hollis, the former head of the agency, was a Soviet spy and
that elements within MI5 had begun a plot to destabilize Harold
Wilson's Labour government in the mid-1970s.

On July 13, the British government commenced proceedings
for criminal contempt against *The Sunday Times* and its editor,
Andrew Neil. The government also won an injunction against
publication of any further extracts of the book, despite Neil's
plea that it was arguing a ludicrous position. The KGB could buy
the book on Fifth Avenue in New York, but it wasn't all right for
the British public to purchase it in London.

There then ensued endless legal nonsense. On July 22, the

newspaper opposed the interim injunction in the high court–and won. The government went to the court of appeal on July 24–the paper lost. On August 13, Neil and his paper went to the law lords in the House of Lords (equivalent to our Supreme Court) and lost. The government got its interim injunction.

In the meantime, naturally, the notoriety had made Wright's book the hottest item in Britain. Hustlers stood beside the roads leading to New York airports to hawk the book at inflated prices to British visitors flying home.

To keep the injunction from becoming permanent, *The Sunday Times* went to the high court on December 21, 1987, and won. The government went to the court of appeal on February 10, 1988, and lost. The government appealed again to the House of Lords. On October 13, 1988, their lordships ruled–in favor of the newspaper–after fifteen months and some $6 million in legal costs spent by the government and the newspapers involved. It was supposed to be a famous victory, but it was hollow if you read the judgments.

Lord Keith, the senior judge of the five law lords, said, "I would stress that I do not base this [ruling] upon any balancing of public interest, nor upon any considerations of freedom of the press, but simply on the view that all possible damage to the interest of the Crown has already been done." In other words, there was no principle involved. It was simply that it was too late to do anything.

Lord Griffiths, saying that *The Sunday Times* was "tainted with Peter Wright's breach of confidence," had an even more remarkable attitude. He said that an editor, if given such accusations or allegations, "should inform the Treasury solicitor, a senior government law officer, that he was in possession of such information and intended to publish it. This would enable the government to apply for an injunction, so that a judge could decide whether the balance came down in favour of preserving secrecy or publication." The law lords, scarcely acknowledging any public interest in the press role of disclosure of public wrongdoing, apparently regarded the press as an arm of government.

The fight is constant. In the 1970s, the government tried to stop *The Sunday Times* from printing the cabinet diaries of Richard Crossman, a former member of a long-past Labour government, on the grounds that they were a breach of confidentiality. When an employee of British Steel gave a TV station documents revealing wrongdoing and incompetence by that company, a court ruled that the documents were confidential to the company and the television people had to hand them back.

In the famous thalidomide case, which really made the reputation of *The Sunday Times* as no longer just a fat staple full of nothing but war remembrances for the landed gentry, the paper ran articles based on company documents showing serious faults in the testing of that drug and its promotion. They were banned by the British courts because the documents were "confidential." The paper fought that legal battle for years and finally won a judgment from a European Community court (not a British one) in Strasbourg that the British ruling was a violation of free speech.

The Thatcher government has now introduced a new Official Secrets Act that will place a lifetime obligation of confidentiality on all MI5 officers. Officers who reveal anything about their duties, even if it is in the public interest, will be liable to prosecution, as will any newspaper that publishes the revelations.

In the *Spycatcher* farce, the government tried to intervene when it quite obviously would do no good to do so. *New York Times* columnist Anthony Lewis said that it reminded him of a scene out of *Mutiny on the Bounty* where Captain Bligh orders a crewman to be given one hundred lashes. After sixty lashes, the sailor doing the beating reports: "The man has died." Captain Bligh says, "I ordered one hundred lashes."

Editor Neil points out that the problem with the British judicial system is that the judges have always gone to the same schools, the same universities and the same clubs–and consequently have the same mindset–as the political ruling elite. That makes them not an independent judiciary. It's not that they are corrupt. It's just that they are out of the same Establishment mold and that's why they make the rulings they do.

In a remarkable speech in Washington in late 1988–remarkable in its pleas for assistance–Neil noted that Britain over the years had contributed, through John Locke and David Hume and Adam Smith and others, to freedom of speech in America.

"Now," he said, "not for the first time in this century, the old country needs a little help. We need some guidance. We need some advice. We need some inspiration. Come over and tell us about the freedom of the press in America and the benefits that flow from it. Come tell us how some of the things the British government is trying to do would be impossible in the United States. We need to shame our authorities into change. We need all the allies we can get. We look to America as the source of inspiration for what a free press should be all about. Help us."

Freedom of the press has been an issue since the invention of printing with movable metal type in the mid-fifteenth century. Governments, being governments, immediately felt threatened by the easy dissemination of information and opinion and quickly began to place restraints on press freedom. One of the first methods used to try to stem the flow of printed opinion was licensing–forbidding the printing or sale of any book without prior official approval.

In 1644, dear old John Milton, in his classic *Areopagitica*, made an early telling criticism of licensing of the press, calling for "the liberty to know, to utter, and to argue freely according to conscience . . ." It was one of the first arguments for freedom of the press, and the essay was influential in Parliament's decision to discontinue licensing in England in 1695.

The end of licensing in England did not mean true press freedom. The law of seditious libel, which banned criticism of government, became the state's prime control over printers. Truth was not a defense. In fact, "the greater the truth, the greater the libel" became the rule, for the argument was that the possibilities of unsettling the state of government were greater as the truth was greater.

In the American colonies, a major precedent in the struggle for freedom of the press was the trial in 1735 of John Peter Zenger, a New York editor accused of seditious libel for criticizing the colonial governor. Zenger was acquitted by a jury after his lawyer argued for the right to print matters "supported with truth."

Later in the eighteenth century, a British court finally freed two printers, who-contrary to law-had printed traditionally secret parliamentary debates. But not for 150 more years was the right to inspect public records and attend public meetings recognized by some legislatures in Europe and North America.

In 1948 the United Nations General Assembly adopted the Universal Declaration of Human Rights, which enunciated the principle that "everyone has the right to freedom of opinion and expression" and to "seek, receive and impart information and ideas through any media and regardless of frontiers." Almost no one pays any attention. Freedom of the press in fact is permitted in a relatively small number of countries, including Canada (hello there, Doug Small), the United States, Britain, some other members of the Commonwealth, though not all, Western Europe and parts of Latin America. Worldwide, there's a continuing drift in most nations towards restricted press systems. Freedom busts out in Poland. Freedom is suppressed in China.

The Americans, perhaps because of their experience with King George III, guard the principle very fiercely. Freedom of the press is guaranteed in the United States by the First Amendment to the Constitution, which states, "Congress shall make no law . . . abridging the freedom of speech, or of the press." But despite that, there are always those who attempt to encroach.

There was an early attempt by Congress to abridge press freedom with the Sedition Act of 1798, which outlawed false, scandalous, or malicious writings about government and its officials. The act was extremely unpopular and was not renewed when it expired in 1901. It wasn't until World War I and passage of the Espionage Act of 1917 (and its seditious libel amendment of 1918) that similar strictures were again placed on the press. A revised Espionage Act was reintroduced during World War II to protect against disclosure of military secrets. But it was never invoked because of the "self-discipline" of the press.

Another limitation on freedom of the press is prior restraint, the cause of the great showdown between press and government in the 1970s. In 1971 the U.S. Justice Department obtained a court order to halt the publication by *The New York Times* and other newspapers of the Pentagon Papers, a secret government study of the U.S. involvement in the Vietnam War–leaked by Daniel Ellsberg. But the U.S. Supreme Court lifted the restraining order, ruling that a government attempt to block news articles prior to publication carried "a heavy burden of presumption against its constitutionality."

The restrictive British libel laws that so intimidate the press were well illustrated by the Profumo case in which Harold Macmillan's government was toppled by two tarts. Fleet Street already knew that the forty-six-year-old war minister, John Profumo, was having an affair with nineteen-year-old party girl Christine Keeler. Profumo, married to prominent actress Valerie Hobson (*Great Expectations, Kind Hearts and Coronets*), was being tipped as a future prime minister. When it was discovered that Keeler was also sleeping with Captain Yevgeny Ivanov, the Soviet assistant naval attaché, the newspapers still held off and instead had a Labour MP ask a question in the House of Commons, leading Profumo to the lie (that there was "no impropriety whatsover" in his personal life) that ruined his career and forced his resignation. The newspapers cashed in on the story; but they didn't break it.

The Canadian example, as always, lies somewhere between the extremes of Britain and the United States. The difference between American society and Canadian society can be seen by their different attitudes to freedom of information legislation. Pushed by consumer activist Ralph Nader, the U.S. government produced freedom of information laws in 1966. After the Watergate scandal revealed the paranoia and secrecy that pervaded the administration of Richard Nixon, the legislation was improved (*i.e*, it became somewhat easier for citizens to wrestle information from their own government). After Ronald Reagan became president, the rules were (surprise!) tightened up again.

As the simple truth that knowledge is power became apparent, there was the gradual push in slower-moving Canada to insist that the public is entitled to share that power with the government and is best able to do so with access to government data. Following an intricate dance that included private members' bills, a federal government Green Paper, draft legislation by one government and subsequent legislation enacted by another government, the Access to Information Act was finally passed in 1982 and came into effect in 1983. (The Americans refer to "freedom of information." Canadians call it "access to information." Ah, there's the rub.)

Canada, building on the American experience, has one improvement. In the U.S., if the government refuses to give you the information requested, you have to take the government to court in hopes of getting the ruling overturned. In Canada, if the same happens, you can take your case to Information Commissioner Inger Hansen. If she finds the case legitimate, *she* takes the government to court and pays the costs.

More information comes out under the American legislation because American reporters are more aggressive at using this law. In fact, there's an indication that in Ottawa requests from the media have gone down since the legislation was introduced.

As it turns out, 48 per cent of all the Canadian requests last year came from businesses–mainly contractors seeking information about bids from competitors. Individual requests made up 27 per cent of the total and media requests just 9 per cent. Differing organizations made up 8 per cent and academics 3 per cent.

Requests under the act in the first year, 1983, numbered just 1,513, increasing to 5,450 in 1987 and 7,301 in 1988. They are expected to top 10,000 in 1989. Of that 1988 total, 5,866 of the requests were dealt with. Some 29 per cent of the Canadians involved got all the information they sought. Thirty-four per cent got "some" of what they wanted. Fourteen per cent of the seekers-after-information were directed elsewhere, and the other categories ranged down to "cabinet confidences": 0.6 per cent.

Timing is indicative of the difference in attitude between Washington and Ottawa. Under the American law, a response to a request must be given in ten days; in Canada, one-tenth the size of the U.S., thirty days. In essence, it usually works out to a forty-five-day to two-month delay before the information trickles out, but the Americans give it to you as soon as they get it. In Ottawa, they tend to wait until the last possible day before releasing it. Those English habits die hard.

"Were it left to me to decide whether we should have a government without newspapers or newspapers without a government," said Thomas Jefferson in 1787, "I should not hesitate for a moment to prefer the latter." And apparently meant it.

The American press is billed as one of the great bulwarks of democracy, dedicated to keeping the government honest. At times, when its white knight image has been a little brighter than usual, it has attracted hordes of enthusiasts.

After the Woodstein twins, the kids from the cop shop, brought down a president of the United States in 1974, the journalism schools of the U.S. and Canada were flooded with applicants, all the preppy youngsters who previously would have gone into law or masters of business administration courses suddenly seeing themselves as incipient Robert Redfords or Dustin Hoffmans with a notebook and a computer terminal. Cowboys were no longer the heroes, nor detectives, nor yuppie stockbrokers. *Reporters*, of all people, were the current idols.

What is interesting about the Watergate scandal is how little time it took for political manipulation, for puffery and bluffery, to gain ascendancy once again, with newspapers openly admitting they were powerless against the skillful and endlessly financed apparatus of government propaganda. For six years after Watergate, governments floundered. Nixon's truncated term was filled by the gormless Gerald Ford, a figure of fun who made Johnny Carson more than he made legislation. Ford was followed by Jimmy Carter (could the world take seriously a president who insisted on being called "Jimmy"?), who immediately destroyed the presidential cachet by walking the Inaugural route and carrying his own suitcase aboard Air Force One.

But once again in 1980, with the advent of the Reagan years, hype and PR and media manipulation crept back–and were, oh, so effective.

It should be no surprise. Reagan from Hollywood and his California slicksters, supreme through his two terms as governor there, were experts in how to stroke and smooth an appreciative Washington press. Michael Deaver, the Nancy Reagan close friend (later convicted of perjury after being charged with trying to make a quick million off his White House contacts) was a master of the photo opportunities that made his cardboard-figure president appear so impressive.

True, the Americans do not have the ingrained class system that so afflicts the Brits and therefore makes authority so, well, authoritative. One could never imagine, under the British system (a state-owned broadcasting service, oppressive libel laws) any English television figure being so cheeky and aggressive to Margaret Thatcher as Dan Rather was in the famous punch-up with George Bush in the 1988 presidential election campaign. Bush was so freaked out by the encounter that, some time later, while being interviewed by "Nightline" host Ted Koppel, he referred to him throughout as "Dan" until a frantic aide slipped him a note. At the finish, Bush apologized to Koppel (can one imagine Maggie Thatcher *apologizing* to a journalist?) for getting the name wrong. "Next time," replied the ever-cool Koppel, "just call me Barbara."

Big-ticket journalists may feel they have the clout to stick it to a presidential candidate, but there's the obverse side. Nothing corresponding to the British Lobby system exists officially in the United States, but press and politicians in Washington manage to achieve much the same chummy result by less formal means. The political handlers are wizards at this game. Because the millionaire broadcasters and columnists feel equal, they want to be let in on the action. The Reagans on arriving in Washington in 1980, coming from show-biz themselves, sensed that.

"The idea of making the press part of your inner circle, or

making them *believe* they were part of the inner circle," noticed Sanford Socolow, executive producer of the "CBS Evening News" during the Cronkite era, "was something that hadn't happened in a long time in Washington." Reagan immediately began to go to the right Georgetown parties. (Jimmy Carter thought it was terrible to go to Georgetown parties, but okay for his chief-of-staff, Hamilton Jordan, and his press secretary, Jody Powell, to pose as ragamuffins on the cover of *Rolling Stone.*)

"It was a very smart move," said Lyn Nofziger, a Reagan insider later acquitted on appeal for using his White House connections for gain. "They were determined to work *with* the Washington establishment, including the press, and not against it. That sensibility came from having operated in the big-league world of California politics and not the boonies of Georgia like the Carter people had."

Nancy Reynolds, long a personal friend of the Reagans and a skillful political organizer in California in the Gipper's early political days there, took a five-month leave of absence from her Washington public relations firm to make sure that the newcomers in the White House met and charmed the right people in Washington.

"It's like marrying into a new family when you move to Washington," Reynolds explained. The Carter people, she said, were invited places but never went and alienated the establishment so much the establishment went after them. "And that creeps into reporting. The impression was that the Carters were hicks. In fact, they entertained very well and were well educated. You never read that, though, because the Washington establishment had already made up its mind about them."

The Washington establishment certainly includes the important press people. Reynolds made every effort to have *Washington Post* owner Katharine Graham and Meg Greenfield, the *Post*'s editorial-page editor, get to know Nancy Reagan. Reagan insiders James Baker and Michael Deaver were available–very–on the social circuit.

ABC News Washington bureau chief George Watson observed that in another time "reporters may have viewed themselves as outsiders. They didn't belong to the inner circle to the degree they do now, when relatively well-paid reporters and government officials can move in the same social circles." In 1985, at the start of Reagan's second term, Watson went to a dinner party with one of his reporters that included the attorney-general of the United States, the Israeli ambassador and a prominent senator. "That happens more than it used to. Today as never before our reporters are part of the town's elite, which seems a reasonable factor in explaining why there is less of an adversarial tone in the coverage" of Washington.

It seems only natural, when one of the million-dollar anchor men is more prized as a Georgetown guest than a vice-president who doesn't know what language Latin Americans speak, and network correspondents at $300,000 make more than the highest politicians.

Of this new cosy relationship with the White House, former *Washington Post* writer William Greider said, "This used to drive me nuts. I thought it was just a waste of time, but they"–referring to his former colleagues and superiors–"*want* to have cabinet officers and important political types in the White House to lunch. It's a perfect Washington symbiosis–those people *want* to come to lunch."

The power lunches were most times held in a conference room down the hall from Katharine Graham's office in the *Post* building in midtown Washington. The guest would be seated at the middle of a long table flanked by either Mrs. Graham or her son Donald (now the publisher) or both. Present would be twenty or so *Post* editors and reporters. The importance of the lunch day's guest could be gauged by the grade of the menu served. Only the varsity squad from Pennsylvania Avenue got the Triple-A meal. Although most lunches were "on the record," Greider emphasized that the sessions were "not about getting news stories. It's about getting to know these people and getting a feel for who they are. The talk may be bullshit, but it takes on a different meaning when said over the intimacy of the luncheon table. The ambience is, 'We're all insiders here.' "

"Stroking"-the modern equivalent of the velvet glove that conceals the iron fist-seems to be the key. Treat the press as partners and they can be extraordinarily-sometimes perilously-cooperative.

In 1908, one of the finest reporters on *The New York Times*, William Bayard Hale, obtained a rare interview with Kaiser Wilhelm II. It went on for two hours, the Kaiser raging against foreign nations, especially Britain. It was in a very belligerent tone, along the lines that part of being a good Christian was the ability to go to war and that a little "jolly good fighting" was good for a nation.

It was such explosive material, David Halberstam explains in *The Powers That Be*, that Hale didn't dare cable it to New York and instead carried it home. His editors and publisher Adolph Ochs looked at the interview and eventually decided it should be shown to President Teddy Roosevelt in Washington. Roosevelt was shocked at the aggressive attitude and said, "I don't believe the Emperor wanted this stuff published. If he did, he's a goose." (As he proved to be.) The president said the *Times*, by killing the interview, could save mankind. And so the prophetic piece, revealing what the Kaiser indeed planned, was killed.

A half-century later, the same powerful newspaper, learning beforehand of President John Kennedy's planned invasion of Cuba at the Bay of Pigs, refrained from printing the news after listening to Washington advice that it would be imperilling national security. Kennedy, swearing that he would never listen to a Washington "expert" again, later confessed to *Times* men that they could have saved him his greatest embarrassment if they had followed their instincts and printed it, thus saving him from his folly.

If treating the press like government team players sometimes works all too well, treating them like lackeys tends to make them a little huffy. The same Kennedy was the darling of the White House press corps for his wit and the glamor of the wife he was cheating on. But as Halberstam recounts, when Kennedy didn't like the critical tone of the network news shows on his performance in the U.S. steel industry's strike crisis, he called

Federal Communications Commission chief Newton Minow and ordered Minow to threaten network executives with suspension of their licenses. Minow (the man who put a phrase into the language by calling American television "a wasteland") ignored the order.

In 1963, Kennedy met with the new publisher of *The New York Times*, thirty-seven-year-old Arthur Ochs Sulzberger, not a confident man, who had held his post only five months. Kennedy was displeased with the *Times* coverage out of Vietnam by Halberstam, then just twenty-nine and later a Pulitzer Prize-winner, one of the finest reporters of his generation and today a best-selling author. The president tried to bully the apprentice publisher about "your young man in Saigon" and suggested transferring him to Rome or Paris. Sulzberger, shaken by the blatant intimidation, immediately cancelled Halberstam's planned holiday so that it would not look as if the *Times* had listened to the advice.

Each country, each bully, has a different approach. Pierre Trudeau of Canada had a different method (leaving aside his use of the War Measures Act). It was essentially intellectual intimidation, he sensing immediately that the awed wretches of the Ottawa Press Gallery–nowhere near as educated as their counterparts in Washington or in the quality British press–were cowed by his erudition and his taste in women, his esoteric wit and his clothes, his worldly manner and his Montreal decadence.

The American press, despite its superior freedom and supposedly legendary vigilance, long turned a blind or an ignorant eye to the interesting case of James Baker III.

Baker, the smartest operator in Washington, a man who plans to be president after George Bush, is ten years younger than the empty suit who now occupies the White House. The two of them have been friends for thirty years, Ivy League products who have passed themselves off as Texans. Baker at least has credentials from the Lone Star State. His grandfather founded one of the largest law firms in Houston, which enabled the sly Baker to polish his gifts at Princeton while retaining his disarming southern drawl.

Bush, born of a Connecticut Brahmin family, his father a long-time senator, himself a product of elite private schools and Yale, and who faked a Texas "residency" via a Houston hotel room, befriended Baker through tennis club connections.

Another friend is Robert Mosbacher, now the commerce secretary (famous mostly because his bosomy flame-haired socialite third wife, Georgette, has solved the eternal female eyebrow problem by having a Terre Haute, Indiana, artist tattoo her *permanent* ones). The three men, all of them early millionaires, determined that they would make George Bush president thirty years hence, knowing that would make them major powers also. (The United States is now governed by Texans who are the president, the secretary of state, the commerce secretary and the chairman of the Senate Finance Committee.)

Baker is as smooth as silk, as cool as the tooled cowboy boots he wore to charm and awe the Brooks Brothers brigade of White House reporters who appreciated his clever leaks and ever-readiness to talk and go on the air for the required sound bites. He was applauded by the political and press insiders for convincing his intellectual inferior, Bush, to pull out of his Republican leadership battle with Ronald Reagan in 1980 in time to sew up the vice-presidential slot (and the Baker timetable for a 1996 shot at the White House).

Conventional wisdom thought he was a genius for then slipping into the role of Reagan's first chief of staff. Even more plaudits came from the Washington press corps when he arranged a clever switch of jobs with Donald Regan. While Regan crashed to earth due to Nancy Reagan's phone barrage and the farce of the Iran-contra Gippergate scandal, Baker became the new treasury secretary for the second Reagan term.

No one in the post-Watergate press, since Baker was such a smooth stroker of the right media buttons, ever cottoned to the fact that–as the world's arbiter over the growing crisis of Third World debts to mainly American banks, and specifically the

panic situation developing in Brazil and Mexico and Argentina–
he had a small problem of his own.

James Baker, the most powerful government financial figure in
the world, held a $2-million personal investment in the Chemical
Bank of America, which was stuck with a lot of South American
debt. Every time he said no to the debtor nations' pleas for relief
from their unpayable loans, the stock of Chemical Bank and its
sisters went up.

It was only when Baker became secretary of state under Bush
that anyone happened to notice this rather large conflict of
interest. Baker himself was apparently oblivious to it. The
Washington press was so charmed and so seduced by this man
who would appear anywhere, any time a camera was present–and
had so many times done a *sub rosa* deal with it for leaks that were
never attributed–that it had never bothered to examine his
fiduciary interest in decisions that kept the banks' wretched
Third World clients chained to their impossible debt loads.

Baker would not be secretary of state today if the lazy press,
suckered by his down-home style and ever-readiness to supply a
quote, had checked on his holdings.

Jim Wright, a honey-voiced slickster from Texas, as speaker of
the House of Representatives was third in line to the presidency
after that thin reed, Vice-President Dan Quayle, in the spring of
1989. He was under investigation by a special ethics committee of
his peers because of a phony job for his wife and a spurious
book-publishing deal, but since the House is heavily Democratic
he was thought able to survive the storm.

What did him in, however, was a story long known but
suppressed by the Washington congressional reporter insiders
who could be equated with the Lobby closed gang.

John Paul Mack was the powerful Jim Wright's closest aide. As
staff director of the Democratic steering and policy committee he
was an influential figure on Capitol Hill. But there was another
side to John Paul Mack. In 1973, he was the manager of a dry
goods store in Annendale, Virginia. A twenty-year-old student

by the name of Pamela Small went into his store to shop for window blinds. Mack took her into the storeroom where the blinds were kept and suddenly beat her over the head with a hammer, slashed her throat and chest with a knife, dumped her in her car and went off to a movie.

Pamela Small miraculously survived and led police to Mack. He was charged with attempted murder and later pleaded guilty to assault "with the intent to maim, disfigure, disable and kill." He was sentenced to eight years in prison, but spent only twenty-seven months in county jail before being paroled. He had a friend in high places: his brother is married to Wright's daughter. Wright, as an important Democrat, wrote a letter of support for Mack during the pre-sentencing investigation, and Wright's offer of a job on his congressional staff was a key reason Mack got out of jail so soon.

John Paul Mack steadily rose in power over the years. He never once apologized or offered a nickel toward his victim's medical bills. Although scarred and traumatized, Pamela Small gained a decent living as a lobbyist on Capitol Hill. Mack was doing much better than Small (being on the payroll at $89,500) when The Washington Post printed his story in May 1989. Mack, Small told the Post, "has got a very powerful, very important job now, and he wouldn't have it if he hadn't tried to kill me. I find that more than a little bizarre." Mack resigned within days of the story's appearance.

What was interesting is that the story did not appear on the front page of the Post or on any of its political pages. It was not written by one of its dozens of political reporters. It appeared on the front page of the Style section.

The Post's ombudsman, Richard Harwood, later informed the paper's readers that the Mack-Small story had been "suppressed" for more than two years by leading journalists in the congressional press gallery. The Fort Worth Star and Telegram broke the story in 1987. But Wright's press secretary, a former Post reporter, warned those Washington reporters who covered Wright that the story was coming and convinced the "biggies" (in Harwood's phrase) that the Mack-Small episode was a "non-story," claiming that the victim refused to talk on the record.

Harwood explained that the story finally appeared in *The Washington Post* because the Style section reporters prevailed over the objections of the congressional reporters-and someone finally had the wit to interview Pamela Small.

3

Mega-Media

In the capitalist world, freedom of the press
represents the freedom to buy the newspapers
and those who edit them, as well as the
freedom to buy, corrupt and mold public
opinion in the interests of the
bourgeoisie. – *Vladimir Ilyich Lenin*

I am in the business of making money, and I
buy more newspapers in order to make more
money to buy more newspapers to make more
money to buy more newspapers.
– *Lord Thomson of Fleet*

We all think that the bad old days of newspapers in bed with political parties was a turn-of-the-century thing, in less sophisticated and more partisan times, when papers in fact were rented out to one party or another. In truth, it wasn't that long ago.

David Halberstam in *The Powers That Be* lays out the incredible story of Kyle Palmer and the *Los Angeles Times*, now one of the better papers extant, but until two decades ago a shameless and shameful travesty of journalism.

Kyle Palmer was the chief political correspondent of the *Times*, a paper that had grown exceedingly rich on real estate manipulation. Owner Harry Chandler had become the largest land baron in southern California, and his descendants used the paper to reward friends (Republicans) and to punish enemies (Democrats, unions, any kind of social-welfare legislation).

In ordinary times, on ordinary newspapers, the title "chief political correspondent" would mean the senior political reporter on the staff who had the most insights, the most wisdom, and the best judgment on the politicians he was paid to cover and assess and criticize and peruse, for the benefit of his readers. Kyle

Palmer, on the Chandlers' Los Angeles sheet, was a hit-man on behalf of the Republican party.

In the 1930s, New York Times reporter Turner Catledge (many years later the paper's managing editor) went out to Los Angeles to cover Upton Sinclair, the Pulitzer Prize-winning author who was running on the socialist ticket for governor of California. As all visiting firemen do, he picked up the local paper, the Los Angeles Times, to find some news about this unusual and well-known candidate. There was scarcely a mention of him, no sign of his schedule or of where and when he might be speaking. So Catledge went to dinner with Palmer, the best-connected newspaperman in the state, and asked where Sinclair was speaking so he could observe him. "Turner," said Palmer, "forget it. We don't go in for that kind of crap that you have back in New York of being obliged to print both sides. We're going to beat this son of a bitch Sinclair any way we can. We're going to kill him." Which the Times, of course, did.

Even as late as 1958, a New York reporter sent to California to do an extensive story about the state's politics, in talking to Palmer, found that he was very cooperative and generous about passing on information about the Republicans. The reporter then asked about the Democrats. "Oh, we don't bother with them," Palmer replied.

Over forty years, Kyle Palmer chose the candidates for the Republicans, laid down party policies, actually floor-managed legislation through the legislature in Sacramento and told governors which bills to sign and which to reject. He and the Times created Richard Nixon. He was the political boss of California, his choices on the ballot listed on the Times editorial page before elections governing the voting of millions of voters. A young reporter from Time who first went to California was told, over and over again, that he should seek out "Mister Republican." The reporter, as Halberstam writes, "was somewhat surprised to find that Mr. Republican was, in fact, a working newspaperman."

About as far as you can get from the partisan Los Angeles Times – philosophically as well as geographically–is The New York

Times. In 1896, when Adolph Ochs bought the floundering *Times* for $75,000 in borrowed money, its circulation was some 9,000, it was $300,000 in debt, was losing $2,500 a week and had a grand total of two telephones and two typewriters. Most of the reporters wrote in longhand and were annoyed by the noise caused by the younger hands who typed.

Although he had never gone to college and aspired to be neither a writer nor a pundit, Ochs was a serious young man who had firm ideas about bringing out a *serious* newspaper. By 1900, despite the Spanish-American War, which was such a godsend to his jingoistic competitors, he had the *Times* in the black at a circulation of 82,000. If his rivals had signed up all the best comic strips of the time, Ochs made it a point of pride that the *Times* would never run comics–which obtains to this day. If the wildly successful papers of his city, Pulitzer's *World* and Hearst's *Telegram*, sold more than 300,000 copies with their yellow journalism, he would put out a dull paper because he liked a dull paper and he sensed that others did so also.

He listed the names of all the store buyers who came to New York to shop, a brilliant decision in retrospect since it helped make the *Times* the important paper of the retail fashion business–so apparent in its success a century later.

There were two other shrewd decisions down over the years that made it the dominant publication it is today. In 1898 the Spanish-American War broke out in Cuba. It was exactly the type of flag-waving spurious exercise in patriotism that Hearst and Pulitzer loved, and they rushed to Cuba with fleets of reporters and photographers and hype artists.

Knowing that he could not compete with the press lords in coverage–his circulation already dropping and his debt-ridden paper in jeopardy–Ochs determined to compete with them in price. Since they were charging two cents an issue, Ochs dropped the price of his far more serious paper from three cents to one cent–without changing his respectable tone.

It was a decision of genius. In a year, his circulation tripled. The Spanish-American War, of all things–so inimical to the *Times'* style–proved to be the making of the paper. Advertising zoomed along with the circulation, and the paper, because it had not compromised its values, became the right one to read for those in government and finance who needed to be told what they needed to know.

The second brilliant stroke that made the *Times* the paper of record came at the start of World War II, under publisher Arthur Sulzberger, son-in-law of Adolph Ochs. The paper, as David Halberstam pointed out in *The Powers That Be*, had in early days been called a paper owned by Jews, edited by Catholics and read by Protestants. Now it was locked into a constant struggle with the New York *Herald Tribune* which seemed to be gaining: the *Times* at 481,000, the *Trib* at 347,000.

In 1942 the U.S. government announced newsprint rationing, and the two rivals took diametrically opposed decisions on how to use their restricted smaller newspapers. Sulzberger thought this was not the time to get greedy, put a tough limit on advertising and decided to go for news.

The *Trib*, always jealous of the *Times'* hold on Manhattan department stores, perceived a chance to pass its longtime rival in advertising lineage. The *Trib's* profits did go up and those of the *Times* did go down and in 1943 the *Trib* won out, for the first time, in department store advertising.

But it was an illusory victory. The *Times*, with its blanket coverage of the war, convinced readers of its more serious nature. With the war over, newsprint rationing was dropped and the *Times*, in a struggle in which only one serious morning paper could survive, drew away easily. By 1950 it was 544,000 to 340,000, and by 1960 it was 686,000 to 352,000. Ball game over.

Even so, there is no reason for a paper to be this hard to read. The *Times* almost shouts at the reader–"We dare you to plough through this!" There is a typographical S-M touch to it: if you the reader want the news and information contained therein, you're going to have to suffer to extract it.

Type jammed up against old-fashioned column rules that even the *Times* of London has long since banished. Headlines that go on forever:

GORBACHEV IS DUE
IN BEIJING TODAY
FOR SUMMIT TALKS

END OF 30-YEAR DROUGHT

**Fate of Cambodia Is Expected
to Be the Major Topic –
Students Await Arrival**

After that, is there any reason to read the story? You've got it all. All, perhaps, but the pomposity of the reportorial bylines, this paper being the repository for pomposity. On the front page one can find over-weening ambition in the form of "Clyde H. Farnsworth" or "Nicholas D. Kristof" or "E.J. Dionne, Jr.," or "John H. Cushman, Jr."–scribes whose desire for attention outweighs their copy.

Columnists can get by with names like James Reston and William Safire and Tom Wicker, but reporters somehow must be known as "David E. Pitt" from Panama or "Esther B. Fein" from Tallin in the U.S.S.R. From Washington, it's "Thomas L. Friedman," from Beirut, "Ihsan A. Hijazi" and from Moscow, "Francis X. Clines." "B. Drummond Ayres Jr.," is reporting from Washington this day. John Cleese has his Ministry of Silly Walks. In my own ministry of journalistic *New York Times* pomposity, B. Drummond Ayres Jr., always comes out the winner. Even the best reporter on the paper, Johnny Apple, goes under the byline of R.W. Apple, Jr.

The February 24, 1989, issue of the *Times* had six stories on the front page. Susan F. Rasky told how the Senate Armed Services Committee had voted 11-9 against John G. Tower's nomination as Secretary of Defense. Nathaniel C. Nash wrote about the Federal Reserve Board's attempt to calm depositor fears by stating that it stands ready to provide cash to any insolvent savings institution. Craig R. Whitney, from London, informed us that British author Salman Rushdie, under death sentence by Ayatollah Khomeini, will never be able to go back to the highly visible and active life he had been leading. Eric N. Berg, from Chicago, explained that Sears, Roebuck and Company was cutting prices by 50 per cent on three-fourths of its inventory in an attempt to revive its sagging profits and rebuild market share.

Only Susan Chira, writing from Tokyo on the burial of Emperor Hirohito, and Martin Tolchin, writing on the probable confirmation of Dr. Louis W. Sullivan as Secretary of Health and Human Services after he apologized for having "misspoken" on the abortion issue, dared to have their bylines appear naked without an initial.

The *Times* is painfully intent on being fair. To such an extent that when a wolf-pack of teen-agers from Harlem gang-raped and beat to near-death a twenty-eight-year-old Yale graduate who was a Wall Street investment banker jogging in Central Park – and white – the paper that boasts "All the News That's Fit to Print" couldn't bear to print in its initial 1989 story that any or all of the young animals were black or Hispanic.

It is ponderous in style, stiff in execution, operated under the belief that in publishing the brilliant Russell Baker, who writes a droll and increasingly cutting column, it has dispensed its obligation to laughter. Only William Safire, among its endless political columnists, has the imagination to realize that wit can actually be involved in a serious political discussion.

It's a given that all great papers (and distinctive papers) are the reflection of a personality at the top. Just as Lord Beaverbrook put his jingoistic stamp on the London *Daily Express* when it was a power, Beland Honderich has had his fingerprints all over *The Toronto Star*. Hearst papers bore the imprint of the bullying William Randolph Hearst just as Joseph Pulitzer was a forceful figure whose name entered the language long before his grandson delighted the supermarket tabloids by getting involved in the messy divorce case with the coke-snorting bride, Roxanne (known as the strumpet who slept with a trumpet).

The *Punch* of Malcolm Muggeridge's day could only have been edited by Muggeridge, just as Peter Newman forcefully put his views and his personality into *Maclean's* as he turned it from a general interest magazine into a newsmagazine. So it is with *The Washington Post*, which has evolved into a very good newspaper, rivalling and sometimes beating the mighty *New York Times*. The *Post* has been the product of two personalities: an editor in Ben Bradlee who is flashy and gutsy and a publisher in Katharine Graham who is shy and diffident but has the sense to back up her editor in times of crisis and showdown.

When James Reston was appointed Washington bureau chief of *The New York Times* in 1953, he became by dint of the position and his talent the most important journalist in town, if not the whole country. Born in Glasgow, at one time the press agent of the Cincinnati Reds, he set out to fill his bureau with the finest young reporters in America. He hired Russell Baker, the paper's shrewd satirist who won the Pulitzer Prize for his book on his childhood. And Anthony Lewis and Tom Wicker, both now regular *Times* columnists. And Neil Sheehan, whose book on the Vietnam non-war, *A Bright Shining Lie*, nine years in the making, was an instant best-seller when it came out in 1989. And Hedrick Smith, who won a Pulitzer for his reporting from Moscow and produced another best-seller in 1988 with a fat, fat book, *The Power Game: How Washington Works*. (Americans like fat books and thin women.)

Always with an eye out for new talent, Reston asked Baker one day if there were any bright new guys in town. "Well, yes," replied the young Baker, "there's this bright guy Ben Bradlee who's just back from Paris." "Bradlee," said Reston. "Yes, I've seen him around. He looks like a bit of a cad."

Ben Bradlee *does* look a bit of a cad, with his slicked-back hair and Franchot Tone looks (rather the precursor of the Los Angeles Lakers' coach Pat Riley), resembling a baddie in an old French movie. But he was born to the purple. (Once, when a journalist friend was seriously ill and in need of blood transfusions, Bradlee wrote to him in the hospital, offering to be the donor, and noting that, further, it would be "blue blood.")

Moneyed and well educated (in the words of his friend Art Buchwald he battled his way up through the school of hard knocks of St. Mark's private school and Harvard), he arrived back in Washington from Paris in 1957 just in time to be made the capital's bureau chief for *Newsweek*. It was his finder's fee for helping *Post* publisher Philip Graham buy *Newsweek*.

He moved into a chic Georgetown townhouse just five doors down from a young Massachusetts senator preparing for a run at the presidency. Jack and Jackie Kennedy and Ben and Antoinette Bradlee made a smashing foursome (not sullied by the fact that Kennedy, apparently unknown to Bradlee, was having a prolonged affair with Mrs. Bradlee's divorced sister). Kennedy and Bradlee, both charming, well-fixed and with an eye for the ankle, were a perfect match. "If Bradlee had been a politician," David Halberstam writes, "he would have been Kennedy and if Kennedy had been a journalist he would have been Bradlee."

For *Newsweek*, always fighting against the superior forces of *Time*, it was a dream connection, Bradlee phoning in time after time on weekly deadline with inside information on what the Kennedys were thinking or eating or doing at a time when the nation, if not the world, was fascinated by the Camelot that had succeeded the dowdy golfer Eisenhower.

In Washington, access is everything and Bradlee–partying with the Kennedys, invited on board their plane while the *Time* men had to go steerage on the press jet–demonstrated the journalistic joys of having friends in high places. *Time* fumed.

When, just two months before his friend Jack Kennedy was assassinated in Dallas, the disturbed Phil Graham took a shotgun and blew his head off (Graham's wife being in another room of their home at the moment), Kay Graham badly needed the strong presence of Ben Bradlee to teach her the newspaper business. In time, they would become the most celebrated duo in American journalism, bringing down a president with his brio and her balls, an editor-publisher relationship that exists, O Lord, in too few newspapers.

Bradlee had style and he invented, for the formerly stodgy *Post*, the most arresting feature of his thick and lucrative paper that operates in an effective monopoly in the fat-cat, recession-proof city with the highest family income (even despite the black slums) of any metropolitan area in the country. It is called Style, and is the most fetching, best-written example of all the "life-style" sections undertaken by all major papers in the knowledge that the news now comes by the idiot box and what newspapers can do is entertain and inform in ways the thirty-second sound-bite experts never can.

Style, laid out beautifully with witty, punster headlines and arch photographs, is to newspapers what Tina Brown's *Vanity Fair* is to magazines. *People* magazine for intellectuals, it features stunningly long profiles on the glitterati. There are ninety staffers in all involved in its production and individual bylines—gifted profile writers and puncturers of show-biz person-alities—may appear only every month or so. It features the best television critic on the continent, Tom Shales, book reviews, gossip, gossip, gossip—which Washington (as well as the super-market check-out counters) loves.

The star of Style, in its early days, was Sally Quinn, a bright and blonde feature writer who could get inside the skin of the most aloof cabinet minister or media star with her highly personal dissections of their male disguises. Her most cele-brated—and highly debated—piece was an interview with the sinister-looking Zbigniew Brzezinski, Richard Nixon's Montreal-born National Security Adviser. She not only suggested in her story that the supremely confident man was making a pass at her, but that his fly was half undone—not, uh, entirely by accident.

The *Post* is heavily (*i.e.*, passionately) Democratic in a town that is overwhelmingly Democratic, and Bradlee, in the face of many raised eyebrows, backed Quinn's version of the events in Brzezinski's office and printed the controversial piece. Before or after, he also became greatly enamored of the winsome blonde, some twenty years his junior, and in a great newsroom scandal that titillated and entertained all Washington, took up with her, ended his "perfect" marriage to the woman that Jackie Kennedy had always said was in fact Jack's ideal, and married Sally and had a child.

One night at the Rock Creek Drive mansion of Ambassador

Allan Gotlieb and wife Sondra (far too late in the night, apparently), I said to Bradlee that I had known Sally briefly when we both covered the Montreal Olympic Games in 1976 and that I was going to get my columns into his paper. "Write me a letter," he rasped and moved rapidly toward the bar. I never did make it into the *Post*. Loose lips sink ships.

On the night of June 17, 1971, Katharine Graham, then the relatively new publisher of *The Washington Post*, was presiding over a party for a retiring *Post* official at her big house on R Street at the top of the Georgetown hill. Executive editor Ben Bradlee at that same moment was in his own Georgetown home feverishly going over the Pentagon Papers with a group of reporters, editors and lawyers. *The New York Times* had published three installments of the classified papers before the U.S. Justice Department had succeeded in stopping publication. Now the *Post* had got hold of the same crucial documents.

Ellis Close, author of *The Press: Inside America's Most Powerful Newspaper Empires–From the Newsrooms to the Bedrooms*, relates how Katharine Graham was called away from her lawn party in the middle of a toast by a phone call from the Bradlee house:

> She finished the toast, picked up the phone, and listened. First, board chairman Fritz Beebe told her the decision would have to be hers. Then, Bradlee, Chalmers Roberts, and a succession of editors and writers said it was vital that the *Post* publish. . . .
>
> She asked Beebe what he would do, and he told her he probably would not publish. The minutes ticked away. She weighed the advice of the lawyers, all urging caution. . . .
>
> Beebe's words unnerved her. . . . Never once had she ignored his advice. Yet all her editors were convinced that morale on the fifth floor would crumble if she said no.
>
> Graham gave the go-ahead, the presses started and the *Post* was one with the *Times*. . . . By month's end both newspapers had won the right to publish.

Most everyone in journalism agrees that the Pentagon Papers decision marked the moment when the *Post* entered the top bracket of American papers–positioning itself for its Watergate triumph.

More and more of the print media these days are carrying the fingerprints of fewer and bigger players, as the communications titans flex their takeover muscles. What is the impetus?

Some fifteen years ago, an interesting book titled *Four Faces of Man* was published in Britain. It was a study of Churchill, as done by four experts. The concept, a shrewd one, was to assess how history would eventually judge the greatest Englishman of his age.

A political analyst wrote how, in time, Churchill might be viewed as a successful or an unsuccessful politician. A military expert looked at his actual record as a war strategist. A literary figure projected how the critics down the ages might regard Churchill as a writer, considering his voluminous output. And, finally, a psychologist gave his judgment on the brilliant statesman in light of his rather unusual childhood.

The boy's father, gifted with a beautiful American wife and a lineage that went back to the first Duke of Marlborough in 1650, was presumed by his promise to be a future prime minister. But Lord Randolph Churchill contracted syphilis, it went to his brain, and the young Winston and his mother sat in the Commons gallery to watch him stumble and stammer in mid-debate and grow mute, his mind gone. He died at only forty-six.

The psychologist contributing to *Four Faces of Man* said that all the studies of men whose fathers died while they were young showed that the experience manifested itself in one of two ways: insatiable ambition or sexual conquest. This is of passing interest, since others whose fathers have died while their sons were young include Pierre Trudeau, John Turner, René Lévesque and Brian Mulroney. We are all shaped by our background.

The past, it seems, also drives the mega-media men who want to take over the global communications scene. All indications are that, as the twenty-first century approaches, there will be perhaps six or eight corporate giants controlling the world's media concerns. One of them is Maxwell Communications Corp. One of them is Rupert Murdoch's News Corporation Ltd. Someone aspiring to these big leagues is Conrad Black, who now is a very big player in the London media world, owns some 185 papers encompassing Canada and the United States and has bought the influential *Jerusalem Post*, which he plans to plant on the streets of New York by satellite transmission.

All three are driven by childhood animosities.

Robert Maxwell is a Czechoslovak Jew who, as a refugee, became a British citizen, had a very good war as a British officer and was decorated for his bravery and daring. He became a loud and notorious Labour MP, widely disliked for his ambition. Having changed his name to disguise his Jewishness, he finally perceived that his dream of becoming Labour leader and prime minister was really not quite on and so proceeded to become a capitalist who would surpass most all capitalists. Beat them at their own game.

"Information," Maxwell says, "is as precious a commodity as energy. The communications industry is merely duplicating what happened to the energy industry fifty years ago." The twenty-first century, he believes, "will be a communications century, and will be dominated by eight or ten or twelve communications companies that are going to play the role of the Seven Sisters in communications. There just aren't that many with the kind of resources required to play communications vertically, from pulp at the foot to satellites at the top—and to play it on a global scale." Of this handful of worldwide media conglomerates he is determined his will be one.

Maxwell, because of his background, knows he will never really be accepted in Britain or some other places (he actually put in a higher bid than Black did for *The Jerusalem Post*, but was rejected) and has gone on a buying spree in the United States, where pedigrees are not quite so important.

The animus that drives Rupert Murdoch, first of all, is that he is Australian. "Part of the Australian character," he has explained, "is wanting to take on the world. It's a hard, huge continent inhabited by a few European descendants with a sense of distance from themselves and their roots. They have a great need to prove themselves."

His investment banker says, "Rupert has been an outsider wherever he's gone." His father, Sir Keith Murdoch, shipped him off at age ten to Geelong Grammar School, an elite boarding school with a military cast. The rebellion came early. He gambled heavily and started an unauthorized student publication.

Sent to Oxford with the usual Australian chip on the shoulder, he declared himself a socialist and had a bust of Lenin prominent in his rooms. (The young Murdoch may not have known, as the older Murdoch might have been amused to find out, that Lenin in a 1920 speech in Moscow demanded: "Why should any man be allowed to buy a printing press and disseminate pernicious opinion calculated to embarrass the government?")

When his father died in 1962 as Murdoch was starting his final year at Oxford, he assumed he would eventually be taking over the three provincial newspapers his father had owned. To his astonishment, Murdoch discovered that his father had never been granted any substantial equity in the Herald and Weekly group and, further, that one of Sir Keith's papers had been sold to his former employers in order to pay death taxes. Murdoch was outraged. "The great driving force in Rupert's life," says his longtime mentor Sir Edward Pickering, "is the feeling that his father was cheated." Another friend adds, "Rupert felt the family was done down. That fire burns inside him still."

Today, his newspapers control 60 per cent of the market in Australia and more than one-third of the market in Britain.

Conrad Black as a youth was sent to Upper Canada College in the center of Toronto, where the sons of the Establishment are supposedly turned into young gentlemen. He hated it and he hated the masters. John Fraser, now the editor of *Saturday Night* magazine, which Black owns, attended UCC with Conrad and in his slim book *Telling Tales* recalls Black's unrelenting hatred of the institution and his constant rebellion.

Conrad Black was expelled from Upper Canada College in the

biggest single scandal in the college's history. With two accom-
plices, he managed to steal a copy of every single final exam and
then sold them to his fellow students–on a sliding scale depending on their family's worth. As much as half the school
population may have been involved. A number of the boys
(presumably those who, for whatever reason, did not buy)
burned him in effigy on his father's front lawn. Fame came
early.

In the past, many newspapers, as we know, were blatant sheets of
propaganda for one political party or the other. That was then
the accepted mode. Today? The corporate giants have their own
agenda. Like governments and politicians, the really big figures in
the media can get to the point where they forget what they are
there for. Early in 1989, the multibillion-dollar forces of Time
Inc. announced a proposed merger with the multibillion-dollar
forces of Warner Communications Inc., the old Warner Bros.
movie outfit that now numbers among its parts, if you can believe
it, Cris-Craft boats. The new giant was supposed to become the
world's largest media conglomerate with a combined value of $18
billion–far surpassing global leader Bertelsmann AG of West
Germany–and has world sales of some $6 billion.

The Time Inc. empire includes *Time* and *Life* and *Fortune* and
People and *Sports Illustrated* and *Money* and has millions of
readers. The announcement of the proposed merger deal with
Warner was made on a Saturday afternoon. Both *Time* and its
chief rival, *Newsweek*, go to press Saturday night. *Newsweek* had
a two-page article on the historic deal. *Time* had nothing.

The *Time* people explained that they wanted to include the
announcement in the same issues of their other weeklies, *People*
and *Sports Illustrated*. The news, as it turned out, wasn't
important. Informing the public wasn't the prime consideration.
Corporate politics came first.

The big conglomerates both dominate and narrow debate.
With the cross ownership between the media and the stock
market–Conrad Black goes from Massey-Ferguson to supermarkets to mines to newspapers, Maclean Hunter goes from maga-

zines to radio to TV-media opinion and moral outlook become increasingly homogeneous.

In 1970, monopoly newspaper chains put out 58 per cent of all copies of newspapers in Canada. By 1980, it was 77 per cent. The single most influential newspaper columnist in Canada, in fact, may be Stewart MacLeod-a name not heavy in Rosedale-who writes a daily column from Ottawa for the 41 Thomson papers in this country.

In 1937 Roy Thomson, he of the Coke-bottle-bottom eye-glasses, bought a Sudbury radio station for $200. That was the basis for his empire that eventually led to his purchase of a title in London that made him Lord Thomson of Fleet. His real fortune, however, came when, with his usual prescience, he invested heavily in North Sea oil, a Canadian bumpkin who could see before the British were held to ransom by OPEC, that he who controlled energy controlled the world. Ownership of undersea oil resources in those days was even better than a private television station.

The Thomson business empire, in restructuring its operations, has surprised some people by selling off all its North Sea oil interests for $700 million. There's a clear reason for it. It's putting that money into its new determination to become a newspaper-information giant. Energy is no longer the most important or profitable concern in the world. Information is.

The newly christened Thomson Corp.-a merger of Thomson Newspapers Ltd. and International Thomson Organization Ltd.-will emerge as the world's most lucrative newspaper-information conglomerate, with profits of $1.4 million each day.

"Knowledge is power," wrote Thomas Hobbes in the Leviathan in 1651, obvious truth to us today. It is not only power, it is extremely profitable power. Robert Maxwell knows it. Conrad Black also knows it. He has shed his tractor factories and supermarkets and Norcen energy concerns to concentrate on information. With newspapers and magazines in North America, Britain, and Israel, he now threatens to move into Europe via Paris.

Pierre Berton certainly knows it. He became the first working journalist in Canada to become a millionaire through his own production of material in newspapers, magazines, television and radio. He sensed the need among Canadians for information about their own supposedly "dull and boring" history and demonstrated it through his railway books and tales of the north that so infuriated academics because they were actually readable.

Peter Newman followed, surely a millionaire now through his love-hate relationship in his books with the Canadian Establishment and his Hudson's Bay Company bonanza that was worth a $500,000 advance from Penguin Books.

Information is power. It's why the purveyors of it are richer than bankers. The sports pages are aflame with the news that Orel Hershiser may now through a multi-year contract be making more money than John Elway or Warren Moon, or even Ben Johnson. But no one blinks that these kings of entertainment have long been surpassed by the Six Million Dollar Man, Dan Rather, or by Diane Sawyer at $2.1 million.

And the instruments of this power? The papers and magazines and television stations–what are they like? Society tends not to worry much about the health of newspapers. In the United States and Canada, the dependence on advertising is the determining factor. In Italy, most newspapers are subsidized by political parties or industrialists. Anthony Sampson notes in *The New Anatomy of Britain* that "while free enterprise may have produced good cars, refrigerators and aircraft, it is much more doubtful whether it has produced good newspapers."

The British read more newspapers than anyone on earth. It is not because the papers are so good; most of them would appal a fourteen-year-old Canadian. It is because the Tight Little Island is so compact (and in one time zone) that the same newspapers can arrive on the same morning from Land's End to John O' Groats. The Brits read twice as many papers per capita as the Americans (though U.S. papers, granted, are much thicker). At the height of its power, the London *Daily Mirror* sold five million copies a day, more than *Pravda* or *Izvestia*.

When foreigners think of British newspapers they always think of *The Times* of London, regarded as the exemplar of what serious journalism is all about. It still is, as someone described it, a sort of parish magazine for the Establishment, publishing obituaries of people no one else has ever heard of, but its reputation as "The Thunderer" has gone with the wind.

For more than two hundred years, *The Times* has lived in a sheltered world created by its own aura. Its circulation, which in 1800 was bigger than that of all its competitors combined, by the 1960s had slipped to 240,000 (in a market of fifty million people) while *The Vancouver Sun*, in comparison, then sold 250,000 papers in a market of some two million.

The Times above all has that mystique, always being more reminiscent of Westminster Abbey than Piccadilly Circus. Its letters to the editor are rather like a private debating chamber. Its social columns are an intriguing guide to Society. "Lady Violet Bonham Carter wishes to express her deep gratitude," read an entry on December 6, 1964, after her life peerage was announced, "for all the generous messages she has received, to which she will reply individually as soon as possible."

There was the famous brief item that appeared after the nude corpse of a woman had been discovered in Hyde Park. The body, reported *The Times*, "had been decapitated, dismembered and disembowelled, but not interfered with."

Though no longer The Thunderer of legend, the paper still likes to give the impression that it is read by everyone who matters. To buttress its 1960s ad campaign declaring that "Top People Read *The Times*," it commissioned a survey of the so-called "top people." Questionnaires were sent to 6,474 people mentioned in *Who's Who*. Sixty-three per cent of them replied and the results showed that 70 per cent of the total read *The Times*, with a breakdown of the professions as follows: "Top Deans and Teachers," 70 per cent; "Top Businessmen," 79 per cent; "Top Civil Servants," 85 per cent; "Top Politicians," 71 per cent; "Top Executives" (administrators in public service), 85 per cent; "Top Professional Men" (in government service), 83 per cent.

The Times doesn't push those figures today. In retrospect, it has never really recovered its early reputation ever since it was at the heart of the pre-war Chamberlain appeasement policy toward Hitler. Geoffrey Dawson, its editor for twenty-nine years, personally cut and edited the despatches of his European correspondents and–in *The Times'* own candid history–confesses the nature of his journalistic approach to the Germans: "I did my utmost, night after night, to keep out of the paper anything that might hurt their susceptibilities."

It brings to mind Humbert Wolfe's lament:

> You cannot hope to bribe or twist
> Thank God, a British journalist:
> But seeing what the man will do
> Unbribed, there's no occasion to.

An indication of the decline of *The Times*, post-war, was that Roy Thomson was able to acquire it. It was one thing for Max Aitken, a brilliant, bullying hustler from New Brunswick, to own the brash and jingoistic London *Daily Express*. For Roy Thomson–son of a barber, peddler of radio sets in northern Ontario, proprietor of the Moose Jaw *Times-Herald* – to own *The Times* was something else. It was the ultimate indication of a tired English Establishment, weary of war and not fit for the aggressive new global economy, surrendering the paper of Lord Northcliffe and Lord Astor and Lord Kemsley and Sir William John Haley to a commoner from Canada who didn't even have a title. Not to worry. He soon bought one. Lord Thomson of Fleet.

Thomson, in the delightful phrase of Anthony Sampson, "enjoyed being brutally frank about money in the way some people enjoy using four-letter words about sex." He was already at the advanced age of fifty-nine when he went to Edinburgh (his great-grandfather came from Scotland) and, with the backing of the Royal Bank, bought *The Scotsman*. He arrived just in time for the advent of commercial television in Scotland, bought 80 per cent of the shares in Scottish Television and became a multimillionaire. On his own much-quoted admission, ownership of a private TV station was "a licence to print your own money."

Thomson's bland greed puzzled the Brits. In the United States, he had papers in the South supporting segregation and others in the North attacking it. "I've got money so I'm a Conservative," he once told a reporter. "If anyone with much money supports Labour, I suspect it's a gimmick."

Lord Burnham of the London *Daily Telegraph* had another question. "Is it a good thing for a man to have the power to sack a hundred editors? I think not." Cecil Harmsworth King (nephew of Lord Northcliffe, who invented modern journalism and died of megalomania) was the most powerful post-war press baron on Fleet Street. His *Daily Mirror* was instrumental in bringing Churchill down. Of Thomson, he said, "At first he said he wanted to buy a hundred newspapers. Now he wants a total of two hundred. This strikes me as a little odd, a little eccentric."

Thomson was odd, granted, but even his paperclip-obsessed mind could not make a profit on *The Times*. The removal of the classified ads that covered the entire front page was one sign of the reality that The Thunderer indeed was gone. The final clue was when the Thomsons, signalling defeat, sold the grand old sheet to yet another colonial, Rupert Murdoch, the "Dirty Digger" from Down Under.

The symbiotic nature of the press and the politicians was never better demonstrated than in the revolution that rendered Fleet Street obsolete. Like all good Australians, Murdoch cannot stand the "poms." He does not try to hide his anglophobia. Anna Murdoch, his beautiful forty-four-year-old second wife, says, "Great Britain will accept you if you're willing to join and play by the rules. Rupert wasn't willing. He went to Great Britain to challenge Fleet Street, not because he loved Great Britain."

Murdoch first burst onto the London scene in 1969 with his purchase of the *News of the World* (popularly known as the *Nudes of the World*), which serves its six million readers a weekly stew of the never-failing English formula of sex, sin and soccer. He then picked up the London *Sun*, a down-at-the-heels tabloid, and transformed it by taking it even further downscale–the first daily in London to feature, on page three every day, topless popsies. The circulation went from 800,000 to four million–proving something about the sexual frustration of the English male–and made it one of the most profitable papers in the world.

Card-carrying members of the stiff-upper-lip set were really discombobulated, however, when the audacious Aussie in 1981 took *The Times* off the hands of the relieved Thomsons, who had proven themselves brilliant in North Sea oil but lousy at running the icon of British journalism. Murdoch, true to his vulgar form, introduced a circulation-aimed lottery gimmick and semi-cleaned-up pieces on sex-starved surgeons.

"He's not in newspapers to make the world a better place," says Sir William Rees-Mogg, former editor of *The Times*. But he remade the British newspaper scene. Fleet Street publishers for decades had been at the mercy of their print unions, which clung stubbornly to hoary featherbedding practices. Some newspapers had eighteen men assigned to presses that required only four. The unions refused to let the owners install the computer terminals that all North American papers had long ago accepted; British papers were still setting type with hot lead.

Murdoch now owns 34 per cent of newspaper circulation in Britain (the *Sun* is the largest-selling daily and the *News of the World* is the largest-selling Sunday paper). He is a great fan of Margaret Thatcher and is not shy about showing it through the slant of his newsprint. Arthur Scargill's coal miners brought down the Edward Heath government but couldn't bend Maggie. She waited them out in a two-year strike and then took on the other unions, bringing in legislation banning secondary picketing–the advantage that Murdoch wanted.

Murdoch, spurning the sacred traditions of Fleet Street, announced he was building a $140-million new newspaper plant at Wapping near the docks in London's east end and would stock it with a reduced workforce, using modern technology. The print unions refused to make any concessions and, while bitter negotiations dragged on, the Wapping plant sat empty for two years.

With the military strategy of a Montgomery, Murdoch set a trap. He announced he was going to start a new tabloid, the *London Post*, which would be printed at Wapping. He ordered computerized typesetting equipment from the United States and recruited outside labor. When everything was in place, he cancelled plans for the new paper and moved his four existing papers to Wapping. The unions went on strike and he fired 6,000 of the strikers. Wapping resembled Beirut, with wild rioting, armies of police, guard dogs and barbed wire, but Murdoch got his papers out, inspiring other British publishers to take on their antiquated unions.

New boy Conrad Black, who had just bought the London *Daily Telegraph* for a price that was a steal, moved to a new site in the Docklands with modern production and printing technology and turned the stodgy paper from a money-loser into what Black says is an "astronomical professional and commercial success."

Black is also a great friend of Mrs. Thatcher, proudly displaying her at the Economic Summit in Toronto in the summer of 1988, at his celebrated annual Hollinger black-tie dinner, which, until this momentous occasion, had always been stag. Maggie dines out on the story, in London, that Conrad is so far to the right of her that he makes her feel like a "wet" (her contemptuous term for the doves she has purged from her cabinet). It is commonly assumed, among those cognizant of Conrad's sumptuous ego, that he can have a spot in the House of Lords whenever he signals the time would be propitious, an event that, at forty-four, would make him the eminent teen-ager among the troglodytes slumbering in that parlor of repose. Lord Black of Wapping would have a faintly erotic air to it.

The biggest secret in Canada is that the third-richest man in the world has three sons called Greasy, Oily and Gassy. K.C. Irving, as we know, owns New Brunswick and, in the most disgraceful monopoly in the country, controls the information that the residents of that backward province receive.

Ninety-year-old K.C. Irving, a man hard to like, has exploited his poor province to build an empire that has made him the world's third-richest non-monarch. *Forbes*, the American business magazine, says that he is worth $10 billion, topped only by two Japanese businessmen with fortunes of $12 billion–real estate magnate Taikichiro Mori and transportation baron Yoshiaki Tsutsumi. He is in the league of Queen Elizabeth, whose assets total $10.4 billion.

Irving, who hides out in Bermuda much of the time to avoid succession duties (he likes to make money out of Canada but he doesn't like to hand any of it back) has willed his fortune to his sons, James, Arthur and Jack, who long ago acquired their nicknames of Greasy, Oily and Gassy. The Irving empire, probably the largest privately owned conglomerate in North America, controls 25 per cent of all the province's timberlands and has a fleet of ships larger than the Canadian navy. Irving owns the largest oil refinery in Canada, trucking lines, automobile dealerships, a shipyard, a tugboat company, pulp and newsprint mills, sawmills, office and apartment buildings, ironworks, home fuel companies–and a security company that may be the fourth largest police force in New Brunswick. The old man is a nineteenth-century industrialist who treats the province like his own plantation.

The man who made his fortune out of Canadian resources has devised a corporate structure that hides his dealings through holding companies incorporated in the tax-free haven of Bermuda. In 1971, the Seafarers' International Union of Canada actually had to abandon a campaign to become certified as the bargaining agent for the crews of six Irving ships because it could not find out the precise ownership of the vessels.

Having a monopoly on the province's gas stations is bad enough. What is worse is that the Irvings own all four of the province's English-language daily newspapers and two of the three English-language television stations. In 1970, the Davey Special Senate Committee on Mass Media called the situation "about as flagrant an example of abusing the public interest as you're likely to find in Canada."

In October 1969, Laurier LaPierre, then the head of McGill's French-Canadian Studies program, addressed a student gathering outside Moncton. He devoted nearly all his speech to the shortcomings of capitalism, the press and K.C. Irving, and to a plea for "decentralized socialism" as a solution to the problems of the Maritimes. In passing, he also mentioned that he was against Maritime union, since he favored less, not more, centralization.

The *Moncton Times* headlined its front-page story "MARITIME UNION WASTE OF TIME AND RESOURCES." It devoted twenty column inches to LaPierre's speech in a story bylined "Staff Special." Of those twenty inches, one inch was devoted to the attack on Irving. Two inches covered the comments on the press. The rest of the article was devoted to Maritime union and economic development, but the economic development was made to appear as simply a variant of the existing economic system, and the word "socialism" did not appear anywhere in the story.

The Saint John *Telegraph-Journal* threw away the final paragraph but otherwise ran the *Moncton Times* account word for word. The Moncton evening paper, *The Moncton Transcript*, of course printed the same piece as its morning sister. The *Evening Times-Globe* in Saint John did the same. The Fredericton *Gleaner* picked up the *Telegraph-Journal* story complete. So far as any New Brunswick reader could tell, here was just another example of some pushy academic from Montreal coming down to tell the locals what to do about Maritime union. The only New Brunswick daily to report the speech reasonably accurately, the one daily to mention socialism and to quote the vigorous criticism of the Irving empire, was the one daily newspaper in the province not owned by K.C. Irving–*L'Evangeline*, the Moncton French-language daily.

In 1974, the New Brunswick Supreme Court ruled that the Irvings had formed a monopoly under the flabby Combines Investigation Act. The following year, indicating the impotence of this country's notoriously weak combines legislation, the appeals division of the New Brunswick Supreme Court overturned the decision. And the Supreme Court of Canada, to its shame, later upheld the reversal.

Canadian newspapers of another year, lest we forget, were also imperfect instruments. Not a few, in fact, were well accustomed to getting into bed with politicians. In the 1940s, the great *Winnipeg Free Press* editor J.W. Dafoe and his Ottawa reporter, Grant Dexter, operated quite openly as a brains trust for Mackenzie King, supplying the prime minister with advice and supportive copy and in return being given access to top government secrets.

Peter Dempson, the Ottawa man for the Toronto *Telegram*, was practically a public relations director for the Diefenbaker government and especially for George Hees. In his memoir, *Assignment Ottawa*, he described the bald-faced pro-Tory slant of his coverage of the 1949 federal campaign, while the Star was doing the same for the Liberals. "The *Telegram* would seize on every opportunity to attack St. Laurent and praise Drew," he wrote. "The *Star* did just the opposite. Journalistic scruples and ethics went out the window."

This led to the most famous headline in *Star* history. In the final days of the campaign, the paper was making much of an alleged secret deal between Conservative leader George Drew and Quebec leader Maurice Duplessis to promise a cabinet spot and the role of Quebec leader to the controversial Camillien Houde, former mayor of Montreal. An enormous, obese figure, Houde had spent time in internment during wartime for his anti-British actions, and the *Star* photographers were ordered to go to all lengths to get unflattering shots of him. On the Saturday before the Monday election, even faithful *Star* readers were startled by a huge Armageddon-like headline that took up a good portion of the front page:

**KEEP CANADA BRITISH
DESTROY DREW'S HOUDE
GOD SAVE THE KING**

Beneath an absolutely revolting picture of Houde was this further instruction to the electorate in the caption: "This man will be one of the rulers of Canada if voters Monday elect George Drew as head of a Conservative government. He is Camillien Houde, isolationist, ex-internee, foe of Britain." The rest of page one was filled with anti-Drew stories. The edition is still used in journalism classes as a wonder of non-journalism.

The election results of course gave the *Star* its wish, but some years later in the 1974 campaign it had a different problem. The paper was editorially backing Robert Stanfield's wage-and-price controls platform, which was (temporarily, as it turned out) opposed by Pierre Trudeau.

A front-page headline read "90-DAY FREEZE IN PM'S SECRET PAY, PRICE PLAN," and the lead of the story stated: "The Liberal cabinet endorsed a secret contingency plan almost a year ago to fight inflation with a short-term freeze of prices and incomes to be followed by controls running up to three years, the *Star* has learned." The story did not name a source and, deep in the copy, quoted a spokesman for the prime minister as saying the plan's existence had been known for months and the government had rejected its use.

The story was phoned in by national editor David Crane to the Toronto newsroom's rewrite desk where Carl Mollins, the Ottawa news editor, was serving as night election editor. "I told him I didn't think it was a legitimate story," remembered Mollins, now an executive editor of *Maclean's*, "and I didn't want to be associated with it because it was based on a conversation with Jim Gillies, who was an active Conservative personally involved in the campaign, but was attributed to unnamed sources." The plan, he further added, was also not secret. Trudeau in a 1973 press conference had said there was a contingency plan for controls but cabinet had decided it wasn't needed.

"I had the impression," Mollins said, "that it was a story requested by someone higher up in the *Star*." Mollins quit the paper.

So, after the election–for the same basic reasons–did Ottawa bureau chief Tony Westell, now head of the Carleton University School of Journalism; reporter Mike Lavoie, now executive producer of CBC's "the fifth estate"; and John Gray, now *The Globe and Mail*'s man in London.

"From its inception in 1892," publisher Joe Atkinson said on his elevation to the paper's presidency in 1957, "the *Star* has been a champion of social and economic reform, a defender of minority rights, a foe of discrimination, a friend of organized labour and a staunch advocate of Canadian nationhood. We shall continue to support these principles with all the vigour at our command."

A staunch advocate, yes, but not always an exemplar of objective journalism. The *Star* through most of its history has backed the Liberal party, often to an extent that is embarrassing to its own journalists. When the *Star*'s interests do not fit the existing political mold, it attempts to change the mold.

In the early 1940s, Atkinson grew disturbed with the Liberals' disregard for civil liberties, highlighted by the internment of the Japanese Canadians. The *Star*, therefore, began to flirt with the CCF as the real party of reform. Atkinson went so far as to try to push a merger between the CCF and the Liberals–just as Beland Honderich when publisher once tried to convince NDP leader David Lewis to join an alliance with the Liberals.

When the CCF became the government in Saskatchewan in 1944 under Tommy Douglas, Honderich, then a *Star* reporter, was sent to the prairies to produce a series on the government that his paper had hailed as a victory for the common man. Honderich's prose was so glowing that the government reprinted his articles and distributed them in pamphlet form.

The *Star*'s affection for the semi-socialists had faded by the time of its notorious conduct in the 1949 federal campaign. In the 1951 Ontario provincial election, the *Star* was hell-bent on defeating new Conservative legislation that would force the sale of the paper by its owners, the Atkinson Foundation. The paper launched into such an open and distorted anti-Tory campaign in its news pages that it went beyond simple endorsement of a political party to declare, for the first time, that it was a Liberal paper–a matter of no great surprise to anyone who could read.

The *Star* likes to make its political statements in the treatment of its page-one stories; it likes its columnists to be reporters/feature writers. It sounds goofy, but tell that to Beland Honderich, the Canadian successor to the Hearsts and the Beaverbrooks of another era. The *Star* is a thoroughly old-fashioned newspaper, old-fashioned in that it is still in the Hearst-Beaverbrook-Kemsley tradition wherein one strong-minded and autocratic proprietor dictates not only the tone but also the content of the paper he owns.

Honderich somehow gets away with it, the *Star* being not only the largest paper in Canada, with a daily circulation of 534,624 and on Saturdays of 796,475 copies, but also the richest. This is partially due to the hegemony of the Liberal party, which has ruled Canada for almost all of this century and to which the Honderich-led *Star* has slavishly adhered, shamefully flouting all those "objective" nostrums drummed into the heads of journalism students.

When the Spanish-American War broke out in 1898, the jingoistic forces of the Hearst and Pulitzer papers filled gunboats with reporters and photographers and illustrators to feed the frenzy. Frederic Remington, a distinguished artist hired by the Hearst organization, complained that in fact there was little action in Cuba. William Randolph Hearst wired back curtly that *he* would supply the war; it was Remington's job to supply the pictures. Honderich runs the *Star* the same way. He uses the newspages the way other papers in the 1980s use editorial pages and columnists to conduct the debate.

There are 247 Honderich jokes around, retailed in every press club in the land when scribes pop a Bud. Why did Honderich build the new *Star* tower at 1 Yonge Street, signalling Toronto's discovery that it had a lakefront? He wanted somewhere to park his submarine. At a *Star* regulation farewell party for a faithful retainer, gimlet-eyed editorial veteran Ray Timson expressed Beland's regrets that the publisher could not be present. "Yeah," said reporter Mike Lavoie, a celebrated wit, now a rising star at "the fifth estate," he being a favorite of Eric Malling, "he's at the iron foundry, getting a heart transplant."

The Honderich manipulation of news in favor of his own political predilections goes beyond his high-minded pronouncements–the *Star* invented the Ontario Press Council, which supposedly reprimands newspapers that do naughty things and offend public perceptions of honesty. When the flamboyant John Bassett, publisher of the flamboyant Toronto *Telegram*, was about to endure a messy and public divorce, after he had fallen in love with a beautiful blonde reporter in his newsroom, Bassett discovered that Beland Honderich–high-minded Beland Honderich from a strict southwestern Ontario Mennonite background–was going through similar divorce turmoil. Bassett phoned his bitter professional rival and suggested that if the *Star* wrote nothing about the juicy Bassett marriage problems, the *Tely* would reciprocate and never mention the Honderich embarrassment. The proud author of the Ontario Press Council agreed. Not a word on either side saw the light of day.

Arch McKenzie was one of the great Canadian Press veterans of Ottawa, a red-faced Scot with strong connections to one of the grand old socialist families of Canada, being the son-in-law of the late Colin Cameron, a fiery radical MP who was one of the finest orators in the Commons. That would make Arch brother-in-law to *Toronto Star* resident cynic Val Sears, who is father of Robin Sears, a former official of Socialist International and one of those, as an NDP headquarters *apparatchik*, who took most of the blame for the party's rather puzzling 1988 election campaign. After decades as a CP "lifer" who ran the Ottawa bureau, McKenzie surprised the trade by accepting a *Star* offer to run that propaganda sheet's Ottawa office. He soon learned the truth as defined by Honderich. "I am very much a directed person," he confessed about his new role. "If you've got an idea, you must sell it to Toronto." Not good enough to discover a story, stumble upon some facts; first of all it must be checked out with 1 Yonge Street to see if it fits the mold.

When the dignified George Bain left the *Globe* after owning for years the bottom left-hand corner column on the editorial page as *the* must read for anyone in Ottawa, he became editorial-page editor of the *Star* and found that his duty, on certain evenings, was to traipse around to some cocktail party and to stand on the front stoop, proofs of the editorial page in hand, until Mr. Honderich could break off the pleasantries and come out to approve them.

Gary Lautens is a *Star* humor columnist who indulges in the saddest of afflictions, journalistic necrophilia–*i.e.*, using helpless innocents, his wife and children, as column fodder. A cheery man of constant good spirits, he puzzled colleagues several years ago by suddenly accepting a Honderich appointment as editor of the paper that has a revolving door of executive appointments.

A columnist as editor? No one thought it would work. The idea, apparently, was that Lautens' eternal optimism would bring more "good news" into the paper. It also meant that he would share direction of the newsroom with Ray Timson, a product of Toronto's east end who had come up the hard way and who has the face of a 3:00 a.m. poker player. The unlikely combination of Lautens and Timson immediately became known, to the staff wits, as "Chuckles and Knuckles."

The strange Lautens appointment, as expected, did not last, Timson being one of the great survivors in newspaper politics. A mistake, naturally, could not be admitted, and so the baby-faced Lautens was "promoted" to the fancy title of "editor emeritus," the world's youngest journalist to assume that one-step-from-the-grave title.

Lautens went back to writing his column. But readers (to their benefit) noticed something. His bite had sharpened. The tales of domestic Dagwood-and-Blondie strife continued, but there was now an edge to his writing. A scornful bitterness toward government stupidity or authoritarian excess was apparent. There was, occasionally, a serious touch of savagery in his copy, an anger that Lautens fans over the years had never detected. His term in Carpet City, learning the truth about corporate newspapering, had made him a better columnist.

The *Star*'s cavalier attitude toward objectivity has attracted the attention of even *The New York Times*. In an article on

November 17, 1988, it was observed that "what has differentiated the *Star*'s coverage has been its habit, acknowledged by all its editors, of giving far more prominence on its news pages to the case against the trade pact than to the case for it."

Beland Honderich, according to the *Times*, considered it his duty to ensure loyalty to the credo established by Joseph Atkinson. The story quoted Honderich as stating that "whether it's overt or not, I think newspapers have a bias, and I think it's better that people should know it," and as acknowledging that the *Star*'s fierce campaign against the free trade proposal had "affected its news coverage."

In a book on "Holy Joe" Atkinson, the founding owner and editor–*J.E. Atkinson of the Star*–author Ross Harkness wrote: "The newspaper stood for certain things and it stood for them in every column from the weather on page one to the Eaton's advertisements on the back page. *Star* reporters always found the evidence to support a crusade."

The *Star* maintains no pretence of detachment once it has decided on a cause. Passionately against free trade, it fulminated against the accord with the United States not only editorially but in other places in the paper. In a six-month period from October 6, 1987, to March 31, 1988, 51 per cent of the *Star*'s stories zeroed in on opposition to the deal or on negative aspects of it. Only 20 per cent dealt with a pro-free trade element–and 29 per cent took neither side. Toronto accountant Kean Bhatacharya, who compiled the figures, filed a complaint with the Ontario Press Council, that toothless beast, which of course dismissed it.

For a paper that uses its news columns so blatantly for its own purposes, the *Star* can be astonishingly prim over what it regards as a breach of ethics. When, in 1971, the Toronto *Telegram* closed its doors, the *Star* made a deal to hire Ron Haggart, the *Tely*'s best columnist and a valuable byline. Shortly before he was to write his first *Star* column, the paper reneged on the agreement, claiming that Haggart had proven himself to be politically partisan because he had written an article in an NDP election booklet before that year's provincial election. *Politically partisan!* The paper that shows no corporate sense of humor may have one after all.

In early 1989, when it came to the paper's attention that Ken Adachi, its sensitive and widely respected book columnist, had plagiarized excerpts from an old Lance Morrow essay in *Time*, Adachi resigned in disgrace. *The Globe and Mail* printed the Adachi prose alongside the Morrow essay, supposedly for comparison but also apparently to beat the *Star*, which planned to do the same. In anticipation, Adachi committed suicide the previous day.

Later in the year, the *Washington Monthly* magazine in a rather playful way noted that the *Star's* Washington man, Bob Hepburn, in listing ten examples of the corruption of the city's mayor, Marion Barry, had used, word for word, three examples from its own pages. It wasn't really a major crime, and Hepburn's friends in the National Press Club rather joked about it, knowing that there but for the grace of God. . . .

But when a Toronto gossip column picked up the long-stale item (Hepburn's column had appeared in early January) in late May, within days Hepburn's weekly column in the *Star* contained a humiliating *mea culpa* ending with the announcement that it would be "the last column I write for *The Toronto Star* on this page for the foreseeable future." It seems rather unnecessary punishment for a minor sin, when the real distortions are being committed by the big boys upstairs.

Beland Honderich's son, John, is a man of sunny disposition and credentials well respected by most anyone he has worked with in journalism. He has a lawyer's degree, he long attempted to distance himself from being seen as his father's toady and, in fact, to his father's displeasure, took a year's sabbatical in Europe to delay the inevitable: his rise to the top. After an interregnum as business editor, he is now the editor, and most everyone who likes him–there are many of us–hope and pray he can make his powerful newspaper a more honest vehicle than his father did.

The senior Honderich has announced that he is allegedly moving himself into retirement, leaving the paper in the hands of two bright chaps who went to school and university together,

David Galloway and David Jolley. The way the Honderich "retirement" announcement explained it, in improbable believability, Galloway and Jolley would alternate each year as the boss of the paper that dominates the province that dominates Canada. And if there is a tie vote between them–as everyone on Bay Street and in the newspaper business said in amusement–guess who would get to cast the deciding vote? The high-minded Mennonite who arranged to keep his divorce out of the public print.

I have twice done a dance of the fireflies with *Star* management over job offers. The clincher came when the gentlemanly (and well-prepared) Borden Spears, then editor, took me to lunch and cited from memory certain Fotheringham columns that–if they had been handed in at the *Star*–would have been rejected until the author had backed up certain allegations. (By which time, of course, they would have been out of date, the targets well in flight behind their lawyers and flacks.)

I thanked him very much for the lunch and returned to *The Vancouver Sun* where a charming publisher, Stuart Keate, and a fearless managing editor, Bill Galt, had the funny old-fashioned idea that the way to run a paper was to hire a columnist you believed in, trust him, and if anyone took serious objection be quite willing to take them on in court. It was a wonderful journalistic marriage.

The essential point was to get that day's column into that day's paper and if it meant a roused-out-of-bed shouting match in the publisher's office between publisher, editor, lawyer and columnist, that's okay as long as we got the slightly altered product to the reader in time for the paper boy to throw it onto the roof or into the bushes beside the front door. The *Star* approach was that if there was anything slightly nervous included, let's hold it out until it's cleansed and bloodless and decaffeinated.

Mine was a fortunate decision. I wouldn't have lasted long, considering the *Star*'s relentless mindset. There may be flakes at the *Star* (*i.e.*, Joey Slinger) but they don't write about politics. Politics is *serious* business at the *Star*.

(I have a theory about Slinger. Joey is sort of a left-over hippie from the sixties who is a hybrid of Woody Allen and Robin Williams and Richard Pryor and William Burroughs in his more lucid moments and I don't think the *Star* brass have the faintest idea of what he's writing about nine columns out of ten. However, marketing experts all, they *assume* someone out there in the great void, Vacuumland as Allan McPhee calls it, does clue in to his stream-of-unconsciousness approach and so they print it–even though they haven't the foggiest. I believe, further, that Slinger shares my view.)

It's always puzzling why newspaper proprietors want to hire journalists who would be completely unsuitable to their papers. John Bassett, when running the Toronto *Tely*, once wanted to hire Pierre Berton, then writing the best column in Canada for the *Star*. Bassett is slightly to the right of Conrad Black. Berton votes NDP and has stated he is not going to leave any of his million bucks to his kids, so they can get a fair start in life.

Berton, who likes Bassett personally, told him he was crazy since they would always argue. "But I love arguing!" Bassett replied. "Exactly," said Berton. "We would spend all our time arguing and there never would be any time for writing."

When there's a strong and forceful publisher with a lot of flair at the wheel, it can be fun to work at a bad paper. This was the case with Bassett and the Toronto *Telegram*. (*The Toronto Star* is not a pleasant place to work, and the *Globe*, under the purges carried out by Megarry, is a very unhappy paper.) Bassett ran the *Tely* like an autocrat, and the passengers aboard had a merry time. Berton once demanded of Bassett in a television interview whether it was true that he used his paper as a personal instrument of power. "Of course," smiled Bassett, turning away wrath. "Why else would you want to own a newspaper?"

He didn't really own it, the Eatons did, but that didn't matter. One Monday morning an enraged Bassett summoned his senior editors to his office. He was apoplectic. On the floor of his office he had the *Tely* spread out beside *The Toronto Star*. Kicking the papers with his foot, he pointed with his toe to a *Star* front-page exclusive and shouted, "*This* is a newspaper." And this, he ranted, while casting a contemptuous shoe on his own paper, "This is the paper that should have had that story on the front page today." He berated his men for fifteen minutes.

When he had run out of insults, *Tely* city editor Doug MacFarlane said quietly, "Mr. Bassett, the reason that story is not on our front page today is because it was on our front page on Saturday."

Bassett never skipped a beat. "Gentlemen," he said, "happiness is having a publisher who is full of shit. Meeting dismissed."

It may not have been the best newspaper in the world at the time, but *The Vancouver Sun* under Don and Sam Cromie in the 1940s and 1950s was more fun than a Marx Brothers night at the opera. The brothers while still under thirty inherited the paper from their father, a health and fitness nut who dropped dead one day while on his miles-long lunch-hour walk. (Decades ahead of his time, he had a gym built into the Sun Tower for the health of the staff, only to discover that the editorial writers used it as their secret drinking haunt.)

Publisher Don was a brilliant eccentric (he hired this computer-stained wretch, for example) who ran the editorial end of affairs while handsome Sam ran the production side and used to take the entire composing room across the street to the Lotus Hotel beer parlor on Friday afternoons.

When Sputnik went up to circle the globe, Don Cromie ordered a *Sun* photographer to go across the harbor to the top of Grouse Mountain (which the Cromies happened to own and hyped endlessly as the site of the *Sun* free ski school). It was all of 5,000 feet high but the publisher somehow thought it might provide a closer view of the world's first space satellite as it passed over Vancouver at the appointed hour. The photographer–was it Deni Eagland or Danny Scott?–obligingly dragged a fingernail across the blank negative and, presto, there was the *Sun* exclusive all over page one next day.

Cromie sent fashion editor Marie Moreau to Cuba to interview Castro and football writer Annis Stukus to Quemoy and Matsu off the China coast when those disputed islands were going to cause World War III. To prepare for the on-the-spot photos to accompany his front-line despatches, the paper had Stukus before he left pose in a helmet huddled in a foxhole dug in the sand of Vancouver's English Bay beach while puzzled bathers looked on.

Globe publisher Roy Megarry, in a rather strange speech to the prestigious Empire Club in Toronto, one of the most-noticed platforms in the Big Lemon, expressed his own frustration with a paper he apparently has not been able to shape into the image he desires.

In a 1989 address about the problems of creating Canadian unity, he confessed that the media, because they are concentrated in Toronto, contribute "to this sense of alienation between various communities that make up Canada." He pointed out the obvious, that the Southam chain is based in Toronto (even though, he failed to add, Toronto is the only major city in which it does not have a paper), that the Thomson chain is based in Toronto, as are *The Toronto Sun* group and *Maclean's* and the CBC and CTV networks.

He then made a strange criticism of his own newspaper: "*The Globe and Mail* – Canada's national newspaper, or Canada's so-called national newspaper, or Canada's self-styled national news-paper–is headquartered in Toronto."

What's important in Canada, he went on, is too often determined by central-Canadian media outlets. His own editors must have been heartened by his next statement:

"Let me give you an example from my own newspaper to make the point. I was in Vancouver two weeks ago and opened up my copy of *The Globe and Mail* to read two front-page stories headed: 'Toronto Courtroom Sees Western-Style Meting Out of Justice'; 'Toronto Catholics Face Year's Wait Before They Can March to the Altar.'

"Fortunately for me, I left town early and did not have to explain to Vancouverites why these earth-shattering events in Toronto were important to them. Or why we had invested tens of millions of dollars to develop a national newspaper that could speed news of these breathtaking events in Toronto to their doorstep."

It was a rather astonishing confession, to any pro in the trade. A publisher head cheese was admitting before an audience of the businessmen who were his subscribers that he was a failure in fashioning his paper to his liking. It was his irritation at the southern Ontario centrism of his paper that apparently led to his sudden sacking of editor-in-chief Norman Webster (whose family owned the paper before the Thomsons) and managing editor Geoffrey Stevens, both superb reporters in the Ottawa milieu.

No one had pointed out to Megarry–and he seems not to have noticed–that his paper is one of the few in the world that defies its origin. Someone arriving tomorrow from Mars on a spaceship would not know where this paper came from, since its lofty and arrogant masthead declares only: *The Globe and Mail*. Other, and more worthy, newspapers declare honestly that they are *The New York Times* or *The Washington Post*. The *Globe*, declaring itself "Canada's National Newspaper," feels it is above geography.

In its schizophrenia, however, it contradicts itself. Toronto stories have no datelines. Lethbridge stories do. Halifax stories do. But Toronto stories (unlike *New York Times* stories from New York which are clearly labelled as coming from New York) are treated as local stories in the paper that pretends to be a national newspaper.

The *Mop and Pail* or the *Grope and Flail*, as those within the trade refer to it, takes itself very seriously, but it can be incredibly obtuse about what goes on in Canada, mainly because it is in truth Toronto's national newspaper and Toronto, like New York, is terribly insular.

Bronwyn Drainie is an intelligent, well-read Toronto broadcaster, the daughter of the CBC's late and brilliant John Drainie. She now writes on cultural and publishing and journalistic affairs for the *Globe*. When Ottawa columnist Charlie Lynch forced the resignation of ACTRA president Dale Goldhawk, who was also the host of "Cross-Country Checkup," because ACTRA strongly opposed the free trade agreement, the cultural nationalists such as Bronwyn Drainie were outraged. As retaliation, she thought she had a hot item. Lynch, she hinted darkly in the *Globe*, had his own conflict of interest because of a "long-standing intimate relationship with a Mulroney adviser." Snigger, snigger.

Lynch has been a columnist for twenty-eight years. He has served in South America, New York, London–where he was an associate of Walter Cronkite and Edward R. Murrow during the London blitz. He landed on the Normandy beaches, and drank with Hemingway in France. He is the dean of the Ottawa Press Gallery. Despite all this, the *Globe* apparently doesn't know that he has been married for two years (he writes about it all the time) to Claudie Mailly, who was the MP for Gatineau and the government deputy whip.

Rosemary Sexton is the new *Globe* social columnist, replacing the celebrated Zena Cherry. In a 1989 despatch from Vancouver, a city that seemed to surprise her in that it possessed not only sidewalks but electric lights, she gushed over the plush homes in Shaughnessy, that provided "spectacular views of the Rocky Mountains looming over the city." She not only was facing the wrong way–west–but has remarkable eyesight. The Rocky Mountains are on the Alberta border, some 700 miles to the east.

Some people in Vancouver have, in fact, been looking east at *The Globe and Mail* and not liking what they are seeing. More than a decade ago, there was born in Vancouver something called The Fraser Institute, a think-tank appealing to those who were somewhat to the right of Ed Broadbent. Unlike the C.D. Howe Institute, which deals in economic issues rather than the direction in which the world should be moving, the Fraser Institute makes no bones about its political orientation. Those of us who are students of the human condition wondered, why Vancouver?–a waystop in intellectual meanderings, according to the Bay Street mindset.

The institute was not taken seriously at first among the local bird-watchers, since it made its right-wing cast so apparent from the start and was reluctant, nay reticent, to reveal its funding. What was apparent, however, was that it was shaped after the many think-tanks in Washington that fuel the debate between what passes for the left wing in the capital and the right wing Republican forces that may have dominated recent presidential elections but have a tough time flailing away in predominantly Democrat Washington.

The new muscle of the conservative movement in the United States did not escape the attention of the business community in Canada. In 1972 the election of Dave Barrett's NDP government in British Columbia caused a frisson of shock to reverberate among good free enterprisers. (Premier Dave Barrett, who was labelled "the Allende of the North" by Wall Street's panicky *Barron's*, used to say that "the trouble with free enterprise is that it is neither free nor enterprising.") Seeking to counter leftish thinking with their own confrontational message, business interests established the Fraser Institute in Vancouver two years after the NDP was sworn into power.

There were just four staffers at inauguration. There are now twenty-one pointy-headed thinkers supported by 1,150 sustaining members—"everyone in corporate Canada from A to Z," according to the institute's executive director, Michael Walker. It receives grants from such as the Ford Foundation and the Donner Foundation. It even markets its own Monopoly-like board game on the joys of capitalism and sells its publications in fifty-two countries.

After some of its more goofy advocacies were laughed at, the Fraser Institute settled down a bit and began a more subtle approach, burrowing into the soft underbelly of its foes rather than bashing them over the head. A sample of the new sophistication—mirroring similar projects in Reagan-era Washington—is the Fraser Institute's decision to take on what so many in the business community see as the enemy: the media. Walker has given a five-year commitment to produce, every month, *On Balance*, a critique of the press, television and radio, and their bias or lack thereof.

The public, of course, would never see such an esoteric item as

On Balance, but those who subscribe to it were intrigued late in 1988 by its study of how the free trade issue was covered by the CBC and *The Globe and Mail*, the latter supposedly the organ of the Establishment.

It's standard wisdom that the mouth-breathers in the Tory back benches have always hated the CBC, thinking it filled with separatists, homosexuals and closet Liberals–partly because the Grits ruled the roost for so much of the century and the Conservatives, as "professional outsiders," felt the Mother Corp. was a captive to government guidance. So, the Fraser Institute screed was even more interesting for government MPs–and types on Bay Street–since it came out just as the *Globe* was making plans to provide items on a daily basis for the planned CBC all-news channel.

The thesis of the *On Balance* study of the two entities–one print, one electronic–is that there had not been balanced treatment of the free trade agreement (FTA). The conclusion of the *On Balance* survey: "In sum, the media examined portrayed the FTA in a negative light. This is reflected by both those quoted by the media and the reporters' commentary. In terms of informing the public on the agreement, the media tended to focus on trivial details rather than providing substance on the issues."

The study didn't even bother with the wildly slanted *Toronto Star*. It concentrated on the state broadcasting service and the "national newspaper." On CBC items on the FTA, it decided (strongly disputed by those journalists mentioned) that Peter Mansbridge and David Halton were "balanced." Not balanced?–Barbara Frum, Bill Cameron, Allen Garr, Wendy Mesley, Terry Milewski, Ann Petrie and on and on.

As for the *Globe*, the institute ignored the editorials, the columnists, and the Report on Business, and looked only at the reporters. It claimed that Hugh Winsor (a former member of the NDP Waffle), Ross Howard and Geoffrey York turned out consistently negative FTA stories, while Christopher Waddell and Jennifer Lewington had been balanced. Overall, the *Globe's* news, like CBC's, was anti-FTA.

Premiers David Peterson and Howard Pawley, both anti-FTA, were given more coverage than such pro-FTA premiers as Robert Bourassa and Don Getty. *On Balance* decided that, in the end, ". . . the national media relied heavily on government sources. The result was that very few external sources were sought to corroborate the government's policy. In fact, very few economists or business representatives–people who generally support the agreement–were interviewed by the national media. By contrast, for positions rejecting free trade, the news media were thorough in obtaining varied sources. Union officials, opposition MPs, workers and person-on-the-street interviews were frequent representatives of the anti-free trade position."

On Balance, in its summation, concluded that "the distribution and positions expressed was [*sic*] the direct result of editorial decisions by the journalists and not due to chance.

The right-wing inherent supposition of left-wing media bias was buttressed by a 1982 survey–long passed around by those who liked the conclusions–by Peter Snow, a faculty member at the University of Western Ontario's graduate school of journalism. Snow, interviewing 118 members of the Parliamentary Press Gallery–both print and broadcast journalists–found that 62 per cent had a university degree and 27 per cent had an annual income of more than $50,000.

Snow's survey showed that the voting record of the Gallery reporters clearly indicated a left-wing preference. The largest section of the gallery (37 per cent) said that it felt closest to the NDP of any of the three federal parties. Liberals drew the support of 17 per cent, with the Conservatives at only 11 per cent. The rest were uncommitted.

When they were asked for whom they usually voted in a federal election, the largest single group to admit to a preference (19 per cent) stated that it voted for the NDP. When asked to place themselves on the political spectrum, 43 per cent described themselves as belonging to the political center, while 42 per cent thought of themselves as being left of center. Just 4 per cent saw themselves as being to the right of center.

According to Snow's survey, a high percentage (85 per cent)

thought that there are some cases in which government owner-ship in the economy is more desirable than private ownership. Two-thirds of the journalists agreed that there should be laws to bring corporations under closer control, but 55 per cent dis-agreed when asked if there should be laws to bring unions under closer control. Some 64 per cent disagreed with the statement that there is too much government ownership of the Canadian economy.

As Ottawa columnist Doug Fisher notes, "It seems to me one can only explain the large scale nastiness of the media assessment of the Mulroney government in terms of a pervasive anti-conservatism in the press. Political reporters, by and large, are for big government. They believe it should dominate our economy, nurture our culture, and control our natural environment. In the U.S. they would be classed as largely liberal, in voting terms, Democrats. Here, a good tag would be social democrats and most would vote Liberal or NDP."

(It would undoubtedly amuse Fisher, who was an NDP MP for seven years before becoming a newspaper columnist, that his old party still rails about "the capitalist press.")

The *Globe*, for all its tradition-founded by Father of Confed-eration George Brown and all that-and its reputation, is in a strange position that cannot be entirely unknown to its owners, the Thomsons, who are allergic to red ink. *The Toronto Star*, filled with department store ads and chauvinist Ontario bombast, is in an unassailable position as the largest and richest paper in Canada. *The Toronto Sun*, fat with ads and ebullience, has liberated the nipple on page three and offers a cornucopia of columnists that no longer-as we used to joke-range from Peter Worthington on the left to Lubor J. Zink on the right. Doug Fisher milks his NDP background, and this scribbler, a card-carrying limousine liberal, tries to keep things sane. The *Sun* easily outsells the *Globe* in Toronto.

The point, however, is no longer that the *Globe* is being squeezed, in one of the rare three-newspaper towns left on this continent, between the success of the tabloid *Sun* and the roller-coaster of the *Star*. The fact is that Toronto is now a four-newspaper town, the daily *Financial Post* coming on as a threat to the *Globe*'s money cow, the Report on Business section.

And so, as the story unfolds, on Boxing Day of 1988 *Globe* publisher Roy Megarry (who seems to have taken the strictures of the Fraser Institute and Peter Snow to heart) spotted editor Norman Webster in the paper's cafeteria, invited him down to his office for a chat and sacked him. When Webster subsequently asked why, Megarry said that he didn't have to tell him. As publisher, I suppose, he didn't have to; a gentleman perhaps might have.

Bad blood had been brewing for some time. Ever since journalist Barbara Yaffe launched a million-dollar lawsuit against Megarry and the *Globe*. When she planned to move to Newfoundland to be married, Webster and managing editor Geoffrey Stevens proposed that she establish a St. John's bureau for the paper. Stevens calls her "one of the best reporters I've ever seen." When Megarry vetoed the idea on economic grounds, the two editors arranged a computer link so Jaffe could file copy on a free-lance basis. Her byline was soon all over the paper.

As a reward for Jaffe's aggressive work and lively writing, Stevens, with the backing of Webster, eventually offered her the *Globe* posting in Vancouver. She sold her house in St. John's and was all ready to set up shop at the other end of the country when Megarry, hearing about the posting, ordered Stevens to cancel the agreement. She promptly sued for breach of a hiring commitment.

Before the case could come to court, Webster was abruptly fired and new editor William Thorsell, an intelligent, handsome bachelor, sacked Stevens early in 1989. There was great anticipation of a showdown between Megarry and his former editors at the trial scheduled for April, since the 900 pages of preliminary testimony given at the examination for discovery made it clear that Jaffe had the goods on Megarry. In a courtroom-steps settlement the day before the juicy trial was to open, the *Globe* agreed to pay Jaffe $67,500.

It was a disappointment for newspaper voyeurs, but there was already plenty of good red claret oozing from the old gray *Globe*. The departures of Webster and Stevens were followed by that of columnist Tom Walkom who had written that the free trade deal wasn't as rosy as painted. Feature writer Judy Steed followed him to the *Star*. Assistant managing editor Shirley Sharzer, the highest-ranking woman on the paper, was offered a demeaning position with a new *Globe* magazine in Vancouver and decided to see a lawyer instead.

An indication of the new direction the paper was taking came when reporter Lorne Slotnick was told that his labor beat would be abolished. In its place would be something called the "workplace" beat, since the paper was no longer interested in coverage of organized labor and a "softer" approach was required. Slotnick requested a new assignment.

Next to go, to the outrage of readers, was the column of David Suzuki, the scientist and television performer whose strong views on the environment were judged to be too political and no longer welcome in the *Globe*'s Science section.

Megarry is described by one *Globe* veteran as "ruthless," by another as "a tinkerer." He has never worked in a newsroom, coming out of a Belfast ghetto to start in Canada as a junior cost accountant and rising to vice-president of corporate development at *The Toronto Star* before taking the top job at the *Globe* in 1978.

His baby is the Report on Business, which is the cash box for the paper and where resources are lavished to the grumbles of the rest of the newsroom. The paper, with or without the help of the Fraser Institute, is clearly being positioned to be more appealing to businessmen now that it is clear the daily *Financial Post* – with the deep pockets of Maclean Hunter, Conrad Black and Rupert Murdoch behind it–is providing growing competition.

Washington is rather unusual–differing from London, Paris, Rome, Tokyo and Moscow–in that the most important newspapers are not necessarily in the capital. *The New York Times*, just off-center in the world's richest city, is the prime example, with the *Los Angeles Times* challenging *The Washington Post* as a very serious paper–reflecting its base in the most populous and most vibrant state.

Ottawa, among its many defects, suffers from the same problem. It was a more interesting town when the *Ottawa Journal*, whatever its cash-starved weaknesses, was in competition with Southam's dominant Ottawa *Citizen*. The country-wide deal-cutting between Southam and the Thomson empire administered premature euthanasia to the *Journal*, creating a vacuum that the *Ottawa Sun* tabloid is now moving into while the nervous *Citizen* offers long-term cut-rate deals to advertisers.

This journalistic black hole is one of the many reasons why few of the important and powerful people in the country take Ottawa seriously. It is that the important and powerful papers–*The Globe and Mail*, *The Toronto Star* and the Montreal *Gazette* – are published elsewhere and land every morning in that parochial little town where civil service pensions and local traffic jams are big news.

The *Citizen* has improved perceptibly since then-publisher Paddy Sherman brought in as editor the intelligent, eccentric Keith Spicer, the former cunning linguist who was the country's first language czar and who, among other things, startled Toronto papers by initiating the highest rates in Canada for book reviews. (It was Spicer, smelling the flowers in an idyllic retreat on Vancouver's False Creek shore, who decided he could no longer live in the city when *The Vancouver Sun* put the death of Glenn Gould on an inside page.) Brian Mulroney, in an imaginative move, has now made him head of the CRTC–though he didn't even own a TV set.

The most popular column in the *Citizen*, however, remains a daily collection of cat-up-a-tree dramas by Dave Brown, claustrophobic items incomprehensible to anyone who has never heard of Bells Corners or Carp, two nearby intellectual reservoirs that make Ottawa what it is (*i.e*, ineluctable).

I've had several close encounters with the infamous Thomson style of management. It was 1958, London, and I was reduced to substitute teaching while waiting for a spot to open up at the Reuters news service. I went to work just up Fleet Street from Reuters, for *Canada News*. Ken Thomson, then apprenticing for his father's lordship, came in one day and struck me as an insecure, shy man.

Canada News was a bizarre little paper. Since it was owned by the Thomsons, everything was on the cheap, and the goofy logistics of producing it were baffling.

Canada News was designed to bring Canadian news to Canadians who lived in Britain, but mainly to the captive audience of Canadian troops stationed on the continent. The *modus operandi* was pure Thomson. Dupes of Canadian Press copy from some Thomson paper in Kirkland Lake or like outpost were *mailed* to London. Our office was in the Edinburgh *Scotsman* building, that solid, serious paper being one of the Thomson chattels.

We would make up the paper and then ship the material to Edinburgh where it was to be printed on *The Scotsman* presses. If a headline was one unit long or a story had to be trimmed an inch, laborious communications between London and Edinburgh (a Thomson budget did not allow telephone expenses) went on until the wee problem was solved. As a result of all the antediluvian fiddling, by the time the paper was printed and shipped to West Germany the poor news-hungry troops would get the Stanley Cup results about the time the World Series started.

The ladies in the office told me about a previous editor, a moody and depressed man–as he had every right to be, attempting to exist in London on a Thomson salary. One Monday morning he did not show up for work. Tuesday he did not show up for work. By Wednesday, the ladies detected a strange odor from an unused closet at the rear of the office. The door was opened and inside was the unhappy editor, hanging from his neck.

I've waited thirty years for a chance meeting with Lord Silverspoon (as one of my sons calls him) at a cocktail party. "Mr. Thomson," I will say, "my name is Fotheringham and we have a former mutual friend."

My second (unfortunate and, I am thankful, brief) term as a Thomson employee ended on an equally bizarre note. We're now talking 1979. The FP newspaper group put together by Calgary oilman and Bing Crosby friend Max Bell by this time included *The Globe and Mail* as well as the *Winnipeg Free Press*, *The Vancouver Sun*, the Calgary *Albertan*, the *Montreal Star* and the Ottawa *Journal*. The FP head office in Toronto decided to start a news service, as its new prestige warranted, and assigned Ted Bolwell to put it together.

Bolwell is an obstreperous Australian, a superb newspaperman who knows makeup and layout as well as the essentials and had been editor of the *Globe*'s magazine, managing editor of *The Toronto Star*, youngest senior editor ever at *Time* and editor of the *New York Post*. He put together the best staff in Ottawa with beautiful, well-equipped offices that were the envy of every other news organization in town, the *Globe* people often dropping around to drool.

The editor was Kevin Doyle, now the editor of *Maclean's*. There was the tough-minded Walter Stewart, now an author. Doug Small, now running the Global TV Ottawa bureau (and newly famous). Carol Goar, now the *Star*'s Ottawa columnist. Mary Janigan, later with *Maclean's*, who had some of the best sources in Canada, which may or may not have something to do with the fact she has been a friend of and is now married to Bay Street millionaire Tom Kierans, son of one of my few heroes. There was talented Dan Turner, the first reporter who used to smoke pot with Margaret Trudeau. There was a member of the ubiquitous Ottawa Van Dusen journalistic ménage, Julie, now in television.

It was a brilliant crew en masse and we were invigorating the long-ailing Ottawa *Journal*. It was a heady time–until Thomson bought out FP. An instant chill went through the office, their cheapo reputation being well known. Would Thomson be willing to support an excellent news service, since they had built their fortune on rip-and-read newspapers–simply tear it off the Canadian Press ticker and paste it up?

Dan Turner grew nervous and started looking around. Other papers courted the prodigious work habits and integrity of Carol Goar. Mary Janigan wondered whether she should jump. Eager to keep the gang together, I phoned Thomson headquarters at Bay and Queen in Toronto, in vain hopes of getting that second meeting with Lord Silverspoon. I was shuffled to St. Clair McCabe, his second-in-command. I said I wanted to come down to Toronto for a chat and, though apparently puzzled at the other end of the phone line, he agreed to the request.

Mr. McCabe, who had risen to his position by toiling faithfully in the Thomson money-making machine for loyal decades, sat behind a large desk at an intimidating distance. I explained my concern. That we had the best staff in Ottawa, with the best offices, but the troops were getting restless. Should they resist the growing offers they were getting from rival concerns? I was here to represent them. Could I go back and give them some reassurance that the news service would be kept intact, fearing that if one of them jumped ship it would set off a signal to the rest?

Mr. McCabe listened patiently and then said, seemingly still puzzled at this outpouring of journalistic passion about standards and *esprit de corps* and excellence, "I really don't understand what you're worried about, Mr. Fotheringale."

I thanked him very much, flew back to Ottawa, told the gang what had transpired and, when Pat O'Callaghan phoned with an offer from Southam, took some holidays and joined them.

Thomson, needless to say, folded the operation within months.

In the realm of flamboyant publishers, a breed out of style somewhat like the three-toed wombat, there are few left in this era of accountants and marketing experts. I have never met Roy Megarry, the rogue elephant in charge of *The Globe and Mail* and wouldn't recognize him if I found him in my soup. One could not say that of Pat O'Callaghan, another Irishman who was a burr under the Southam blanket. As publisher of *The Edmonton Journal* and then the *Calgary Herald* in the heady days of the oil patch, no one could ever mistake him for anything but a *publisher*, who always regarded an editor as a bit of a bothersome annoyance and had a grip on his papers right down to personally touring the composing room to dish out tickets to the Oilers, or the Flames, games.

The most interesting publisher in the country at the moment is Doug Creighton of the ever-expanding Toronto Sun group. This is not only because he signs my paycheque (though perhaps it's interesting that he *does* sign my paycheque) but because he is the last major publisher to come out of the newsroom.

A former cop-shop reporter at the long-dead *Toronto Telegram*, he still combs his hair with an egg-beater and somehow looks, whatever the tailor, as if he's slept in his clothes. There's the gift. He relates to the grunts down on the floor, front shop or back shop. Among his humorous idiosyncrasies that, one suspects, do not entirely amuse the Maclean Hunter guardians of the counting house who now own his newspaper, he holds his annual meeting each year–with assorted camp followers–in unusual places: one year on a cruise ship in the Caribbean, another year in London, in 1989 in Israel.

Included in the guest list that may stretch to ninety bodies are composing-room foremen from Calgary and head photographers from Edmonton and their wives, with the expected result in morale. Because he's from the newsroom, he understands the newsroom, unlike Megarry of the *Globe* who, discharged managing editor Geoffrey Stevens has testified, used to complain when he saw reporters sitting around talking to one another instead of–this is an assembly line, isn't it?–being back at the lathe.

Since the war there have been only six daily newspapers started in major North American cities (*USA Today* being excluded, it being a national, no-base paper.) They are *Newsday* on the Long Island fringe of New York, *The Toronto Sun*, *Edmonton Sun*, *Calgary Sun*, *Ottawa Sun* and the *Sun*-owned

Financial Post business daily. Creighton is now threatening to open a paper in Washington, which would serve the Americans right, since they wanted free trade.

Creighton has succeeded John Turner as the regular luncheon fixture at Winston's, the restaurant off Bay Street that Peter Newman dubbed "the day-care center for the Establishment." At his permanent table, first on the right past the entrance, he runs up a sumptuous expense account, one of the reasons why the economy of Toronto is so vibrant.

No one ever sees Ken Thomson, the Calvin Coolidge of publishing, except for those who get up early enough in the morning in Rosedale to see him walk his dog (some neighbors have seen him walk his dog *twice* in a morning, the sign of either an extremely incontinent pet or a man with not much to do). No one dares approach Conrad Black in person, for fear of being impaled on his vocabulary. The Southam clan seems in some confusion. Therefore it's heartening, and pleasant, and amusing to find in charge of a growing newspaper chain someone who is actually a live human being, is made mock of by his cartoonists for his martini habits, has few pretences and still remembers when he used to be in the cop-shop.

After the antsy Peter Worthington was abruptly amputated from the editorship of *The Toronto Sun* and after his successor Barbara Amiel had taken her cleavage off to London, *Sun* publisher Paul Godfrey and his boss Doug Creighton tried to convince me to become the new editor. I told them they were daft, that our philosophies were diametrically opposed and that the hang-all-jaywalkers element in the Tory back-bench in Ottawa would soon be bringing a return-to-capital-punishment bill to the Commons and I didn't happen to believe in state-sponsored murder and I would just have to resign since the paper felt differently.

It was one of the few examples of a rush of common sense to the head, and it was to the great advancement of all mankind that I eventually accepted a lesser role, where the Uzis are not quite on target.

4

Agents of Influence

All writers are vain, selfish and lazy, and at the
bottom of their motives there lies a mystery.
Writing a book is a horrible, exhausting
struggle, like a long bout of some painful
illness. One would never undertake such a
thing if one was not driven on by some demon
whom one can neither resist nor understand.
For all one knows that demon is simply the
same instinct that makes a baby squall for
attention. And yet it is also true that one can
write nothing readable unless one constantly
struggles to efface one's own personality. Good
prose is like a window pane. – *George Orwell*

Implicit in the love-hate relationship between press and politicians is a marriage–a marriage of convenience between two partners who need each other. The politicians need the press for coverage, to manipulate them, to use them as a twisted mirror. The press need the politicians, for they are the meal ticket, the reason for existence.

As in even the best of marriages, there is the sexual tension. There are the promiscuous types in the media, who figuratively get in bed with their sources, never to betray them, the pleasures–*i.e.*, useful leaks–delivered regularly. At the other end of the scale are the virginal types who never go near the politicians, never touch them, never want to have anything to do with them.

It is a most necessary sexual/journalism role and (not being an attitudinal virgin myself) much to be recommended. I.F. Stone, the great Washington journalist, was the finest example, a radical and original thinker who never went near the White House, never went to a press conference or a cocktail party. All he did was sit at home and, to put out his *I.F. Stone's Newsletter*, read government documents and releases and tables and charts–wherein he found government lies and obfuscations and camouflages and, eventually, the truth.

There is the myth that today's journalists are voracious, man-eating types, cynical and callous, who destroy reputations and devour small children. They are, in fact, pussycats when it comes to some of the assassins of bygone days. Sixty years or so before Bob Woodward and Carl Bernstein were breaking the Watergate story, the phenomenon of the investigative journalist burst upon the U.S. scene. Leonard Downie, Jr.'s, book *The New Muckrakers* tells us that, in that golden age of aggressive, committed journalism, an astonished nation learned of widespread corruption in government and private business–particularly in the largely unregulated oil, railroad, banking, insurance and food-processing industries.

From the turn of the century until about 1912, Lincoln Steffens achieved fame as the most prominent muckraker. He was followed by Upton Sinclair, David Graham Phillips, Ida Tarbell, Ray Stannard Baker and others. Newspapers of the time did not reach beyond their local circulations. So this new breed of journalists wrote their exposés of monopoly practices, bribery, conflicts of interest, election rigging, stock manipulation, racketeering, abuse of labor and health dangers in books and newly popular national magazines, such as *Collier's*, *McClure's* and *Cosmopolitan*, that for the first time were reaching millions of rapt readers across America.

These reporters created the climate for Teddy Roosevelt's trust-busting introduction of the landmark Pure Food and Drug Act and a law that provided for popular election of the U.S. Senate.

At first a champion and a friend of Steffens and other gutsy journalists, President Roosevelt once safe in power began to have a different view of the sweeping investigations these reporters were coming up with. David Graham Phillips produced a series in *Cosmopolitan* (hello there, Helen Gurley Brown), entitled "The Treason in the Senate," in which he accused a number of powerful senators, including Roosevelt's trusted allies, of being mere messengers of large corporations to which they were tied by the wallet.

In an impassioned 1906 speech, Roosevelt set out to discredit "these reckless journalists" and by happenstance christened them by comparing them to the Man with the Muckrake in John Bunyan's *Pilgrim's Progress*. Bunyan was warning against a too narrow concentration on worldly concerns, to the exclusion of the spiritual, when he wrote about "the man who could look no way but downward, with a muckrake in his hands; who was offered a celestial crown for his muckrake, but who would neither look up nor regard the crown he was offered, but continued to rake to himself the filth of the floor."

Downie records that the angry Roosevelt, who in full flight could be both scathing and eloquent, had his own interpretation of Bunyan and told his listeners that the Man with the Muckrake

> typifies the man who in this life consistently refuses to see aught that is lofty, and fixes his eyes with solemn intentness only on that which is vile and debasing. Now, it is very necessary that we should not flinch from seeing what is vile and debasing. There is filth on the floor, and it must be scraped up with the muckrake; and there are times and places where this service is most needed of all the services that can be performed. But the man who never does anything else, who never thinks or speaks or writes save of his feats with the muckrake, speedily becomes, not a help to society, not an incitement to good, but one of the potent forces of evil.

(Can we imagine George Bush speaking this way?)

Whether this presidential reproof had much effect on readers is hard to determine. World War I intruded, and tough investigative reporting practically disappeared for sixty years–through the Depression, another world war and the McCarthy era.

Earlier in the century, Westbrook Pegler, though not a muckraker *per se*, was a powerful force in American journalism, as influential in his day as Jack Anderson and George F. Will are now, as well read as Walter Lippmann or Walter Winchell. As someone wrote as a compliment to H.L. Mencken, the words "on the other hand" never once crossed his typewriter. When Pegler died in 1969 at the age of seventy-four, younger readers who had never heard of him were probably puzzled that *The New York Times* would lead off his obituary on the front page and continue it inside for almost an entire page.

At the height of his powers, when he was carried in 186 papers in the 1940s, Pegler had, as we say, a definite point of view. He won a Pulitzer Prize in 1941 for his exposés of labor union corruption, articles that helped ship George Scalise, president of the Building Service Employees International Union in New York to Sing Sing prison for a ten-to-twenty-year term. (Scalise complained that he had been "Peglerized.") But Pegler's fame, in a columning career that lasted twenty-nine years–from 1933 to 1962–came from his rage.

In the early days of the New Deal, he was a supporter of Franklin Roosevelt, but by 1936, after FDR tried to pack the Supreme Court and introduced welfare legislation, Pegler turned on this "feeble-minded fuehrer" and wrote, "It is regrettable that Guiseppe Zangara hit the wrong man when he shot at Roosevelt in Miami"–a reference to a 1933 assassination attempt in which Chicago Mayor Anton Cermak was killed.

To Pegler, Eleanor Roosevelt was "La Boca Grande,"–the big mouth–and President Harry Truman was "a thin-lipped hater." A man of indiscriminate distastes, Pegler was dismissed for a time by his Hearst employers after remarking that a Hearst newspaper resembled "a screaming woman running down the street with her throat cut"–a description that, fifty years later, fits exactly the worst of the Rupert Murdoch penny dreadfuls that infest what is left of Fleet Street.

Pegler, as all bright young men do, entered newspapering through the sportswriting dodge, because he had noticed that "big salaries in newspapers usually were paid to sports men." Like some others we know, he drifted out of boredom into political commentary, and his first nationally syndicated column, in 1933, created a sensation for its defense of lynching.

"As one member of the rabble," it began, "I will admit that I said, 'Fine, that is swell,' when the papers came up that day telling of the lynching of two men who killed the young fellow in California, and that I haven't changed my mind yet for all the storm of right-mindedness which has blown up since."

He survived the storm, though losing such friends as fellow columnist Heywood Broun, founder of the Newspaper Guild, who called Pegler "the light-heavyweight champion of the upperdog."

Pegler raged on, FDR's vice-president, Henry Wallace, becoming "Old Bubblehead" and assistant Secretary of State A.A. Berle, Jr., a "blood-thirsty bull twirp." Justice Felix Frankfurter of the U.S. Supreme Court, an intellect revered to this day, was a "fatuous windbag," while Fiorello La Guardia, the reform mayor of New York, was "the little padrone of the Bolsheviki." It was clear the newspaper house lawyers were more lenient than those I have known.

J. Edgar Hoover, that bachelor *poseur* who was the fierce FBI chief, was "a nightclub fly-cop" and–my favorite description–fellow columnist Walter Winchell was "a gent's-room journalist."

Pegler's anger delighted and entertained his readers but, as with all love-hate relationships with employers who like you until you touch on sacred ground, there were some places he could not tread. He had attacked members of the Hearst organization by name, including William Randolph Hearst, Jr., Frank Conniff, who was the national editor, and the celebrated Bob Considine, a famous Hearst columnist. (He also was hard on himself: one New Year's Day column consisted solely of "I will never mix gin, beer and whiskey again"–repeated fifty times.)

But an attack on President Dwight Eisenhower and Henry Luce, the Republican-loving owner of *Time*, was killed. So was a column that began, "There is something wormy about our State Department."

After Pegler's unflattering references to the John Kennedy

White House were killed, Hearst terminated his contract on the grounds that "too many irreconcilable differences on vital matters have existed between the parties to continue a workable relationship."

In a 1962 speech to the ultra-conservative Christian Crusade in Tulsa, Oklahoma, Pegler said, "Much of our daily press is now under a coercion as nasty and snarling and menacing as Hitler's was in the first year of his reign. I will not speak of other newspapers, but of recent alarming experiences in the Hearst organization. I received insolent, arrogant warnings from King Features [his syndication service] that nothing unfavorable to the Kennedy Administration or offensive to any member of the Kennedy family will be allowed out of New York where the censors sit."

The strange link between the Establishment and its recorders manifests itself in differing ways. Pegler was allowed to be an entertaining magpie until his venom proved too bothersome and embarrassing for his employers, in their desire to ingratiate themselves with a new and exceedingly popular president.

There was a different *modus vivendi* between the Establishment and the greatest journalist of this century, Walter Lippmann. Unlike Pegler, who railed against the established order from the outside, Lippmann got into bed with it and not so much seduced it as raped it. He not only was clearly the most powerful columnist in the world, he was arguably one of the most powerful men in the world between the two world wars and beyond the second one. He did not have to seek interviews; prime ministers and presidents and kings sought audiences with him. He did not see himself as an adversary of government and politicians. He was above all that–he sought to help *them* solve their problems. He is a story.

Lippmann was a towering figure. No journalist anywhere, before or since, had his influence on world affairs. His sway came because he was not from journalism. In David Halberstam's phrase, "He was a journalist who had never covered a story, had never worked in a city room, and had never rushed to a fire." He did not come from the ambience of *The Front Page*, but from academe. He studied under George Santayana at Harvard. When the great William James, that university's emeritus philosophy professor, first read the prodigy's article in a student publication, he walked across the Harvard Yard to the freshman dorm to meet a youth so brilliant.

Lippmann's classmate John Reed later chronicled the Russian Revolution–much later the inspiration for Warren Beatty's movie *Reds*. It was predicted that Lippmann, then still at Harvard, would become secretary of state one day or, at the very least, governor of New York. Theodore Roosevelt said he was the most brilliant young man of his generation. He did not get his famous column until he was forty-two (anyone who is given a column before age thirty-six is spoiled/doomed by early success). Unlike Pegler, who eventually was discarded by powerful publishers when he displeased them, the cerebral Lippmann devised a different route: he would burrow into the soft underbelly of the established order.

He had extraordinary influence, almost impossible to believe in this era of the Information Explosion. An earnest socialist when young, he apprenticed under the original "muckraker" journalist Steffens. But Lippmann, abandoning his socialist ideals, became a conspirator with Teddy Roosevelt. He was crucial in formulating Woodrow Wilson's Fourteen Points. He helped the American ambassador avert a war with Mexico. He personally coached both Wendell Willkie and Dwight Eisenhower as they tried for the White House.

He openly (*i.e.*, secretly) plotted with key senators in Washington for diplomatic recognition of the Soviet Union, for Lend-Lease with Britain, and for approval of the Marshall Plan. John Kennedy and Lyndon Johnson sought him out for advice as they tried to wrestle with the problem of being president. Lippmann, as the psychiatrist who had the world on his couch, informed them and advised them. He had a unique status unknown to any journalist before him, and never to be matched.

Along with his brilliant mind, he had another advantage. When his nation reluctantly accepted world leadership after

World War II, Lippmann was already in his mid-fifties, a widely travelled man who every year had European monarchs and prime ministers changing their schedules so they could accommodate his visits. He had reached emeritus age by most journalistic judgments, but it was almost as if he had spent his entire life preparing for this period of opportunity, a man who had more experience than any secretary of state and so was able to advise them.

Pat Carney, a journalist before she plunged into politics, once pointed out to me that a reporter is the most interrupted person in the world. The phone is always ringing. You seldom have a straight ten minutes of thinking time. A crisis always intrudes. Lippmann, unlike his colleagues, had complete control of his life. Mere news events never intruded.

At the start of every year, he knew his entire schedule for the following twelve months. He had mapped out when he would be in Washington, when he would go to New York for two weeks of theater. He knew when he would go to Maine to escape the summer heat and when he and his wife would host their two annual parties. He knew all the dates of his annual tour of Europe. (Bruce Hutchison, the dean of Canadian journalism, as Lippmann was the dean of the American variety, has much the same routine, doing his annual sounding of Harvard, Washington and Ottawa on a regulated pattern. He also does not cover fires.)

It was not that Lippmann was omniscient. The portrait drawn by Ronald Steel in *Walter Lippmann and the American Century* shows him as a man who could at times be terribly wrong in his judgments, despite the stupendous reputation history has given him. Of Franklin Roosevelt, he wrote to a friend in 1931 that "I am now satisfied that he just doesn't happen to have a very good mind, that he never really comes to grips with a problem which has any large dimensions, and that above all the controlling element in almost every case is political advantage. He has never thought much, or understood much, about the great subjects which must concern the next President." Lippmann labelled him little more than a "kind of amiable boy scout."

He was not above being a hypocrite, and a bit of a cad, in his personal life. When in his late forties–despite the great success of his column–Lippmann was restless and contemplated the many offers to become a professor at Harvard, Amherst or Columbia. His marriage, to a woman not interested in politics, had developed into a stale ritual–the beach house in Florida, the country home, Broadway first nights. In his book, A *Preface to Morals*, he wrote that "as the glow of passion cools, it is discovered that no instinctive and preordained affinity is present."

His best friend was Hamilton Fish Armstrong, a fellow intellectual who greatly admired Lippmann. They dined twice a week at their New York club and talked every day on the phone. He had toured abroad with Armstrong and his wife, Helen, a woman he liked for her sharp tongue and quick wit. One night, with Lippmann's wife out of town, Armstrong had to attend a meeting and asked his best friend if he would take Mrs. Armstrong somewhere for dinner. Lippmann took her to the Rainbow Room of the newly built Rockefeller Center. They talked and talked, danced, dined again a few nights later and Lippmann–the most respected and dignified journalist in the world–found himself, after twenty years of marriage, in a passionate affair with the wife of his best friend.

They arranged to meet in Europe that summer. But Lippmann's intensely romantic letters (he was writing up to four a week) just missed Mrs. Armstrong in Kitzbühel in Austria. The hotel, which was where the Armstrongs always stayed, mistakenly sent the four love letters to Armstrong's office in New York. Although they were clearly addressed to Helen Armstrong, the secretary recognized Lippmann's handwriting and, suspecting something–she had never liked Helen–opened the first one and handed it over to Armstrong.

The lovers were unveiled, but Lippmann could not face informing his wife of the news. The man who advised presidents could not tell his wife the truth. He asked her father, a gentle man who was a former clergyman, to break the news to her. He never saw her again. In the divorce settlement, he willingly gave her everything he had–the two country houses, their Manhattan residence, all his savings, to be taken from his income over the next five years.

He married Mrs. Armstrong, and New York society of course divided over the public scandal. Dinner invitations were arranged so that Lippmann and Armstrong would never meet. Lippmann, knowing the tragedy could never be abridged, attempted to write Armstrong a letter of explanation. Armstrong refused to accept the letter–hand-delivered by a relative–let alone read it. As editor of *Foreign Affairs*, he never again allowed Lippmann's name to appear in the influential magazine. It was not until thirty years later that the two aging men, embarrassingly close to one another at a New York party, finally spoke.

Hamilton Fish Armstrong was a gentleman to the grave. When he died in 1973, among his papers was a packet of letters with a note attached that they were to be sent to Helen. When Mrs. Lippmann opened the packet she found the four letters, three of them unopened, with the note: "I read only the first three lines of one of these." And so Helen Armstrong Lippmann finally read the love letters the world's finest journalist had written to her thirty-six years previously.

Britain, because of its class structure, never had one journalist with the overwhelming power of Lippmann, who acted (as do London press barons) in consort with national leaders in the background–but also wrote a column out front. In London, the Rothermeres and the Northcliffes and the Beaverbrooks schemed behind the curtains; hired hands displayed the bylines.

The most famous byline, both pre-war and wartime, was that of the incomparable Cassandra of the brash *Daily Mirror*, the tabloid with five-million-a-day circulation that boosted Churchill into the prime ministership before the war and then helped toss him out as soon as the war was over. Cassandra was William Neil Connor, a man of choleric temperament. He was a medical and mental problem: suffering physically and spiritually from high blood pressure.

Connor's father was Irish and worked in the Admiralty. His mother was from Aberdeen–a good mixture of Celtic flair (and flare). On leaving school he was rejected by the Royal Navy as "not up to optical standard." He wandered through the licking of stamps, minor clerical work and junior accountancy in various offices until he drifted into advertising, eventually writing copy for the J. Walter Thompson giant. It is greatly amusing that the most powerful British journalist of his day–epitomizing all that was down-home English pluck and common sense–learned the power and value of words while writing hype for American proprietors who in those days were so far ahead in that new art.

He moved from there into journalism and swiftly progressed, in the words of his *Daily Mirror* boss, Hugh Cudlipp (writing in his book on the *Mirror, Publish and be Damned!*), "in the only profession where big-scale, incessant rudeness (skilfully written) is highly paid." Connor and Cudlipp joined the paper on the same day in 1935, the latter recalling later that, on first meeting, "I felt that I was involved in an extremely unpleasant motor crash; even the exchange of orthodox civilities, the casual 'Good Morning,' was accompanied by the awful din of screeching mental brakes. It has never been a question of What Makes Connor Tick, but What Makes Connor Clang."

His admirers used to say that he could make his column purr or bark, nuzzle or bite, canter or gallop, soothe or repel. Cassandra became an enormous Fleet Street success story on the most commercially successful newspaper in the world.

The *Daily Mirror* was the perfect platform for his bluster. On the day the Germans attacked Poland on September 1, 1939, there appeared on the front page of the *Mirror* just one symbol: the head of a determined lion. On September 4, Cassandra produced a page that had screaming headlines:

WANTED!
For Murder . . . For Kidnapping . . .
For Theft and for Arson
ADOLF HITLER
Alias Adolf Schicklegruber

Accompanied by a full-face and side-view of the criminal variety and similar excited text, the page ended with:

THIS RECKLESS CRIMINAL IS WANTED
–DEAD OR ALIVE!

The cheeky tab at this stage caught perfectly the mood of the British public. It was clear of panic, defeatism and gloom and its editorial on Dunkirk just had one large headline:

BLOODY
MARVELLOUS

Cassandra only slipped once. The most disgraceful subservience of the British press to the Establishment came in 1936 in the abdication crisis when the weak-faced King Edward, a sartorial dandy but nobbled by the twice-divorced American opportunist Wallis Simpson, was putting the entire future of the monarchy in peril. The New York press had been retailing for months the juicy news about the smitten king. He had bought Mrs. Simpson a $125,000 emerald necklace one day; another day, reported another American paper, "One gift is believed to have been a big black sedan. The King ordered two, and only one was delivered to him."

The American press eagerly reported that when the official six-month mourning period for King George V was over, Mrs. Simpson was on the Mediterranean cruise that Edward VIII took aboard the yacht *Nahlin* with the covering camouflage of the minister of war, Duff Cooper, and Lady Diana Cooper. There were the reports from the Hotel Bristol in Vienna of Edward stopping at a shop on the Kaerntnerstrasse and buying copious supplies of silk stockings, underwear and clothing.

None of it appeared in the British press. Geoffrey Dawson, editor of *The Times*, conferred privately with the archbishop of Canterbury over the crisis. The opposing factions pursued Churchill and Beaverbrook – who silenced his papers. The Thunderer, which had remained silent on the rise of the Nazi menace, further forfeited its great reputation by waffling over the decision to be first to denounce the smitten one's intentions.

In December, with the news that Mrs. Simpson's latest divorce had been made official–four months after the American press had been telling American readers what was going on–Fleet Street finally came out of the closet.

The fiercely proletarian *Mirror*, for once, got caught on the wrong side of the issue. The paper demanded of the prime minister, in its usual restrained tones: "THE NATION INSISTS ON KNOWING THE KING'S FULL DEMANDS AND CONDITIONS. THE COUNTRY WILL GIVE YOU THE VERDICT."

Cassandra leapt in with a defence for the king who gave up his throne for love (as was claimed, not entirely surprising those close to the scene who suspected he never had the craw for the job anyway). His column was titled "I accuse!" and, as Cudlipp reports, began with these words: "I am writing about what I regard as the biggest put-up job of all time. I accuse leaders of the Church of England of putting our King in a position from which it was almost impossible to retreat. I accuse the Prime Minister and his Government of manoeuvring, with smooth and match-less guile, to a desperate situation where humiliation is the only answer."

As it happened, the *Mirror* backed the wrong horse this time. The Church and the cabinet, in a showdown with the king, won. Prime Minister Baldwin prevailed, the weak man abdicated and the public, in its great common sense, accepted the verdict. Curiously enough, though the paper had misjudged public opinion this time, its circulation increased more than that of any other newspaper during the crisis, and it kept secure that increase after the crisis subsided and the doomed couple went off to an aimless drifting life of cocktail-party exile.

Cassandra–and the *Mirror* - never missed again. Of the Coronation celebrations for King George VI, he wrote:

> The latest insult to the unemployed has been announced by the Minister of Labour, Mr. Ernest Brown.
>
> He proposes that the Unemployment Assistance

Board should make special Coronation payments of 2s. 6d. to all persons who were unemployed during the week ending May 8 next.

Half a crown! What a contemptible gesture! They will fill their stomachs all right. They will have a good time on thirty pence. The whole nation will be united at this gladsome time and not a word of complaint will come from the great army of workless gratefully clutching their half crowns. Oh nuts!

When the *Mirror* published a photograph of a greyhound that had been allowed to starve to death and the dog-loving English wrote endless letters of protest, Cassandra decided to address the matter in his column.

"I wish to protest about the disgusting picture you published," wrote one reader. "This is cheap sensation at its worst. My two children who saw the picture were quite upset by its horror and ugliness. As I cannot allow gruesome illustrations like this to be left lying about the house I have asked my news-agent to stop sending the *Daily Mirror*."

Cassandra, father of three who lived in an old country rectory in Berkshire, wrote: "Well, we have lost a reader. But we can take it, and we are not very downhearted by losing the attention of a mind so monumental in its stupidity and bigotry. We are going to publish more of those pictures, and if we lose another handful of readers, well, that will be just too bad."

The traumatic episode killed off for the *Mirror* untold thousands of shawled female subscribers in Bognor Regis, Bath and Clacton-under-Mud but–by happenstance–launched it onto its unsurpassed urban triumph.

Cassandra took on everyone. Of the medical profession: "Of course I'm biased. I'm agin' doctors. I don't like 'em. For one thing their mumbo-jumbo, their smooth, lying inefficiency, and their blunt assumption that the disease-laden clients have the mentality of sick cattle. They are traders in the most valuable commodity we have–life itself." Cassandra decided that the General Medical Council was "unparalleled in bigotry and autocracy" and described the ordinary doctor as a man with "neither the wit nor the means to break into big money."

After helping to drive out Neville Chamberlain and install Churchill as the wartime leader, Cassandra soon became the hero of the British troops in exposing the idiotic orders requiring polished boots and drill parade. His popularity increased even more as soldiers and their wives mailed him further instances of bureaucratic goofiness.

Certain people were not amused, however, as he persisted: "I see that an MP is to ask why dances are permitted to be held in the premises of the Ministry of Information. What's wrong with dancing in the Ministry of Information? I think the whole thing should be turned into one vast dance-hall staffed by scores of red-hot mommas. . . . All play and no work in the Bloomsbury Taj Mahal would be a decisive blow for our cause."

He particularly liked sticking it to the home secretary, Herbert Morrison, who (Cassandra knew, and Morrison, uncomfortably, also knew) had written for the *Mirror* before the war. Now Morrison, as an orthodox socialist, closed the *Daily Worker*, the newspaper of the British Communist party. "What is the sense of gagging the *Daily Worker* any longer?" asked Cassandra when the Russians had been forced by Hitler's betrayal to enter the war on the side of the Allies.

The other most popular feature of the most popular paper in the world was the cartoonist Zec. Born a Cockney, trained at St. Martin's School of Art, Philip Zec was brought to the *Mirror* by Cassandra and they worked in the same office at the paper. Zec was as blunt as the columnist, and his heavy, dark drawings shocked people. He had Neville Chamberlain as a lugubrious pianist, with Hitler peeping out from under the lid, and the caption: "Don't shoot the pianist, he's doing his best." When Hitler in 1941 announced that he was feeling "fresher than ever, for Spring is coming," Zec drew a Nazi jackboot crunching a cluster of daffodils into the earth.

In 1942 the *Mirror* cartoonist began a series on a single theme, black-market activities and waste that were hampering the war effort. Tankers were being sunk by German submarines at an alarming rate and the death toll among merchant seamen was horrendous. The British government had just authorized an increase of one penny in the price of petrol, but Zec wanted to shock the public into a realization of its wastefulness. He produced a powerful drawing of a torpedoed sailor adrift on a raft on a black and angry sea–a stark scene emphasizing the horror of U-boat warfare. As a caption, he had written: "Petrol Is Dearer Now."

He showed it to Cassandra, who thought it brilliant but advised that it needed a stronger caption to dramatize the extra penny charge. And so when the most controversial cartoon of the war appeared the next morning the caption read: " 'The price of petrol has been increased by one penny.'–Official."

It was enormously popular with the public and the Mirror was inundated with requests for reproductions. But the government was outraged, there was an uproar in the Commons with cabinet ministers claiming that Zec's intention was not to admonish the public to conserve petrol by portraying the heavy cost in terms of human life but, instead, was an attempt to tell merchant seamen they were endangering their lives so that fatter profits could be made by the oil cartels.

The War Office complained to the cabinet that the Mirror was destroying morale, and Churchill ordered an investigation into the identity of all the shareholders in the newspaper. At the Home Office, Herbert Morrison saw the chance to strike. Harry Guy Bartholomew, as a director of the paper, and editor Cecil Thomas were ordered to appear in his office. Hugh Cudlipp's book details what happened based on notes kept by Thomas.

Morrison opened by saying that what he had to tell them was the unanimous decision of the cabinet. He produced a dossier on critical Mirror editorials. The Zec cartoon was "worthy of Goebbels at his best." It was clear, said Morrison, that the Mirror's wish for a drive in war production was camouflage to hide the real intent to bring down the government and society, to get the public depressed so that Britain would make peace by agreement.

Morrison reminded his silent listeners that he had closed one paper and said it would be a long time before it was opened. "And that goes for you, too. You might bear that in mind. If you are closed, it will be for a long time." No further warning would be given. "We shall act with a speed that will surprise you."

Bartholomew's only remark was that the cartoon had been so popular that there had been thousands of requests for it and did the government plan to stop the showing of it. "You had better get them back," was the cabinet minister's advice.

Morrison went immediately to the House of Commons to announce that action had been taken, citing Regulation 2D, which provided "for instantaneous suppression of a newspaper on the edict of the home secretary"–adding that a warning had been issued. To buttress his case, he quoted, rather out of context, a recent *Mirror* editorial that had stated ". . . the accepted tip for Army leadership would, in plain truth, be this: All who aspire to mislead others in war should be brass-buttoned boneheads, socially prejudiced, arrogant and fussy. A tendency to heart disease, apoplexy, diabetes and high blood pressure is desirable in the highest posts. . . ."

On Fleet Street, the *Mirror* was not liked–both for its success and for its cheekiness–but all its competitors recognized the threat the government was brandishing and rose to the national debate over freedom of the press. Morrison was silenced, however, by a fellow politician. In the emergency debate in the Commons, MP Fred Bellenger (a future war minister) rose to read long passages of something written during World War I. It was a passionate denunciation of soldiers being forced to go out and kill.

It turned out to have been written by Herbert Morrison. Herbert Morrison was a pacifist in that war, while Bellenger and Churchill and the others around them had fought. This was the man who had suppressed the *Daily Worker* for saying that this war should not be fought at all and who as cabinet mouthpiece was now threatening to suppress the *Mirror* for insisting that the war be fought efficiently. There was never heard again any talk about closing newspapers.

The *Mirror*, the only paper in Fleet Street to be hit by bombs

("The only British newspaper during the war to get into trouble with both sides," said Cudlipp) had the last laugh. When German High Command papers were examined by the Allies after the war, it was found that the Nazis had issued an order that all *Mirror* directors were to be immediately arrested when London was occupied.

Cassandra? During the closing-of-the-*Mirror* debate, the House of Lords rose ponderously to the question, and the lord chancellor, Viscount Simon, said, "I observe that the articles in the *Daily Mirror* which in some quarters have roused most offence are signed by the *nom de plume* of Cassandra. I do not need to remind those of your Lordships who maintain a memory of the Greek tragedians that Cassandra came to a very sticky end."

Cassandra, perhaps sick of the whole thing, within days joined up. "I cannot and will not change my policy," he wrote. "I am still a comparatively young man and I propose to see whether the rifle is a better weapon than the printed word." He returned to his bully pulpit five years later and began his first column:

"As I was saying when I was interrupted, it is a powerful hard thing to please all the people all the time."

Canadian journalism, because of its infancy, has never had one figure with the stature of a Lippmann or the national impact of a Cassandra. It had, however, Blair Fraser and Bruce Hutchison.

Blair Fraser was the last of the "Establishment" reporters. Peter Newman, while always fascinated with men of wealth and power, was an outsider, pinning the wings of the flies with his rich phrases. Peter Gzowski and Robert Fulford and Ken Lefolii delighted in tilting at windmills. Ralph Allen was always the man from Oxbow, Saskatchewan, a captive of no one. Berton bashed at everyone and everything before deciding that he wanted to be the readable historian that the detested academics could no longer ignore.

But Fraser typified a breed of journalist still found somewhat in the United States but extinct in Canada: well-bred, well-educated, more comfortable in the right type of club and on the right tennis court than in the press club or at the weekend in-house hockey match or softball game. (Jeffrey Simpson and John Fraser, of the younger breed, aspire to the Fraser ideal, but the days are not the same.)

Fraser was the quintessential Ottawa insider journalist. A cultured and discreet man, he shared the societal values of the senior civil servants he had to cover. In the post-war years, Canada had a dedicated, superbly confident mandarinate that suited the country's position then as an important "middle power" in the world.

Fraser, as *Maclean's* man in Ottawa, fitted in perfectly. His style of journalism was the opposite of loner Bruce Hutchison's. Fraser belonged to the exclusive fishing clubs that distinguished the upper elite of the Ottawa deputy ministers, drank with them at the Rideau Club, respected their confidences and established the best contacts in town. He never betrayed a secret in that incestuous little capital that has its own tribal rites (*i.e.*, if you don't play bridge or ski cross-country, it's tough breaking in). Even Fraser's untimely death, in a canoeing accident on a rugged stream, was viscerally connected with the Ottawa ethic.

On May 12, 1968, Blair Fraser was probably the most respected journalist in Canada. He had been Ottawa editor of *Maclean's* since 1943. In 1951 and again in 1961 he had won the Governor-General's Award for the best articles written by a Canadian anywhere in the world. In a troubled time at the magazine he took over as *Maclean's* editor in 1960 and then was overseas editor during 1961-62. He was known throughout the country for his thoughtful radio and television commentary. He travelled China, the Middle East, India, Africa, Europe, Australia–he had been everywhere. His book *The Search for Identity* summed up his convictions and analyzed the events that shaped Canada's post-war emergence as a middle power.

Fraser was for nearly twenty years one of a tightly knit group of eight men who made high adventure out of canoe trips from Ottawa and the Gatineau, reaching across northern Manitoba and Saskatchewan all the way to the Northwest Territories. Their purpose was not only to follow the old routes of the fur trade and exploration but also to get the flavor and the meaning of the wilderness. The group included Dr. Omond Solandt, a senior figure in the Ottawa defence firmament, several Americans and, as ready replacements, eager experts in white-water canoeing.

On this blissful spring Sunday morning, the long Ottawa winter finally over and the rivers finally free of ice, four of the canoeists set out. The Petawawa River, a major tributary of the Ottawa River along the border of Algonquin Provincial Park, was in full flood. They had all run the river before and looked forward with excitement to Rollway Rapids, a dangerous half-mile stretch of white water, rocks and spume. Rollway in days past was where logs had been rolled down the banks to be carried by high water to the Ottawa River and on to the mills below.

Whatever the reason–the spring run-off with the higher than usual water-level or the shifting river bed–expert canoeists Fraser in the stern and his longtime partner Elliott Rodger in the bow missed their turn into the portage and found themselves drawn into the throat of the main rapids. Their canoe quickly swamped, they tumbled helplessly down the cold water of the half-mile of rapids. Fraser was hurled head first into a rock. He was fifty-nine.

One of the moving eulogies was from Pierre Trudeau, who had been among Fraser's canoeing companions the year before on the Petawawa. In cruel irony, Blair Fraser, the best-connected journalist in Ottawa, died just three weeks after Pierre Trudeau was sworn in as prime minister of Canada.

Bruce Hutchison, still writing his column at the age of eighty-eight, is the most remarkable figure in Canadian journalism. Starting out in his teen-age years as a sportswriter, at twenty he sold fiction to *The Saturday Evening Post*. He regularly sold both articles and cartoons to the popular New York magazines. At twenty-four he was the youngest member of the Victoria Press Gallery and at twenty-five was in Ottawa meeting Mackenzie

King. His initial major book, *The Unknown Country*, was a national success as the first popular expression of the Canadian ethos.

He wrote regularly for all the mass circulation magazines–*Life*, the *Atlantic*, *Reader's Digest* and *Maclean's*. Every week, from 1919 to 1975, he produced a piece on Canadian affairs for *The Christian Science Monitor*. He travelled to West Germany to talk with government economic experts about that country's remarkable post-war miracle and went to Japan to do a series on its recovery. In Washington, he visited with Walter Lippmann, Mike Mansfield and Ben Bradlee.

The books continued to roll out–*The Fraser*, *The Incredible Canadian* (Mackenzie King, true); *Canada: Tomorrow's Giant* (not quite true); *The Struggle for the Border*; *Mr. Prime Minister*. Three Governor-General's awards and two Bowater awards. Two President's medals and three National Newspaper awards. Honorary degrees, for the high school graduate, stretching from the University of British Columbia to Yale. When the Royal Society of the Arts in London struck a silver medal for the best journalist in the Commonwealth outside the United Kingdom, the first winner, by unanimous vote, was Bruce Hutchison.

Hutchison never bothered going to Harvard. As a matter of fact, he never bothered going to any university. Canada's most literate journalist is the I.F. Stone of Canadian scribbling, a man who knows that distance encourages perspective, that the more you stay away from other journalists the more chance you have of discovering something new.

He learned some of the advantages of distance early on, as a bookish and non-drinking nineteen-year-old high school graduate covering the British Columbia Legislature for his Victoria paper against the competition of the hardened veterans sent over from Vancouver for the mainland newspaper and news services. Viewed as a bookish rustic, Hutchison declined to enter into the spirit of things at a sumptuous political banquet in the legislative buildings. By the end of the bibulous evening, as Hutchison has explained, the entire press gallery "lay down on the floor and went to sleep, which led me to conclude they were drunk."

Aware of his colleagues' deadlines, aware of their tenuous employment prospects if this momentous affair was not reported, the only sober journalist in Victoria sat down at his typewriter and turned out, in rapid fashion, six different stories to cover for the six stiffs laid out on the floor before him – each story with its own twist, depending on its destination: one sensational paper, one Tory paper, one Grit paper, etc., Hutchison knowing, in those days, just what prejudiced slant to put on each piece of copy. He marched down to the midnight ferry headed for Vancouver, despatched his six versions of the same story, while his mates slumbered on the cold floor – and saved six jobs.

In his memoirs, *The Far Side of the Street*, he described another "splendid occasion, indeed an event of international solemnity," which was sponsored by the provincial government to mark the resumption of liquor sales in British Columbia after wartime Prohibition – and to entertain the still-deprived legislators of Washington State.

> The guests and their ladies arrived at the Union Club in full evening dress and with a prolonged thirst, soon quenched by the government's preliminary cocktails. No pain was visible as the eminent assemblage seated itself around a vast and glittering table in celebration of the ancient friendship between Canada and the United States. All the arrangements were perfect, the food delicious, the wines of finest vintage. Predictably but, alas, unpredicted, the fraternal spirit could not be maintained.
>
> Senator J.W. de B. Farris, British Columbia's peerless orator, rising to deliver a message of the continental brotherhood and howled down by rival orators; John Oliver, host and premier, who drank no alcohol, surveying the scene in unbelief and horror, his white beard twitching; a distinguished statesman from the northern hinterland bestriding the table to make his voice heard above the tumult, collapsing among the broken glasses, face and hands cut, his blood staining

the napery; carried insensible across the street to his room in the hotel where his jovial friends summoned an undertaker who removed the corpse, to wake with a scream next morning on a marble slab; the ladies in the club leaping up, one after the other, with squeaks of alarm as if mouse-bitten; an esteemed labour member of the Legislature found crawling under the table to pinch female legs and, forcibly ejected, sleeping peacefully in the gutter of Humboldt Street; Charlie and I, cold sober, viewing our betters in judicious neutrality and reporting their behaviour with a decent minimum of truth—so ended a night of unrecorded North American history.

The narrowest line in journalism is the line between exploiting your sources (without ever destroying them) and being captured by them. Bruce Hutchison explained in his memoirs how he would be called in the Ottawa Press Gallery by Lester Pearson who was having problems with a particular speech. The elegant phrase-maker who is now the icon of Canadian journalism would go down to Pearson's office, craft a more graceful piece of text than Pearson's men could manage—and then sit in the Press Gallery on delivery and write a critique of it for his unknowing readers. It was another age, with other standards.

Politicians, even as late as 1957, had power over certain senior journalists and some journalists had access and a friendship that would be unheard of today. In that year, John Diefenbaker won his famous minority government decision from the voters, ending the Liberal rule that stretched back to the 1930s, and defeating the neophyte Liberal leader Pearson. When Parliament resumed, Pearson—in the first speech he had ever made in the House of Commons—was persuaded by Grit plotter Jack Pickersgill to try an outrageous ploy: demand that the Tories, since they clearly lacked a mandate to govern, resign immediately and turn the reins over to the Liberals.

The naive Pearson, once he had agreed to go along with the goofy scheme, arranged time for a nationally televised speech on the CBC and, through loyal Liberal reporter Grant Dexter, commanded that Hutchison be the interviewer.

Hutch, in Washington at the time preparing for an interview with the great Dean Acheson, told Dexter he couldn't do it. Pearson insisted, Dexter passed on the insistence, and Hutchison had to cancel the interview and fly to Ottawa just in time to enter the Commons Press Gallery and catch Pearson making his ludicrous proposal. On hearing it, the Commons burst into astonished laughter, and Dief, who always knew how to kick a guy when he was down, destroyed the humiliated Pearson with a searing denunciation that had the Tory troops whooping and bouncing in glee. The sheer effrontery of the Pearson proposal, yet another example of Liberal arrogance, led of course to the Dief electoral triumph of 1958, then the largest majority in the country's history.

After the debacle of the speech, Hutchison and Dexter—as they did so easily—went to Pearson's office and found him crushed and despondent, the victim of the greater "wisdom" of Pickersgill and Louis St. Laurent. He hadn't even told his own caucus what he had planned to propose to the Conservatives.

The television spectacle still awaited, and Pearson had no idea what he could say. As Hutchison candidly admits in his memoirs, he sketched out a few ideas on the back of an envelope and then he, Pearson and Dexter—with the other insider, Blair Fraser, squeezing into the car (Pearson drove)—rode out to the CBC studio together to patch together thirty minutes of explication. Peter Mansbridge and Barbara Frum, not to mention Dougie Small, would have been rather perplexed.

These days, "The Hat," as those of us who love him refer to him, slouches into Washington or Ottawa on his yearly reconnaissance forays beneath the fedora that actually expired in the forties and makes him appear a baddie in a John le Carré mystery. He has a double whisky at the press club, sucks on his pipe, playing the innocent from the bush (he should have received an Academy Award long ago), and when you pick up his column a week later it is clear he has been conferring with all the heavies in town a young journalist never gets near.

This has been the sly-virgin motif that Hutch has maintained so successfully since he was a pup. How could a chap simultaneously act as editor of both the *Victoria Daily Times* and the *Winnipeg Free Press* (and later editorial director of *The Vancouver Sun*) while hidden deep in the rain forests of Vancouver Island? At one time his only links with the outside world were a beat-up mantel radio and a phone in a gas station two miles down the road from his cottage.

While siring an Olympic sprinter who is now a Victoria judge, Hutch had a better idea: let the world beat a path to his door. Down a remote country trail came a constant stream of visitors to trade wisdom: Henry Brandon of *The Times* of London, Max Freedman from Washington and Blair Fraser and Peter Newman; American statesmen such as Scoop Jackson, Livingston Merchant, William Bundy and George Ball. The chief justice of the British Columbia Supreme Court, J.O. Wilson, was a frequent guest and was forthwith directed to wood-chopping detail.

"Since youth," Hutchison has confessed, "I have felt a horror of crowds, or argument, of making decisions, while criticizing the men who had to make them. Instead of responsible power (assuming that I could have gained it) I sought irresponsible privacy, the one thing worth buying and now outside the reach of anybody but a millionaire, who generally doesn't want, deserve or appreciate it."

5

The Revolving Door Problem

Woe unto you, scribes and Pharisees,
hypocrites! – *Matthew 23:23*

The indubitable truth is that the politicians and the press have
more in common with one another (and unconsciously prefer it
that way) than they do with members of the garden variety
unwashed. If you stumble into Nate's Steak House, down Rideau
Street from the zoo act on Parliament Hill, most any evening you
will find Press Gallery regulars trading lies and gossip with MPs
and the lower level of junior cabinet ministers who cannot find
elsewhere the winsome ambience that has made the town the
Athens of the North. This strange rapport develops because the
press and the politicians, like penitentiary inmates and their
guards, are imprisoned in an artificial atmosphere that bears no
resemblance to real life. This is especially true in the bogus cities
that are too often built to contain government, towns that
otherwise have no reason for existence. We're talking Ottawa, of
course, Washington, Canberra, Brasilia.

The stifling little lumber village of Bytown, on a mosquito-
ridden swampland, was chosen by Queen Victoria only to detour
around the competing bids of Hochelaga and Ticonderoga. The
original capital of the United States, Philadelphia, was moved to
another fetid lowland on the Potomac mainly because George
Washington owned a lot of land in the vicinity and knew it
would be profitable. Canberra, an arid retreat in isolated dry hills
in a country that has the most beautiful beaches in the world, was
chosen as a site equidistant between Sydney and Melbourne so as
to negate the rivalry between the two demanding applicants.

Brasilia was created in forlorn wilderness so as to win somebody architectural prizes and enrich the airlines because of the government bureaucrats who cannot wait to get out of the place on weekends and jet to the sea–and civilization.

In all four artificially created capitals (sites by steroids), the predictable has happened. A recession-proof populace, isolated from reality, exists in an upper-middle-class dream sequence, actually believing that this existence mirrors the national reality. There are no slums in Ottawa, no unemployed lobbyists in Washington (the fact that Washington is now the murder capital of the U.S. as well as the political capital provides useful practice in ignoring unpleasant facts right under one's nose). No ill-dressed people in Brasilia, nary a bag-lady at an intersection in Canberra. It is Dreamland, where all prospects please and nothing is vile.

It has nothing to do with jolting legislators, reminding lawmakers, hinting to journalists, how most Canadians, or Americans, or Australians, or Brazilians live. I used to get into passionate debates with Charlie Lynch over my mild printed critiques of Ottawa as the sumphole of the mind. He would declaim heatedly that it, in fact, was the Venice of the Tundra, a wondrous spot where he could, on leaving his office in summer, be at his cottage on his lake in the Gatineau Hills in Quebec in, on a hard day, twenty minutes.

Exactly. That's the problem. Ottawa is a very safe town for a politician–small, comfortable, sleepy. The high point of the entire year? A hijacker's bus is stuck in the mud of the Parliament Hill lawn. (You had to know the guy was demented in the first place, demanding that the bus bound for New York go to *Ottawa* instead.)

Even more dangerous to the body politic is that Ottawa is an extremely pleasant resting spot for journalists, the couch potato ideal for scribblers who wish to sink among the cushions of the middle class. It doesn't have the traffic problems of Toronto, or the political tensions of Montreal. (Vancouver is too far away from anywhere to be a threat to anything.)

As in Washington, where the Ivy League-bred and Brooks

Brothers-clothed aspirants to the newspaper suites adopt the Georgetown camouflage of the politicians and bureaucrats and diplomats they are assigned to cover, the long-term Ottawa journalist–who does not want to move because it is so pleasant, as God knows–is in constant danger of becoming part of the furniture, the wallpaper behind the action. Long-range acquaintance with either atmosphere is dangerous, fostering the illusion that you really know what is going on.

It's why the most volatile (*i.e.*, interesting) politicians in Ottawa over the years have been the ones from Quebec, proving the veracity of Jean Marchand's comment that the best thing about Ottawa was the railway station that pointed to Montreal. Western Canadian and Atlantic province MPs, by contrast, have their home bases so far away (particularly because of the arcane transportation problems in getting out of Ottawa) that they tend to hunker down in the nation's supposed capital, sharing bachelor flats and drinking too much, while wife and kiddies suffer afar.

(MPs from Ontario, which really isn't part of Canada, simply drive home on Friday, returning on Monday, members of the famous Tuesday-to-Thursday Club.)

Press and politicians find each other in Nate's Steak House, Mike Duffy picking up the gossip from the gossips in the Liberal caucus, Hugh Winsor tapping his Tory sources, the politicians in return asking if it is true about the absolutely filthy joke Mulroney chief-of-staff Stanley Hartt told at the stag for former Mulroney speechwriter L. Ian MacDonald before his marriage to the winsome Lisa Van Dusen, one of the many winsome daughters of Diefenbaker loyalist Tom Van Dusen who is now in the Mulroney entourage. Like, it's not as if Ottawa is incestuous. No more than Washington. No more than Canberra. No more than Brasilia. . . .

In all three countries I have worked in, it has been the after five o'clock socializing that has provided the best transfer of information from politician to journalist, with the public unaware of the connection. In Britain, it is based (as is most everything, still) on class. The Beatles may have liberated the lower classes with the bad accents in the world of entertainment and movies (Michael Caine with that thinly disguised Cockney accent could not have succeeded in Hollywood if the Beatles had not conquered the United States first. Cary Grant, the supposed epitome of sophistication, was born Archie Leach and surpassed because he perfected a plummy accent; Caine didn't have to disguise his roots, thanks to the Fab Four.) But a non-upper-crust accent still doesn't work in British political journalism.

Thanks to their accents, graduates from Oxford and Cambridge continue to come down to London on graduation and move right into coveted jobs on the quality papers–*The Times, The Observer, The Daily Telegraph*, to a lesser extent *The Guardian* and now *The Independent*–becoming correspondents, commentators, critics on the arts pages and in the political columns, because their connections give them access to information.

In Washington, where accents don't count, addresses take their place. It's hard to get ahead at *The Washington Post* if you don't live in Georgetown, the ten-block square at the end of Pennsylvania Avenue bounded at its lower reach by the Potomac and its upper by the Dumbarton Oaks estate where the skeleton of the United Nations was mapped out by the winning nations in 1944. Katharine Graham, who, when her brilliant and manic-depressive husband blew his head off with a shotgun at age forty-nine, did not know how to write a cheque and is now the richest woman in America as owner of *The Washington Post* and *Newsweek*, lives at the very top of the Georgetown hill on R Street.

Her Pulitzer Prize-winning and now millionaire reporter Bob Woodward lives a martini throw away down on Q Street. Ben Bradlee, her editor, who traded girls with his close friend Jack Kennedy, and made young cop-shop reporters Woodward and Carl Bernstein into the national heroes of Watergate by backing them all the way, lives just down the hill on N Street, where the rock music from his big parties wafts over the lawn into the balcony of *Maclean's* bureau chief Marci McDonald, who lives just along the street from where John Mitchell, the Nixon attorney-general who spent time in the crowbar hotel after Watergate, died of a heart attack on the sidewalk outside his place the other day. You get the picture.

Woodward, of course, knows better than most the value of social and personal connections. His book *Veil* was based entirely on his personal and private conversations with CIA chief William Casey, who in some strange (or perhaps not-so-strange) symbiotic relationship between an Iran-contra super-schemer and the No. 1 investigative reporter of our time revealed more to Woodward than to Congress. To the extent that Woodward, in his book's dramatic dénouement, has a dying Casey confessing all after the reporter had somehow smuggled himself into his hospital room.

Mrs. Casey denies to this day that Woodward could possibly have got into the room. Woodward says he will not identify the people who helped get him into the room—which to some of his critics is the only way he can prove his actual presence in the death ward. Woodward has a pretty good batting average. It would be rather improbable if he began faking things at this stage. What we do know is that he understands the social connections.

The myth, in the public mind, is that the "adversaries"–the press and the politicians–lead different lives, encountering one another only in the scrum outside Question Period or in the television interview. In reality, because they share the same values–power, for example–they frequent the same watering holes, the same restaurants and (with the Bigfoot Journalists) the same parties.

Information is power, and the most powerful journalists know the asset a well-set table and a well-selected guest list can be in collecting information–and demonstrating clout. Knowlton Nash of the CBC has long known the political uses–in both CBC politics (of which there is nothing more byzantine) and political politics–of a selectively selected guest list at a Christmas cocktail party.

Barbara Frum is known to her public as a tough and demanding host, first on the "As It Happens" radio inquisition that made her name, and then as the expensively dressed host of "The Journal." In Toronto, she performs another role. She is a power broker. She sifts and selects who is important. Ascendancy, and the opposite, on the popularity scale can be judged by who can be seen at the Frum dinner table.

With husband Murray, a merry-eyed man who grew bored with being a dentist and became a wealthy developer instead, she has a Ron Thom-designed wood-and-glass home in a bosky dell in Don Mills that is the only house in Toronto that looks as if it is in British Columbia. It is full of expensive African art, and the dinner parties have a guest list that is pure cream.

Barbara is the den-mother-cum-traffic-cop among the town's personalities in broadcasting, journalism, the book industry and the arts world in general. Has someone wounded Larry Zolf's sensibilities? She is on the phone, advising as to apologies, the extent of the hurt, the suggestions for damage control. Why did Adrienne Clarkson and McClelland & Stewart part company? Barbara knows the details immediately. She mediates feuds, has all the hot new gossip, watches who's on the way up and who's on the way down and generally knows everything that's going on. Which is the mark of a good journalist, of course.

Her connections–hence her power–were perfectly demonstrated early in 1989 when it became known that *Globe and Mail* publisher Roy Megarry had bumped into editor-in-chief Norman Webster in the paper's cafeteria on Boxing Day, taken him into his office and fired him. Within weeks, an all-star cast was summoned to the Frum home on a Saturday night to meet the relatively unknown successor: William Thorsell, who had established a reputation for himself on *The Edmonton Journal* editorial page before returning to the *Globe* as an editorial writer.

There was the natural curiosity about the new Megarry pick, particularly considering the controversy that had followed the sacking of Webster, proud, wealthy and a good journalist, who had been a Rhodes Scholar, whose family had owned the *Globe* and whose uncle was still listed on the masthead as honorary chairman. Frum knew who wanted to meet Thorsell and check him out. The king is dead, long live the new king and Frum had him at her dinner party.

There was the cerebral Marcel Masse, back in the Communications portfolio he never should have left, after his non-communicative venture in the oil patch as Energy minister. In his first stint in the role, the Toronto culture crowd was alive with the story that he had never heard of either Margaret Atwood or Wayne and Shuster—a rumor possibly (and understandably) half-true. The Toronto literati now approve of him.

There were the Gotliebs, Allan and Sondra, just in from his Harvard chores filling the Mackenzie King Chair of Canadian studies to do some house-hunting in the most dreadful house-hunting market in North America, Sondra of course making the prints with one of her tossed-off remarks that they couldn't find anything they liked for less than $1 million–undoubtedly true but a comment, like those of Yogi Berra, that will always follow her around.

There was Hal Jackman, he of the ferocious eyebrows, another of the celebrated Tories along with John Bassett and Dalton Camp who could never get elected to Parliament on their way to the prime ministership, the voters proving stubborn. Jackman is now occupied with raising the money for Toronto's new opera-ballet house.

Conrad Black, of course, was present, armed with his orotund vocabulary and stories of his close friend Maggie Thatcher. This was a tricky bit of Frum stick-handling, because also present at the gathering was close friend Robert Fulford, who had a most interesting description of Black in the book he wrote after he and Conrad swiftly parted company when the latter bought *Saturday Night* where Fulford had been the long-time editor:

> Black turned out to be an extremely uncommon millionaire, not so much in the content of his conversation as in his manner. He was more theatrical than any other businessman of my acquaintance. His personality had a staged, directed feel to it. It was also

oddly familiar. Where had I seen it before, a large, handsome man with a supercilious and condescending manner and a baroque vocabulary? Of course: Orson Welles in *Citizen Kane*. I was talking to Citizen Black.

Who else? Margaret Atwood, naturally, the high priestess of cultural nationalism, and her man, author Graeme Gibson. Robert Campeau, the millionaire developer who now owns New York's beloved Bloomingdale's. The fashionable Ostrys, bureaucrat supreme Bernie who now heads TVOntario and Ottawa mandarin supreme Sylvia.

Mulroney chief-of-staff Stanley Hartt was down from Ottawa for the thrash: Frum can throw a wide net. Peter Mansbridge and new bride Wendy Mesley, a rising CBC star. Writer George Jonas, who shares his political philosophy with Barbara Amiel.

The mix demonstrated the Frum style: a minister or two from government, heavy hitters from the book world, money men, broadcasting faces, developers, one judge, an architect, someone from music–all to impress with the muscle of the arts community at a time when the beleaguered *Globe* is apparently shifting even more to business news with feared results for coverage of the cultural field.

There was David Crombie, the tiny perfect one, who might have survived in Ottawa if he had ever been given Masse's Communications portfolio. Peter Herrndorf, the big guy with the big mustache who as publisher of *Toronto Life* is heavily into Stratford and good works. From the NDP there was Gerry Caplan, the co-author with the Tories' Hugh Segal and the Liberals' Senator Michael Kirby of the hilarious election campaign book that posits the false conclusion they are political rivals.

The list stretches on and on, power people who need to know the new chap on the block who can tilt his paper in ways that could be beneficial, or harmful, to those who are perusing him this evening. Toronto, like New York, likes to concentrate its power among as few people as possible. It's easier to keep track that way. Concentration on Wall Street and Bay Street means fewer and fewer firms, more and more giants. If you want to know where power is in Toronto, go to a Barbara Frum party.

Who is the jailer? And who is the jailee? Barbara Frum hosts Brian Mulroney's chief-of-staff and the minister responsible for the CBC. Who benefits more? The politicians and political operators down from Ottawa who hear the beefs and polemics from the Toronto media crowd? Or the power journalists and publishers who have a new feel-all around the excuse of Thorsell-for those close to Mulroney? It's a symbiotic relationship. The Stockholm Syndrome.

To every rule, there are exceptions, of course. Probably the best investigative reporter in Canada is John Sawatsky. He almost threw me into a faint, too many decades ago, when he showed up in my *Vancouver Sun* office from his Simon Fraser University studies, offering to do research on weekends and in his spare time. I explained that I had the world's finest researcher, Marilyn Stusiak, and couldn't afford a second one. He didn't want or expect money, he replied, he just wanted to do it for the experience. Having learned that the Vancouver Newspaper Guild had just negotiated a new contract guaranteeing that all employees-however old and however uninterested in a rainy February holiday-would get a day off on their birthday, I almost expired at the sight of a reporter who was obviously going to succeed.

I think Sawatsky now a trifle overuses his journalism students as bird-dogs to collect a lot of his material, but he is a credit to his craft and his books become more powerful with each outing. Because he's a virgin-he works outside the system.

Don McGillivray, the Southam News Ottawa columnist, is also a virgin, despite his Established Order employer. He works out of the Southam office on the fifth floor overlooking one of the more surreal landscapes in the western world, the Sparks Street Mall. And he never leaves the office. He has voluminous files, a superb memory, a quiet private humor-and a great distaste for how Ottawa works. "McGoo," as his fellow workers call him, automatically turns down party invitations, does not go to receptions, does not socialize. He bangs out the column that so infuriates Brian Mulroney and he never misses a deadline and the column, landing in the Southam mothership computer, is never a word too long or a word too short. McGoo is a virgin. The promiscuous ones know who they are.

This author knows something about the dangers, because I invented Brian Mulroney. It was the autumn of 1975 and Robert Standstill, figuring three straight defeats to Pierre Trudeau were enough, announced to his party that he wished out and would it please arrange a leadership convention to pick his successor. I wrote a column–in fact it was the second one I had done on the back page of *Maclean's*. I said that Paul Hellyer was too stubborn and Jack Horner was too dumb and Joe Clark was too young (the next time I ran into Clark, in Toronto's Terminal Two, he pointed out that he in fact is two months younger than Mulroney).

I noted that you did not have to be too bright to figure out that the Tories would never become a real force in the country until they found a leader from Quebec who was fluently bilingual. I pointed out that they had one if they only woke up, he being someone I had never met at that moment but whose track record I had been watching. Young and lively, with a beautiful wife and a reputation from working on the union racket-busting Cliche Commission, he seemed worth the gamble. I dubbed him "The Candidate from Whimsy."

A while later, the world's most efficient English secretary, Miss Framsham, buzzed–this being *The Vancouver Sun*–and said, "There's a Mr. Mulroney on the line from Montreal."

I picked up the phone and, dispensing with preliminaries, asked, "When did you decide to run?"

The voice on the other end of the line said, "The second time I read it in your column."

It was a great relationship while it lasted, between this Protestant boy from Northern Ireland and Mulroney, a Catholic boy from the other end of the Emerald Isle, and both loving a laugh and a touch of the gargle on occasion (as he did then, though no longer), and many the lunch was spent in his haunt in the Maritime Bar in the Ritz-Carlton across from his office on Sherbrooke and there was great damage done to the truth.

It took the Tories, of course, until 1983 to take my sound advice, and when my invention moved into 24 Sussex Drive, I was a frequent guest with mutual friends and parties and the rest. There was an unwise acceptance to a weekend at Harrington Lake, the prime ministerial retreat in the Gatineau across the river in Quebec, with the wine and cold chicken arriving by motor launch for lunch in the private cabin, and things were getting rather too close.

My journalistic colleagues, while envying the open and easy access, began to wonder about the effect on the objectivity. They were correct. I *was* getting too close. When the chance came to remove to a safe distance in Washington for the first four years of the Mulroney regime to launder myself, the opportunity was grasped.

The world of politics has many ways of exerting pressure on those who are paid to write about it. Bruce Phillips, before he became a CTV star and then press officer at the Canadian Embassy in Washington and then director of communications in the PMO, was the Southam newspaper chain's correspondent in Washington. Phillips is a large morose man with a vicious wit and a reputation for laziness. Nonetheless, he was a superb reporter. Charles Lynch, then chief of the Southam news service, says Phillips was the best correspondent he has ever seen, doing a brilliant series from South Africa that was years ahead of its time, and fine work in covering America.

It was the time of the Vietnam War, and the United States was torn with the debate on its involvement. Phillips' despatches made it quite clear he thought it an insane venture, doomed to failure. The tone of his reporting did not please the conservative Southam publishers, especially in the chain's western Canadian papers. Criticism of the official Washington position and descriptions of the growing revolution on U.S. campuses against the war did not go over well. Phillips, as a good correspondent who had established his credentials, persisted in writing it as he saw it.

If a sulker, Phillips is gregarious (he usually ends up as president of whatever golf club he belongs to). One night, he organized a "Canada Night" at the National Press Club in Washington, going to a great deal of trouble to entertain the foreign journalists who were guests and to publicize his country.

There was plenty of strong liquid, so much so that there was a supply left over, which Phillips decided to store in his Southam office in the same building, not wanting it to go to waste. Having consumed his share and the evening being rather late, he relaxed on the couch in his office, covered his face with newspapers and went off to the land of Nod.

As the fates would have it, one Arthur Moscarella, publisher of Southam's Vancouver *Province*, happened to be in town and thought it would be a good idea to drop around and check out the Southam office. Moscarella came up through advertising and was a strong-minded man when it came to how newspapers should be run.

He walked into the office the next morning, to find a large hulk, still far from death, stretched out on the couch covered by newspapers. He tugged at a shoe that was protruding. "Bruce," he said.

From beneath the newspapers came a muffled, "Fuck off."

"Bruce," the publisher said, "it's Arthur Moscarella."

From beneath the pile came the reply. "Fuck off, Arthur Moscarella."

Bruce Phillips left the employ of the Southam newspapers.

Some two decades later, this here scribbler, in agreement with Southam News, for whom I was toiling in the Ottawa office, moved to Washington to write a column from there. I learned to love it–a nice little house and garden in delightful old George-town, a little slice of London in the most important city in the world. A well-outfitted Southam office in the National Press Building, two blocks from the White House, the most beautiful press club extant just one floor above our office.

One day I received a call from Toronto from Brian Butters, who had been my office mate in Washington before moving into management to handle communications in the Southam head office on Bloor Street. As part of the plan to shake up Southam's stuffy image, he explained, it was planned to hold the annual directors' meeting in Ottawa this year, this year being 1987. Would I come up and be the speaker at the dinner?

I laughed. Butters laughed. It wasn't really a request, as we both knew. It was a command performance. I was to sing for my supper. Butters explained that it would be just "family"–Southam directors and their wives, publishers and editors of the company's papers that stretch from Montreal to Vancouver. Southam has always been noted for this approach. The organization treats its correspondents well and everyone knows everyone else, writers often staying with other Southam brethren in their homes when abroad.

As the Ottawa date approached, I enquired several times for further details and an exact guest list, but Butters was busy and distracted with other work. He knew my act well, and I thought I knew what was expected of me: after a spell in Washington, to pass on to the closed meeting of Southam brass my candid thoughts on what I had found. A member of the "family" to be flown up to give an honest assessment.

At the pre-dinner cocktails on the patio of the National Arts Centre, I thought it a little puzzling when I spotted the scrumptious Tory minister Barbara McDougall, who will be the female challenger for 24 Sussex Drive when Mr. Mulroney leaves, but she advised she was just there for drinks and wouldn't be at dinner. Bruce Phillips loomed through the crowd of a hundred or so, but that could be explained away, I reasoned, since he was a close golfing buddy of Butters, both of them being addicted to that strange boring sport wherein middle-aged and middle-class men get to dress like pimps.

The guest list, as it turned out later, contained more puzzling additions. To wit, American Ambassador to Canada Thomas Niles, a man I had never met. Free trade was much in the air (one of the reasons I thought I was invited to a family affair), and I told my audience of what I assumed were insiders that it was a fact, pleasant or not, that Peter Murphy, the Washington negotiator up against our sweet-tempered Simon Reisman, had an inoperable brain tumor. It did not affect his day-to-day work but, I added, brain tumors are brain tumors and if something happened I suggested that the Canadian public–in assessing how serious Washington really was about the negotiations–would wonder what the Americans were doing putting the whole ball of wax in the hands of a guy who had this problem. It was a comment meant for Canadian ears, but it turned out that two pairs of American ears were listening.

I wound up with a line that I thought most of the audience was somewhat familiar with since I had made it in print. That I was not one of those Canadians who moaned over the fact that Americans are ignorant of–as they are–and uninterested in–as they also are–Canada. When I would get worried, I explained, was if the United States *did* get interested in Canada, because I recalled all those countries the U.S. had become interested in: Chile, Vietnam, Nicaragua, Lebanon, Libya, Grenada. "Let's keep that ignorance flying!" I advised as a closer.

Mrs. Thomas Niles, who was seated next to Paddy Sherman, the Southam vice-president in charge of all newspaper operations, hissed, "I don't mind coming to dinner, but I resent being the dessert." As I finished, Mr. and Mrs. Niles broke the *Guinness Book of Records* mark for the forty-foot dash to the door.

A pleasant woman I had never met who identified herself as Mrs. John Fisher, which would make her the wife of the fairly recent new president of Southam Inc., came up and said how much she enjoyed the speech. But John Fisher–as the Nileses sped off into the night–walked over to J. Patrick O'Callaghan, then publisher of the *Calgary Herald* and previously chairman of the publishers' committee that oversees Southam News, and said, "I didn't know Fotheringham was like that."

"You should have asked me," replied O'Callaghan who was then and is today a good friend. "I hired him."

Phillips, Butters and I ended up in one of our rooms at the

Four Seasons. Phillips, as usual, was morose and mordant. Butters simply sat and looked at the floor. It was clear that a brave plan had seriously gone wrong.

I received a stiff note from Paddy Sherman, pointing out the diplomatic rudeness of talking about brain tumors in the presence of foreign dignitaries. This rather puzzled me, since I had not been informed that foreign dignitaries were to be present. Butters, in deep despair that his former office mate might have cost him his job, mumbled that I probably wouldn't have changed the speech anyway if forewarned about Niles. I thought it over and allowed as to how he was possibly correct.

Months later, Nicholas Hills, as general manager of Southam News in Ottawa my nominal boss, came down to Washington and requested lunch. He had been a personal friend for years along with his lovely and vibrant wife, Lana. We proceeded with our usual bibulous lunch in the Celadon restaurant deep within the bowels of the Marriott Hotel on Pennsylvania Avenue next door to the National Press Building–a lunch filled with high tales and much laughter.

Nick Hills is an interesting rogue, a rollicking character with a news sense matched by few journalists in the country. The morning after the celebrated evening when Sondra Gotlieb slapped her social secretary, Connie Connor, on the steps of the ambassadorial residence in Washington, there seemed little interest in the story in the Southam News office in Ottawa. When Hills arrived, he immediately sensed the import of what had happened–he said it was "a Greek tragedy, in a way," which it has proven to be for a bright lady–and ordered his less perceptive staff to get cracking on the story.

Hills arrived in this country from England as a "draft dodger" who could not abide Britain's 1956 Suez action. A product of a reasonable birth in what is now the stockbroker belt in Sussex south of London, he went to the same Balham typing school that produced Peter Sellers. He is short, rotund (less today than previously), disputatious and given to bullying waiters (a common English xenophobic trait). One of the great Canadian journalism stories of all time is about Hills and Jack Webster setting fire to a waiter in the best restaurant in Winnipeg, which, being Winnipeg, was in St. Boniface.

It is typical Hills that, on arriving in Toronto and unable to find a job, he inserted a classified ad in a journalism trade magazine specifying that he was a bright young reporter who would "go anywhere, work for anyone, for any price." He received twenty-seven replies. His brashness and his energy and ambition made him, at the unusual age of thirty, news editor of Southam's now-dead *Winnipeg Tribune*.

Hills became a minor star at Southam, establishing a western Canadian bureau based in Vancouver, where we first became buddies, and ranging across the prairies for stories, where he became friends with such as Ed Schreyer and other political figures. He was stationed in London and given the Eastern European beat, covering Moscow and the Solidarity story in Poland and the Pope's historic visit to his homeland. After seven years as general manager of Southam News in Ottawa, where he energized the service, hired some women and saw his disciples win seven National Newspaper Awards, he was rewarded with his present post as editor-in-chief of *The Vancouver Sun* in a city he loves.

Over the years our friendship flourished–with the usual flaring catfights destined between personal friends who share professional relationships, sometimes one on the top, sometimes the other. In 1984, after encouraging the Washington move, happy in a new marriage, he had me detour a Bahamas holiday to fly to his wife's blissful family retreat in Westwell, Kent, to preside as godfather at his new daughter's christening. In 1987, though I was in Winnipeg on the way to Los Angeles, he argued successfully that I had to travel via Ottawa to deliver the speech before all our comrades at his fiftieth birthday. I digress.

We are now finishing lunch at the Marriott. With a large grin on his face (which was sporting a new regimental mustache that makes him appear to be either a retired British major or a publican), he handed across the luncheon table an envelope. Its opening passage detailed that ". . . this will confirm that your salaried employment with Southam News will end on December 31, 1988."

I didn't bother to wait for the deadline and moved to the *Financial Post/Toronto Sun* group.

And I still haven't met Mr. Niles.

Peter C. Newman, who is intrigued by men in power and therefore had been keeping his eye on the young Brian Mulroney for some time, is accused by other journalists of being in the pre-convention group that prepared Mulroney for his crucial (and, as it turned out, disappointing) speech at the 1976 Conservative leadership convention that he lost to boyhood rival Joe Clark.

Newman now has a unique deal with the prime minister. He has open access to candid conversations between the two of them on a regular basis–on the understanding that nothing will be published in a book until Mulroney leaves office. In effect, Newman is getting the inside on the life-in-power story of Mulroney. It undoubtedly will be a great book. But Newman, in his columns and journalism, rarely says anything very openly critical of Mulroney.

One suspects that Mulroney–always seeking approval–will not be happy with the finished product, just as Conrad Black, who had given Newman similar access to his inner self, was enraged at the contents when the Newman book on him eventually appeared. They are no longer friends.

Mulroney, because he is such a media freak, and because he is so thin-skinned about criticism, embraces with a sometimes suffocating hug those journalists who are sympathetic to him. (I once asked him, in a tape-recorded interview, why he was so thin-skinned. He lowered his head, thought for some time and then replied, softly, "Because I'm Irish, I guess." The honesty of it surprised me, being Irish myself, and rather charmed me. Recognizing one's weaknesses is the first step to wisdom.) And so he hires those scribes (often in most inappropriate roles) who have been sympathetic to him. That's crazy, as a matter of fact;

they would be more useful to him outside the wall, pushing his case in the public prints.

When he was in his depression after losing the first time to the Joe Clark he did not respect and was in his drinking period, one reporter who did not desert him was Bill Fox of *The Toronto Star*. A rough-hewn type from a rough northern Ontario town–as Mulroney was from rough-and-ready Baie Comeau–bilingual, a bit of a carouser himself, Fox recognized another small-town boy, perhaps more polished and with a law degree, but still with small-town insecurities. Mulroney never forgot that fealty and, once prime minister, made the hot-tempered Fox his press secretary.

As the Fox assistant, he hired Michel Gratton, an exuberant former rock singer who wrote a column for *Le Droit* and dressed as if motorcycle gangs were still in vogue. Once, on a Mulroney visit to the White House, an American reporter leaned over and asked why Mulroney's bodyguards stood so close to him; Reagan's Secret Service agents, as he pointed out, tried to blend in with the drapes. Those aren't bodyguards, we had to explain. Those are his two press secretaries.

In all, Mulroney hired eight journalists for his office in the first six years after winning the leadership. In addition, he brought in the bright and polite Marc Lortie from External Affairs as press secretary. On the outside, about the only two he managed to seduce–if temporarily–were Fotheringham and Newman.

He hired, as speechwriter, L. Ian MacDonald, a handsome, rather arch Montreal *Gazette* columnist with impeccable Westmount connections and contacts. "L. Ian," cracked Nick Auf der Maur, another roistering Mulroney pal, "has never met a rich man he didn't like." L. Ian (the moniker is not entirely an affectation–he devised it to distinguish himself from another Ian MacDonald on the *Gazette* who toiled on the sports pages) has the air of a man from another era, preferably F. Scott Fitzgerald's, and gave Mulroney the necessary gossip from the salons of Montreal and the Ritz-Carlton while the rough duo of Fox and Gratton worked the beer circuit in the press clubs.

He hired Ian Anderson, an aloof young man from *Maclean's*

who disappeared into some black hole of disinformation once such bulldozers as Fox and Bruce Phillips appeared. He hired Luc Lavoie, a Quebec TV reporter who worked on Parliament Hill, and steadily promoted him after new chief-of-staff Derek Burney cleaned out the PMO and Fox left for "consulting" (becoming even more affluent with his new connections) and Gratton went back to journalism after some unfortunate acrimony as to who did what to whom in some lady's flat, one of those issues that, in the milltown-with-mosquitoes that is Ottawa, wipes nuclear talks and wars and deficits from the headlines.

He hired Jacques Labrie, and Gilbert Lavoie. The two Lavoies and Labrie all come from Rimouski, which happens to be on the south shore of the St. Lawrence, right across the river from Baie Comeau. Mulroney likes his securities, can read sympathies acutely. He knows that his fortune rests on Quebec and therefore insists on being well plugged into and having good relations with the Francophone portion of the Ottawa Press Gallery. (The press is as bifurcated as the country of which he is prime minister. The Quebec reporters sit in their own enclave today in this officially bilingual country just as they did when I first walked into the Gallery almost a quarter of a century ago.) Gratton, Luc Lavoie and Gilbert Lavoie all were great favorites of this embattled, resentful (because out-numbered, because of funny, Waspish Ottawa) Francophone gang who regularly gather at one particular end of the bar at the National Press Club.

Richard Ericson has spent six years studying the relationship between reporters and their sources. He is a professor in the University of Toronto's Centre of Criminology and Department of Sociology, and co-author, with Patricia Baranek and Janet Chan, of *Negotiating Control: A Study of News Sources*. An earlier work, *Visualizing Deviance*, looked at news organizations. The final of the three volumes, *Acknowledging Order*, will examine how the differing media, whether print or broadcast, treat the same news.

The authors have a good historical perspective. Before there were such things as newspapers and radio and television, the courts and public executions and such humiliations as pillories were the ways of spotlighting behavior that was contrary to the accepted order. By the end of the last century, the public morality play had shifted to popular newspapers with their sensational rape-and-read crime dramas. But when the community institutions began to lose their influence over common values, they point out, the law and its media allies assumed the role of ethical educators.

Their essential point is that the media create consensus in society. News, they maintain, is moral drama–the resolution of the conflict between the good guys and the bad guys is always filtered in the media through an object of authority: the police chief, the corporate executive. Thus, the press is getting the public to support an elite view of the social order.

Sources and reporters, in the words of Ericson *et al*, are involved in a "dance of secrecy and revelation." The dance has interested the authors since they began their research in 1982, focusing principally on *The Globe and Mail* and the Toronto CBC station. Most of their financing came through grants from the Social Sciences and Humanities Research Council of Canada (the longer the name, the heftier the grant).

Negotiating Control demonstrates how interwoven are the lives of journalists and their sources. We see it all the time. Bodies and personalities and names are easily interchangeable. It is, in fact, an efficient industry, the skills required in each field complementary, enabling the practitioners to go over the wall with ease–and apparently with clear conscience.

The dance of politicians and press involves, as could be expected, seduction. It's an unequal encounter, because one side has most of the weapons. The weapons are money and security and normal hours. They are used by the politicians in the supposed "battle" with the press, the money coming from the taxpayer to hire away talented reporters who otherwise would be informing the taxpayer about the nefarious deeds of politicians. It is a most sleazy romance.

John Ferguson is a tall, shambling chap with a permanent limp from a youthful motorcycle accident. He has an infectious laugh and is very stubborn, the despair of his companions who would like to end an editorial conference before the cows come home. Probably because of those disparate qualities, he was in Doug Fisher's eyes the best reporter in Ottawa. I thought so too, at one time, and when Nick Hills, then general manager of Southam News, was casting around for new talent to burnish his own energetic image, I recommended that he talk to Ferguson, a Canadian Press stalwart whom Hills, being new to Ottawa, had never met.

"Why should I hire him?" he asked. "Simply because he's the best reporter in Ottawa," I replied. Hills, a man who likes such sweeping generalizations, immediately phoned Ferguson and invited him to drop around for a job interview. They got along swimmingly and had agreed to have a second meeting until Ferguson, as things were being wrapped up, said that there was one thing he should bring up, one thing that Hills as his prospective boss should know.

Hills, fearing the worst, suspecting some evil secret that might doom the match, with sinking heart asked what it was. "You should know," said the earnest Ferguson, "that I don't know how to drive a car."

Hills collapsed in laughter, his raucous cackle that has emptied many a restaurant in full throttle. He laughed so hard that Ferguson, feeling insulted, expressed his irritation. Hills, from being doubled over, straightened up and screamed, "Neither can I! You're hired!"

Ferguson lived up to my boasts, enlivening morning planning sessions in Hills' office with twenty-minute defenses of indefensible positions and graduating to the post of economics columnist. He had a solid reputation in and out of the trade.

In early 1989 those lovely people from Canada Post, who can't deliver your mail but don't mind spending your money telling you how and why they can't deliver, phoned Ferguson and asked him over for a talk, just as Nick Hills had done a half-dozen years earlier. They offered him a grandiose title, some $100,000, a car and all the perks that government can offer. In the going market in the private world of journalism, Ferguson would have been in the $60,000-$70,000 range at Southam News.

So we have this strange perversion of sanity. The people who don't want the truth out, the people who essentially are in the business of propaganda, can afford to pay more for a talented man than can the people in the private sector who want the guy to reveal the truth to the public–the same public that is now providing his wages as he goes over the wall.

There is a major debate going on beside the Potomac, as the Bush administration tries to find its feet, over the "revolving door" problem. It is the debate–which killed off John Tower as George Bush's choice for defense minister–over people moving into government and then out and in again, whether in journalism or what, to their benefit and against the commonweal.

The argument is particularly heated in the media, where White House aides suddenly reappear on television panel shows as great experts. There is the countering argument that the public is better served if, in fact, a journalist puts in some time behind the walls, learns something of how the operation operates, and then returns to the media to give the public the benefit of his increased understanding of the problems of governing and government.

In Canada, Richard Gwyn is the best example of this genre–for good or bad. He has tremendous contacts in government and works the official sources rather than the press clubs, realizing that social contacts are in fact probably the most productive in the search for real information.

Gwyn, who followed the brilliance of the icon-smashing Peter Newman and the solid, sensible and calm Anthony Westell in the *Star* Ottawa column, sees himself in his present reincarnation in London as the successor to the remarkable Mark Gayn, the paper's globe-trotting international sage for decades, a man who could read Russian and spoke a half-dozen languages. A man who has a good dry-gin sense of humor in private and likes to laugh when relaxed but never cracks a smile in print, Gwyn came to journalism by a most unusual route. Son of an English military father, he was sent to Sandhurst, the upper-class factory consigned to producing good Brit officers with the requisite stiff upper and perhaps a stiff lower. Gwyn hated it and, a short time before graduation, told his father so. Gwyn senior swallowed his pride and, as was the requirement, paid a goodly sum to buy his son's way out of his commission.

It was 1954 and Richard Gwyn headed for Canada. He peddled magazines door-to-door and worked on the trains running from Montreal to the Maritimes, selling soft drinks, sandwiches and pillows to the passengers. He almost perished in a crazy attempt to sail a boat into the Caribbean hurricane season. He worked for the penurious United Press International in Halifax, covering the Springhill mine disaster by phone, since UPI couldn't afford to send him a hundred miles to one of the biggest stories of the decade. In Newfoundland, he found his bride, Sandra, one of the most felicitous writers in Canadian journalism, and eventually fetched up working for *Time* magazine in Montreal.

Gwyn's real boost in journalism, however, came when he was attracted to the most attractive minister in the Pierre Trudeau government: Eric Kierans, a passionate Irishman who was a self-made millionaire out of Montreal and was years ahead of his time as communications minister. I recall him explaining, over a drink, that soon door-to-door mail delivery would be gone and everyone on the block would have to go down to the corner to a group mailbox. That was about 1970: the storm burst two decades later.

Richard, as Kierans' executive assistant, would phone each time through Vancouver and pluck my brain and we would exchange lies and gossip–as all visiting firemen do–in the dining room of the Devonshire Hotel, owned by the delightful bandit Coley Hall and run by a sharp-eyed Geordie, Moira Fitzpatrick, who knew which Howe Street rounders should be seated well away from the marks they had rooked, and which Supreme Court judges who liked the noon-hour gargle should be secreted in the back room separate from the criminal lawyers who would be appearing before them that afternoon.

Gwyn's success, on taking over the *Star* column, rested on that invaluable tenure with Kierans. As a key shover and maker at an Ottawa time of much innovation and excitement, working for a guy he worshipped who was constantly stirring the pot, Gwyn plugged himself into the incestuous, tight gang of middle-management Trudeaucrats who ran that town and, with their hand-me-down successors, still run it–as the faceless ones of Westminster run Britain and the people who drive Volvos and live in Georgetown still run Washington.

To find out where the real power rests in Washington and how influence is traded, don't read the front pages or the editorial pages. Read the social pages. That's where you find out who nests with whom. That advice was given many years ago by Felix Frankfurter, arguably the most brilliant U.S. Supreme Court judge of this century, to the young Joseph Rauh before Rauh became the most famous civil rights lawyer in the United States, friend to Adlai Stevenson, fruitful in the Kennedys' rise, and authority (if he cared to tell) on where all the bodies are buried. Frankfurter's advice is as good now as it was then, for Washington and any other capital you could name.

Bob Hepburn, *The Toronto Star* correspondent in Washington, was hated by Ambassador Allan Gotlieb. Hepburn, of course, was instructed to bash Gotlieb at every turn (which he did with relish, to the puzzlement of outsiders) because Gotlieb–appointed by a Liberal called Trudeau–now worked for a Conservative named Mulroney. So he had to be a baddie in the *Star*'s eyes. Gotlieb banned Hepburn from every ambassadorial party and would grow almost apoplectic at the mention of his name. However, Richard Gwyn, also of *The Toronto Star*, when he came to Washington from London, would stay at the ambassadorial mansion on Rock Creek Drive, as a house guest of Allan and Sondra Gotlieb, close personal friends of Richard and Sandra Gwyn. Read the social pages.

Gwyn, now that he has been unleashed from the tightly controlled domestic coverage of the *Star*, wherein Liberals can do no wrong, is writing stronger and more confident stuff on the world stage. Distance has its great advantages. It is easier to bash

Canada as a country, and to make pronouncements on China, than it is to sit in Ottawa and pronounce that the Grits in fact are dolts and the Tories are, occasionally, quite clever. This used to be called, in the newspapering trade, "Afghanistanism"–anyone could be an expert on it since no one ever went there. After a war broke out and reporters actually became familiar with the place, the phrase dropped out of use. At any rate, Gwyn is now more useful to the reader, travelling a lot and writing about world events, than he was in Ottawa where he had to keep one eye on the current party line at 1 Yonge Street.

The natural successor to Gwyn as the purveyor of the established line is Jeffrey Simpson, an intelligent and ambitious young man who fashions himself as a clone of George F. Will, a cerebral chap who takes himself terribly seriously. Simpson affects the manner of an Ivy League version of the usual grubby Ottawa journalist. He summers at a second home in Vermont. He is so earnest in print that Peter Gzowski, as emcee of an authors' party in Ottawa, brought down the house by introducing Simpson as "*The Globe and Mail*'s humor columnist."

Simpson's real ambition is to join External Affairs, which is why he dresses the yuppie Rockcliffe way he does and why, like Gwyn, he never writes anything that would prevent him from being invited to any place in town. When the rogue publisher Roy Megarry suddenly sacked Simpson's friends, editor Norman Webster and managing editor Geoffrey Stevens, despite his anger and his carefully crafted public pronouncement about his disquiet, Simpson did not express clear outrage in his column–that might have been yanked by the publisher on grounds of insubordination but would have demonstrated to his colleagues his guts. (When the elegant George Bain, after his long years gracing the same column, was forced out by the *Globe*, the same publisher killed Bain's farewell column in which he explained, however obliquely, that he was being forced out.)

Like Gwyn, Simpson can never really be pinned down to any one position. He does not come down on one side or the other of free trade; he explains the options. He does not really say what he thinks of Brian Mulroney as a person or a prime minister. He offers you some ways of viewing him. He waits, like Gwyn, to see which way the wind of public opinion is shifting, then attempts to get ahead of the wind. It is not the Lubor J. Zink style of column-writing, or the Marjorie Nichols style, or that of his sartorial idol, George F. Will. It is accurate, well done, and careful.

If you must know, the most useful Ottawa columnist to a reader is Doug Fisher, a large baleful man who (for some strange reason that has always puzzled me) does not like me. He is from Thunder Bay, an outpost that also produced the late Bora Laskin, Bruce Phillips, ambassador to the U.S. Derek Burney and Paul Weiler, the Harvard-based law professor who–I tell him–found a way to break up Canada. He was the genius who, as a constitutional adviser, invented the "notwithstanding clause" that Robert Bourassa so misused in the Quebec sign-language dispute, convincing the rest of Canada that enough was enough and that the ghost of René Lévesque could take his province to whatever oblivion it wanted to go. So much for Thunder Bay. I digress.

Fisher, who first achieved fame by upsetting the tyrant of the Pearson government, C.D. Howe, in the Port Arthur riding in 1957 is by profession a librarian. It is his gift and his defeat. After seven years as an NDP Member of Parliament, he stumbled into journalism–a very intelligent man who doesn't know how to write.

He reads a book a day. He watches Question Period every day on the tube. He reads *Hansard*–one of the very few Ottawa journalists who do. He follows committees, peruses mind-glazing documents on forests, Indians and amateur sport (three of his abiding interests) and keeps up with all the inside gossip on drinking and infidelity and caucus back-biting by shrewd schmoozing with veteran MPs in the West Block cafeteria in the mornings. Fisher never goes to cocktail parties, never socializes, never goes to the Press Club; he taps what Canada is thinking over coffee with guys from Red Deer and red-neck eastern Ontario who tell him what The Larynx That Walks Like a Man really said in caucus this morning.

The Fisher problem–it doesn't disturb those of us who are information freaks, but does those who would like their information organized in a manner that can be understood–is that he has never been in a newsroom. Never subject to some foul-mouthed city editor who has thrown back to him six times an eight-paragraph story on a traffic accident because the "lead" is in the wrong place.

Fisher wouldn't know a lead if he found one in his soup. He is a librarian by training, and so he simply piles the factoids and opinions one on top of the other, as if he were building a brick wall. Often, a reader will find the sentence with which he should have started the column half-way through, or perhaps buried two-thirds down in the type. I could do it, any desk man on any paper could do it: Fisher's column in *The Toronto Sun* could be improved 50 per cent with ten minutes' work with a strong pencil. Such is life. It's not my job to improve the work of my more serious competitors.

Fisher has been involved in a strange circumstance which surprised, as well as some of us, no doubt himself. A faithful socialist since riding a tank in World War II, he worked on being an objective observer in his column after ending his time as an NDP MP. Over the years, with his fairness and honest opinions, he has become less and less thought of as "former NDP MP Doug Fisher." But when Brian Mulroney came to power in 1984, Fisher appeared somewhat to lord it over the young whipper-snappers in the Ottawa Press Gallery with his early knowledge of Mulroney–having first observed him as a university student involved in arranging a Confederation conference at Laval University.

He had been taken with Mulroney's self-assured and ambitious manner then, and he advised his readers (and the professional mockers in the Gallery) that there was more to this guy than they thought. Later, he raved over the neophyte prime minister's early months in office, in effect advertising that Doug Fisher had been correct in his earlier judgment. Now, boasting is not Doug Fisher's style; he clumps around Ottawa with an ailing hip, dressing somewhat like a polyester garage sale, and the sudden outburst of partisanship from a good socialist to a Tory PM struck the Young Turks in the Gallery as somewhat ludicrous. Middle-aged Young Turk and professional Mulroney-hater Claire Hoy, whose wardrobe Fisher could adopt if a foot shorter, took outrage in hand one day to brand Fisher "an aging Tory toady." This appeared in the pages of the paper that was then their mutual employer–The Toronto Sun.

Fisher, ailing hip and all, suddenly appeared in the Press Gallery–scene of many a debauch–sought out Hoy, picked him up by the soiled lapels and threatened further grievous harm. It was probably the most exciting thing that happened in the Ottawa Press Gallery (if not all of Ottawa) that year.

Fisher has four sons. Their names are Matthew, Mark, Luke–and Tobias. One day I asked Toby, who works with his father on the column, the obvious question: how he came to be Tobias rather than John. His dad, he explained, was out of town when he was born; Mother got the chance to name him.

The Ottawa Press Gallery annual dinner is a raucous black-tie affair, invitations to which politicians, top businessmen and out-of-town publishers vie for. Before the satirical show, which carves up the most prominent of those present, the dinner speeches by the prime minister, leader of the opposition, leader of the NDP, governor-general and president of the Gallery compete in high insults. In 1989 Gallery president Luc Lavoie (later a Mulroney aide) made his predictions for the coming year, one of them being that "Doug Fisher is going to leave politics and enter journalism." It brought the loudest gleeful ovation of the evening, crushing two Fisher sons, who had followed their father into newspapering and were present. Until that ovation they had had no idea of the depth of the Gallery's feeling toward Fisher for his championing of Mulroney.

In Washington, where showbiz has crossed into government, and vice versa, the crossing-the-wall game has been perfected by a group of insiders who are equally at home in either camp.

The cleverest columnist in Washington, William Safire of The New York Times, was a wordsmith for Richard Nixon. So was

Diane Sawyer, the new millionaire on ABC. Bill Moyers, the press secretary for Lyndon Johnson, moved on as editor of *Newsday* and is now the highly respected commentator on PBS. Even John Chancellor, the NBC commentator, worked for government as head of the "Voice of America."

Henry Grunwald, the long-time managing editor of *Time*, is now the American ambassador to Austria. Lesley Stahl of CBS once worked for New York mayor John Lindsay. Ben Bradlee, executive editor of *The Washington Post* was a U.S. press attaché in Paris in the early 1950s.

It is a very cosy fit. One never has to leave Washington: just flip to the other side. George Will, the erudite syndicated columnist for the *Post* and *Newsweek*, who once taught at Toronto's York University, got his start in the capital as an aide to Gordon Allott, a Republican senator from Colorado.

Will, who frequently took Nancy Reagan to lunch, had a lofty view of the relationship on the eve of Ronald Reagan's inauguration. "Is journalistic duty compatible with feelings of friendship between journalists and those political people who do the work of democracy?" he proffered in a 1981 column. His answer? "Yep. A journalist's duty is to see politicians steadily and see them whole. To have intelligent sympathy for them, it helps to know a few as friends. . . ."

Will's "intelligent sympathy," as it turned out, led to his coaching Reagan before one of the crucial campaign debates with Jimmy Carter–a small fact he didn't disclose subsequently in writing about the Reagan debate performance. Whoops! Once caught out, he confessed in print that it had been somewhat of a mistake. He was never taken quite so seriously in Washington thereafter–but he continued to take Nancy to lunch.

Carl Rowan, the black columnist and gun-control advocate who raised more than eyebrows when he shot and wounded a beery teenager who invaded his swimming pool, is a former ambassador to Finland and a former director of the U.S. Information Agency. Pierre Salinger, who was John Kennedy's press secretary, is the trench-coated foreign correspondent for

ABC News. The president of CBS News, David Burke, is a former aide to Senator Teddy Kennedy.

It's a movable feast. Seymour Hersh, the first, most famous investigative reporter who uncovered the My Lai massacre, once wrote speeches for Eugene McCarthy. The feast becomes self-serving. Leslie Gelb moved from a Capitol Hill position to *The New York Times* and back to the Carter administration before going back to the *Times*–where he replaced Richard Burt, his successor as national security correspondent, who was moving into the State Department job Gelb had just vacated. It is incest, twice-compounded. With the public on the outside.

Early in 1989, in the "ethics" debate then consuming Congress, there was great press palaver over the some $9 million paid out each year by special interests to members of Congress for speechmaking. Was it, in fact, "protection money," which is a nice name for bribery? There is so much money floating around Washington, with so many companies and organizations so interested in upcoming government legislation, that any Congressman can, two or three nights a week, line his pockets with a standard rote speech to groups only too eager to pay to listen, sort of, to him.

Transactions of this sort are prohibited by conflict-of-interest laws, if proven. The Washington press regularly prints the totals that various politicians receive each year in "honoraria." It makes good reading.

What is not printed, however, is the loot received by prominent journalists for the same sort of service. The top Washington names are in great demand among the thousands of corporations and trade associations with vital interests in public affairs and public policies. They routinely offer large honoraria–$2,000 to $20,000 for a single speech.

For the big-name journalists, the income from the lecture circuit can be astounding. Hugh Sidey of *Time* magazine (known as "Hugh Sidestep" in the trade) and syndicated columnist Jack Anderson each make an estimated $500,000 a year from their speeches. William Safire, according to a Washington magazine, takes in about $200,000 from ten or twelve appearances a year.

The most influential column in the world today is the Evans and Novak syndicated piece. Rowland Evans and Robert Novak regularly, for $25,000 and up, hold closed seminars for companies wanting to buy their expertise and their insider tips.

For the right fee, a convention can "rent" an entire panel from the television programs so popular in Washington–"The McLaughlin Group" and "Washington Week in Review." A new enterprise, Women at the Top, provides trade associations with panels of successful women, including television's Ann Compton, Rita Braver and Judy Woodruff and such business and political figures as Marcia Carlucci of Coopers and Lybrand, wife of the U.S. defense secretary; Deborah Dingell of General Motors, wife of the chairman of the House Energy and Commerce Committee; and Heather Gradison, chairman of the Interstate Commerce Commission.

There's an interesting question here. The superstars of journalism, of course, are above any thoughts of compromise or intimidation. But would the same assumption of intellectual virginity be granted to a Pentagon reporter making $18,000 a year for speeches to defense contractors?

One of these same contractors announced that "with the inauguration of the Bush-Quayle team, we are pleased to announce a new LTV team" to deliver commentary on a Washington radio station five nights a week. It is composed of David Gergen of *U.S. News & World Report*, Margaret Warner of *Newsweek*, columnist Mark Shields, ex-*New York Times* reporter Hedrick Smith and Haynes Johnson of *The Washington Post*. Their sponsor happens to be the same company that paid John Tower, the failed defense secretary nominee, $246,000 in "consulting fees" over the previous two years.

It raises the obvious query. Should moonlighting celebrity journalists make public disclosures of their income from corporations, trade associations and lobbies?

David Broder is, in this writer's myopic view, the best political commentator in Washington. In early 1989, after another presidential election that realigned loyalties, he made a speech at

Washington's National Press Club (the site – just two blocks from the White House – where Walter Cronkite's mother was mugged one night as she left an evening event).

Broder, a very serious journalist, expressed concern about the increasing cosiness between journalists and politicians in Washington. What he found really worrisome was the growing tendency for journalists to "dabble in politics," either as closet strategists or as temporary government appointees. Or, for government officials, whether press agents or policy-makers, to go through the revolving door and emerge as prominent commentators and news executives. There is a virulent strain creeping into the professional gene pool. The "switch-hitters" they are called, leading Broder to the observation that "the incessant bed-hopping between the two is doing damage to the image of independence we cultivate and cherish."

The response to Broder's eminently sensible cautions? Great whining and moaning from those pinged. Safire of The New York Times, who has won a Pulitzer Prize for his column writing after being a flack for Nixon and Spiro Agnew, wrote, "Tainted I ain't." The ponderous Carl Rowan, who worked for both the Kennedy and the Lyndon Johnson administrations, also complained loudly.

Right-wing columnist and TV commentator Patrick Buchanan, an eager press-basher for Nixon, Agnew and Ronald Reagan, jumped all over Broder for even suggesting improprieties. It was Buchanan, then supposedly a journalist, who joined fellow columnist George F. Will in rehearsing Reagan for his election debate, one of the more remarkable outrages of the cross-dressers.

What Broder warned about was this very blurring of the line between politicians and journalists. The First Amendment of the American Constitution gave journalists a special immunity from government regulation because the Founding Fathers believed that a free press, however flawed, would be a healthy check on government.

"If we are to defend that privilege," Broder noted in his speech, "we better make it clear we are not part of government, and not part of a Washington Insiders' clique where politicians, publicists and journalists are easily interchangeable parts. Once we lose our distinctive identity, it will not be long before we lose our freedom."

Has the "interchangeable parts" phenomenon taken root in Canada? Aileen McCabe, an aide in the Trudeau prime ministerial office, is now the Southam News correspondent in the Middle East. Terry Wills of *The Globe and Mail* becomes an executive assistant to Donald Macdonald in the Trudeau cabinet and then emerges as the Montreal *Gazette* bureau chief. Former MPs Doug Fisher and Paul Hellyer become newspaper columnists. CBC television broadcasters Fraser Kelly and Larry Stout become partners in a lobbying firm that will court the same sources they once interviewed. What of *The Toronto Star* practice of running on its op-ed page regular contributions from non-journalists Jimmy Coutts, Gerry Caplan and Hugh Segal? The apparent assumption is that this will provide a balanced point of view from the Liberals, the NDP and the Conservatives. But each one is filled with that certainty of judgment that marks all political zealots. As Broder points out, journalists are brought up to be skeptical of certainties and are taught early in the newsroom, "If you think your mother loves you, check it."

The party affiliations of Segal, Caplan and Coutts are so known and the partisan bias so obvious that this is–by American standards–a rather primitive example of cross-over. These guys are too clearly labelled to be convincing as journalists. The cross-over is not yet, in Canada, the art form it has become in Washington.

6

The Glass Menagerie

The truly serious criticisms of television can all
be reduced ultimately to the proposition that it
shouldn't have been invented in the first
place–and I agree.
−*network executive Reuven Frank*

When television is good, nothing is better. But
when television is bad, nothing is worse. I
invite you to sit down in front of your TV set
and keep your eyes glued to that set until the
station signs off. I can assure you that you will
observe a vast wasteland.–*Newton Minow*

Dallas changed everything. It changed, forever, not only the
consumers of news but also the collectors of news. Until the day
the president was murdered, the American networks had been
poor second cousins to radio and newspapers in delivering the
news. Nightly newscasts were only fifteen minutes long, and
news specials were reserved for major events.

The Kennedy assassination created a new hunger for TV news
and, almost overnight, made television the preeminent medium
for information. According to the Nielsen ratings, 96 per cent of
U.S. households watched assassination news that weekend as the
three networks–ABC, CBS and NBC–carried an unprecedented
forty-one hours and eighteen minutes of coverage. The average
viewer watched for thirty-two hours, or nearly nine hours a day,
from the time of the assassination to midnight Monday, the day
Kennedy was buried.

There are few reporters of any age who have actually heard
Teletypes sound ten bells. They may have heard three bells in

the wire rooms of newspapers–signalling that an important story was about to zing over the wire. Or, perhaps, five bells–warning that something really important, such as the resignation of a cabinet minister, was happening. Ten incessant bells on the old machines were reserved for the biggest of stories: the end of a world war, a cataclysmic disaster. Or the assassination of a president.

NBC correspondent Bill Ryan was preparing the 2:00 p.m. network radio newscast on November 22, 1963, in the New York studio when an unnerved staffer burst into his office, shouting, "Get back to TV right away! The president has been shot!"

It was 1:45 p.m., Eastern Standard Time, and NBC was "down" for its daily noon-to-2:00 p.m. break for local affiliates. Technicians had to rig a hasty patchwork network of telephone lines before NBC could tell the United States and the world that John F. Kennedy had been felled by an assassin's bullets in Dallas.

Even then, NBC couldn't tell an anxious nation if Kennedy was alive or dead, because it didn't know. In 1963, there were no satellite linkups, no microwave relays, no instant live pictures, no you-heard-it-first reports from on-the-scene correspondents.

Seated in a closet-sized studio, Ryan and Chet Huntley scrambled not only to report the news, but to learn it, reading verbatim from Associated Press bulletins fed to them by technicians crouched at their feet.

A phone patch to NBC correspondent Robert MacNeil (the Halifax native now the wordstruck wordsmith of the "MacNeil-Lehrer NewsHour") at Parkland Hospital in Dallas failed because of overloaded circuits, so anchorman Frank McGee, phone to his ear, passed along news from MacNeil, bit by precious bit. When MacNeil abandoned the phone to learn fresh news, a helpful medical student kept the line open.

There was no videotape and no film, so Ryan held up AP wirephotos of Kennedy's motorcade through the crowded Dallas streets. A visibly shaken Huntley, one of the coolest men on television, stuttered and stumbled as he recalled the day eighteen years earlier when President Franklin D. Roosevelt had died.

It was Ryan who read the AP flash that Kennedy was dead. "It's jarring," he told Associated Press on the twenty-fifth anniversary of the event, "when somebody comes up to you and says, 'You're the one who told me President Kennedy was dead.'" What Ryan, McGee, Huntley, David Brinkley and millions of others couldn't know was that from that day on television was changed forever.

Ryan, now sixty-one and host of a public TV magazine show in Morgantown, West Virginia, on looking back at the NBC tapes of that momentous weekend, was struck by the lack of technical sophistication. "We didn't even have a regular news studio. We had to go to what they called the flash studio, 5-HN in New York, a little room where they had one black-and-white camera set up. It wasn't like today, where you could punch up the whole world by satellite in a minute and a half."

Bill Ryan was on air until 11:30 that night and showed no emotion until he walked out of the studio and "just fell apart. Obviously, it was a momentous story. I was desperately trying to concentrate on getting it right. All other thoughts were out of my head. I got off the air and I cried like hell, my one emotional outburst of the weekend."

As Bill Ryan's staffer was hearing those fatal ten bells on the Teletype, I was sitting at the back of *The Vancouver Sun* newsroom and happened to see Barry Broadfoot as he wandered from the wire room over to the news desk and was waved away. He was a known trouble-maker and the serious people were approaching the second edition deadline.

Broadfoot had given up on being one of the best raucous reporters on a raucous, *Front Page*-style paper and had settled into a role as the office cynic and gossip-monger, and so, since what he had learned in the wire room had been dismissed as just another Broadfoot smart-ass remark, he walked blithely away. He passed my desk and remarked off-handedly that Kennedy had been shot. No one looked up. It was Broadfoot.

(It was good for Broadfoot and newspapers, needless to say, that his distaste for his trade led him in frustration to his highly successful next career as an oral biographer of the Depression prairie years from whence he came and other oral histories, leading up to his book on the Soviet Union.)

This day, however, being November 22, 1963, no one took the professional cynic Barry Broadfoot seriously until I suddenly saw a human explosion far down the newsroom where the decisions were made. A copy boy had relayed the ten bells message, and the newsroom was in a panic. I watched the wirephoto coming across showing Jackie Kennedy, on the plane on the way back to Washington from Dallas while Lyndon Johnson was sworn in, the blood from the shattered brain of her husband prominent on the lap of her suit. She had coldly rejected offers to be cleaned up, declaring that she wanted the American public to see the evidence of what some madman had done.

I worked furiously all day during the special editions to help, went home and then–like Bill Ryan–broke into uncontrollable sobs when I walked in the door and saw my wife.

In 1989 we are much better equipped to cater to the public desire, the unconscious *demand* for the news *now*. The paradox is that as the public knows more of what is going on, it realizes less. Since Kennedy in Dallas, since the *Challenger* explosion off Florida, it demands–and expects–its news instantaneously. If television had not existed, Lee Harvey Oswald would be alive today. His simple Sunday move from one jail to another would have been a routine thing; it became, perforce, because of the events of the weekend, a "photo opportunity," with the flanking Dallas detectives in their sheriff hats now so familiar to genera‑ tions of TV flashback fans almost brandishing Oswald before the TV cameras and making him an obvious target for the demented Jack Ruby who wanted his fifteen minutes of fame.

Dallas was the first major event that changed television and the rest of the media forever, it was the first assassination of a world figure captured on television, and Oswald became the first person murdered live on television while the world watched.

After that, it became almost "routine"–as the White House press corps realized they had to cover everything every hour since they had become the "death watch." And so Bobby Kennedy was gunned down with live cameras in tow and George

Wallace and Gerald Ford and Ronald Reagan outside the Washington Hilton with John Hinckley, Jr. But Oswald (or Oswald's killer) began it all, and we merely follow the inevitability of the insanity.

The ultimate was reached in the spring of 1989 when the mothers of Lancashire, watching on television the Football Association Cup semi-final between their Liverpool lads and Nottingham Forest in the "neutral" ground of Sheffield's Hillsborough Stadium, could see their young children–taking the front row for better viewing–crushed to death before their eyes, courtesy of zoom lenses, as a beery mob turned the fenced-in crowd into a pen of death for ninety-five.

Dallas made television the most important member of the press corps. Those of us in the pencil press tried to ignore (and resist) that reality for some time–but no one now denies it.

There are differences, granted, between a TV camera and a reporter with his note-book (now his tape-recorder). The camera can't analyze, it has no memory and without help can't remind viewers of contradictions between past and present behavior. It can't capture certain kinds of integrity, though it can expose, show, obvious signs of insincerity (hello there, Brian Mulroney).

But there are similarities too. Just as politicians are helped if the press corps likes them, so are they helped if the TV camera likes them (as it does not like Joe Clark). Just as politicians are more successful if they can understand and subtly manipulate the press, so the better they do if they have learned how to manipulate TV.

If it was Kennedy's death that marked the start of the television age, it was his presidency that introduced the presidential manipulation of a medium that would soon surpass the press as the most influential factor in politics. Kennedy liked television, and television quite obviously liked him. Even more important, Kennedy, as the first television president, instinctively understood the medium. Early on, he asked press secretary Pierre Salinger to find out how many fireside chats Franklin Roosevelt had given. He planned to use them as a guide, since people always remembered them. Salinger soon found that the reason they were so memorable was because there were so few of them, perhaps one or two a year. That was Kennedy's point: people thought FDR had been on all the time yet he had carefully rationed these broadcasts. JFK knew that television was a far more powerful medium than radio, and he didn't want to become a bore on the tube, resisting his aides' pleas that he go on the air more often.

Long after a bitter Lyndon Johnson had voluntarily given up the White House, a CBS crew went to Johnson City, Texas, to film his televised memoirs. The first of two presidents to be driven from office by the press, LBJ seemed in a relaxed mood one day during the shooting and, in a break, a senior producer asked him what had changed in politics between his time in the presidency and his first going to Congress some thirty years earlier. Johnson suddenly turned vehement. "You guys," he said. "All you guys in the media. All of politics has changed because of you. You've broken all the machines and the ties between us in Congress and the city machines. You've given us a new kind of people," he said with some contempt. "Teddy. Tunney. They're your creations, your puppets. No machine could ever create a Teddy Kennedy. Only you guys. They're all yours. Your product."

If Teddy Kennedy was the product, Jack Kennedy was the pioneer. It is by now standard wisdom, taught in any academic course on television, that the surveys of radio listeners taken immediately after the first Kennedy-Nixon presidential debate came up with Nixon as the winner. By ear, on logic and argument and issues, Nixon appeared superior. It was on television, where a sallow, sweating Nixon with the wrong makeup looked so dreadful up against the clean good looks of the relatively unknown Kennedy, that the newcomer triumphed.

Kennedy had just come from campaigning in a convertible in California. Nixon was exhausted, had lost some twenty pounds and his suit and shirt sagged on his frame. On the way to the studio, he banged a bad knee on a car door and turned even more gray. The result was so devastating to Nixon (a politician who had wasted the experience of eight years as vice-president against an underdog) that there wasn't another presidential debate for sixteen years: the candidates saw that there was simply too much to lose.

The Nixon forces blamed the disaster on the CBS producer of the debate, Don Hewitt-now famous as the brains behind "60 Minutes." David Halberstam reports that years later, when Nixon was thinking about running again, he appeared on a CBS show produced by Hewitt and asked him several questions about makeup. The producer told him the best makeup in the world was a natural tan. Hewitt pondered later whether he might have been the inspiration for the presidential retreats in San Clemente, California, and Key Biscayne, Florida.

Kennedy was the first television president (as Pierre Trudeau was the first television prime minister). Neither one of them could have been elected without television. In *The Powers That Be* David Halberstam has explained how Kennedy, on taking office, instinctively realized that television producers loved film and perceived how the White House, in effect, could get into the business of producing its own shows, its own television spectaculars-especially on his foreign trips. The nation watched in fascination his forays to Paris and the Berlin Wall and Ireland and elsewhere, while the network journalists, no longer critics, became part of the pageantry, spear-carriers in the spectacle.

Kennedy understood, says Halberstam, that the farther he was away from Washington, the less knowledgeable about local conditions were the camp followers of the press and the more dependent they had to be on the president's aides for information. Halberstam, who made his reputation by refuting the official military line in Vietnam, discerned that the Kennedy era -which lasted only three years-transformed the role of the network journalist: "the ability to get on the air, which was crucial to any reporter's career, grew precisely as the ability to analyze diminished."

The Bay of Pigs, in a strange way, was proof of the power of television. It was a complete disaster and totally John Kennedy's fault. But it wasn't a *televised* disaster and the printed reports were rather fuzzy, since the government of course controlled all the information on it. But Kennedy's response to it was televised, and the new president stood before the American people and accepted full responsibility, projecting with perfect control and giving almost no details under the guise of national security. His popularity soared–after a monumental blunder.

A year later during the Cuban Missile Crisis he used television to bind the nation together. He realized the spectacular potential of the space shots, and the entire country paused before TV sets, even at work, when lift-off took place in Florida.

Both Lyndon Johnson and Richard Nixon, neither of them the natural television performer that Kennedy was, studied and tried to copy how he had exploited the networks. The result was that there was a tremendous zoom in the power of the president–as opposed to the importance of the Congress that, in the genius of the American system, is supposed to check the clout of the president. Television unbalanced the balance between the executive branch and the legislative branch. Fred Friendly, a Kennedy believer in 1960 and the television producer who helped the new president perfect his TV image, within a decade was so discouraged at what had happened that he called it "an electronic presidency." When his old associate Walter Cronkite decided to accompany Nixon on a clearly spurious trip to the Middle East in 1974, Friendly complained to Cronkite that his presence on the junket–quite obviously–was raising the importance of the trip.

Walter was to blame for it all. Uncle Walter. The man who year after year was voted "the most trusted man in America" in popularity polls. Walter, who convinced Lyndon Johnson not to run again for the White House because Walter had gone to Saigon, had seen the military and government lies at first hand and had come out against the war. If he had lost Walter, as LBJ conceded, he knew he had lost Middle America and there was no more future for him in Washington.

Walter Cronkite, because of his avuncular nature, because of his obvious integrity, made the supper-time anchorman into a man of incredible power and influence. (The Americans like their summing-up pronouncements on the world at 6:00 p.m. There was a tremendous fuss, recall, when Canadians–who supposedly liked their version at 11:00 p.m. with Lorne Greene and Earl Cameron and Stanley Burke and Knowlton Nash–were informed that the Canadian Broadcorping Castration was to move the evening news to 10:00 p.m., thus improving the sex life of the entire nation–perhaps the subliminal reason for the complaints.) I digress.

Cronkite followed Huntley and Brinkley and, with his obvious patriotic, gung-ho, moist-eyed coverage of the first American space shots when the American people so badly needed an answer to the early Soviet advances, turned the anchorman into a TV icon, a man whose power went beyond that of a mere mortal.

In the crucial ratings wars that govern U.S. commercial television, senior network executives slowly realized that their fat salaries and limos and expense-account lunches depended on the unimpeachable, visibly honest anchorman who brought in the viewers.

There were two divergent factors at work here. Just as the power of the anchormen was increasing, the audience for the three American networks was decreasing. Cable TV was finally making the advances that had long been apparent in certain Canadian jurisdictions (Victoria with a cable penetration of some 95 per cent has overtaken Vancouver as the most-cableized city in the world). Independent stations were becoming more independent. Satellites, offering all-sports and all-porn channels, fragmented the audiences still more.

No more was the time when 95 per cent of the American viewers were tuned, during prime time, to either NBC, CBS or ABC. By 1981, the three networks' share of viewers had dropped to 84 per cent. It is expected by some experts to drop, by 1990, as low as 59 per cent.

The one area, however, where the networks could still dominate was in news–which is much cheaper to produce than entertainment, the sit-coms that make up "the wasteland" of the most misused medium in history.

A good news operation that attracted viewers became essential to shore up the entertainment portion of the schedule, which is where the *real* money in television is reaped. All the studies show that if the couch potatoes regard favorably a network's news approach, they are more likely to have a high opinion of the network's whole programming schedule. If Walter had a faithful following at 7:00 p.m., it meant that the faithful were more likely to stick with the CBS offerings that followed in prime time.

So it was, after Walter, that the network executives realized that his successor was worth millions not only to whoever it might be, but also to the network–and undoubtedly their own jobs. Whoever followed Cronkite, as Barbara Matusow explained in *The Evening Stars: The Making of the Network News Anchor*, "was likely to become the single most important employee in the entire organization, the linchpin holding the network and its nervous affiliates together." And so, nervous CBS made Dan Rather television's first Six Million Dollar Man.

Rather, in truth, is a twit. The better choice would have been the calm and calming Roger Mudd, a natural successor to the soothing, trustworthy Cronkite. Rather is not liked by many of his staff or trusted by his employers. Very few people in the business really believe his story of being mugged by two men late at night when, walking home in Manhattan, he supposedly was accosted by two gentlemen who demanded, "What's the frequency, Kenneth?"–an in-joke in New York that still raises eyebrows.

His apparent unprofessionalism–and ego–was proven when, piqued because an overtime sports broadcast intruded on his news show, he walked off the set, leaving the screen black. (Cronkite, the pro, asked for his opinion, said, "I would have fired him.") The tightly wound Rather, discovering to his panic at a glitzy TV cocktail party that NBC rival Tom Brokaw was also present, was so intent on keeping his eye on his handsome adversary while also bussing important CBS wives that he nervously planted a large wet kiss on the cheek of one of his executive-suite bosses.

Rather-thanks to Walter-became the watershed, the anchor who became more important than the network, the tail that wagged the dog. While Cronkite ran his own program, he stayed away from the politics of his division. Rather-as befitted his multimillion-dollar salary-became the "managing editor" of the CBS Evening News, thanks to a clause in his contract that gave him power over the hirings and firings and assignments, and a say over personnel.

The reason was clear. An anchorman on a multimillion-dollar contract wanted assurance that he could do something about it if he felt his performance was being impaired by a hostile producer or a lazy line-up editor. In earlier days the editorial product on the network news was a result of tugging and arguing among producers, anchormen, correspondents and senior executives. Now, the superstar had almost complete control.

The outcome in the race for ratings? The other networks had to produce their own superstars. Instead of news people, we have entertainers reading the news. Thus, ABC pays Diane Sawyer $2 million to leave CBS. In desperation at losing a pretty face, CBS then pays Connie Chung $1.2 million to leave NBC. To replace Chung, NBC then reaches to CNN for the beautiful Mary Alice Williams. To make sure that it will not suffer in the coiffure league, NBC also gives a new four-year contract to Maria Shriver, the daughter of the Kennedy family's Eunice Kennedy Shriver and the wife of muscleman Arnold Schwarzenegger.

It's infotainment. It's why Mark Starowicz, the boss of "The Journal," made such a puzzling bad decision by originally opening the CBC showcase show with two female hosts, Mary Lou Finlay as well as Barbara Frum. If the rationale was to attract more female viewers or bow to feminism, it was a predictable flop. For one entire season very few women in Canada actually listened to "The Journal." Instead, it was a nightly fashion critique: Mary Lou's hair against Barbara's hair, Barbara's shoulder pads *vs.* Mary Lou's lipstick, Barbara's beaded sweaters up against Mary Lou's dresses. It was the subject of every office water fountain conversation each morning. The CBC brass, which let Knowlton

Nash read the news for years wearing smoked glasses, thus ruining the one necessity of an anchorman–eye contact with the viewer–finally saw the obvious and moved Finlay.

Trudeau, like Kennedy, realized that politics is an extended version of show-biz and, it being that, knew television was better at displaying it than dull print. Print, in the Trudeaumania phase of 1968, couldn't possibly do justice to his trampoline bounces or the double-flips off the diving board so artfully orchestrated by his handlers who nudged the TV cameramen to the "private" gymnastics of the Liberal leadership candidate who supposedly was just working out on his daily routine. Television, not print, implanted in the minds of Canadian voters the pubescent maidens intent on kissing a man old enough to be their father (and who eventually married one of them).

Because of television, Robert Standstill didn't stand a chance in 1968. If there had not been TV, only print, he probably would have won, with his print-oriented, more serious message.

Pierre Trudeau became known as a master of TV, since the medium obviously liked him and suited him. But the reputation rested on specific dramatic moments: his besting of Daniel Johnson at a federal-provincial conference that first alerted the public to this brilliant maverick; his refusing to flee from rioters' bottles at the election-eve St. Jean Baptiste stand; his "just watch me" confrontation with CBC reporter Tim Ralfe; his steely address to the nation on the War Measures Act.

Kennedy had mastered the greatest art of television, in the words of Halberstam, "appearing to be spontaneous without in fact being spontaneous." Jimmy Coutts, the long-time acolyte of Pierre Trudeau, once confessed that Trudeau's greatest gift in politics was that he was a consummate actor. He would appear in the House of Commons for Question Period as one day a bully, one day a clown, another an aloof patrician, next week foul-mouthed, the next time a precise intellectual. The Opposition never knew what to expect, explained Coutts, and was kept continually off guard as to which of a dozen Trudeaus they would encounter on any particular day.

Politicians now have to be actors on TV (as opposed to being actors in a church basement). The most successful politicians have always been actors. Those that can't project a stage presence–fail. Canadians were astonished to find out that John Turner, returning to politics after nine years on Bay Street, in fact couldn't talk in an intelligible manner. Especially up against the mellifluous large-vocabularied Brian Mulroney, who while a university student would ask his friends visiting Montreal to bring him back dictionaries, because he wanted to learn a new word every day.

Ed Broadbent got on TV so much because he mastered the ability to deliver the thirty-second sound bite–and the ten-second sound "phrase," two entirely different but essential tricks. When reporters followed Ronald Reagan to the border between South Korea and North Korea, they noticed that Reagan choreographer Michael Deaver even had hashmarks laid down on the floor of the border patrol station where Reagan was to stand, so as to provide the best TV angle against the backdrop of North Korean guards and battlements.

George Bush does not project well on television, with that crooked mouth and the whiney voice (reminding every American woman, so goes the line, of her first husband). He knows all of the above, and so he restricts the time he spends on TV as much as possible. He prefers to invite small, select groups of journalists to the White House for quiet lunches and drinks, relying on his patrician charm and good manners to win over the doubters–provided the palaver is off the record.

Even the intellectual hit-man of the column-writing (i.e., calumny) trade, William Safire of The New York Times, fell for the trap, gushing about the access as he was invited to dinner while the Bushes' dog, Millie, was emitting puppies, the apparent highlight of an intimate evening. (The brainy Safire, the Nixon speech-writer who put into Spiro Agnew's mouth the "nattering nabobs of negativism" attack on the Washington press, is annoying because he is actually a nice guy. "This is Fotheringham," he would introduce me at Georgetown soirées, "the most brilliant columnist in Canada." I would say, "That's only because

I'm the only Canadian columnist you've ever met." He would say, "That's true." At least he was honest.) The better U.S. papers now forbid their men to attend the Bush strokings unless they can emerge with real live news.

Bush knows he is an awkward figure on television, and Maggie Hilda Roberts, daughter of a grocer in a lower-middle-class family in the drab Lincolnshire town of Grantham, knew she would never make it to the top of Conservative politics with a grocer's daughter's accent. The plummy, pseudo-Establishment voice of Maggie Thatcher that we hear is a completely manufactured one, recognized as such by the toffs at the top but sufficiently phony to pass muster in the stockbroker belt where she gets her votes.

It's essentially a game, a deadly serious game, but a game nonetheless. To the televiewer home in Dubuque or Swift Current, Sam Donaldson seems such a fearless, gutsy reporter yelling rude questions to the president of the United States, poor man, as he hustles to his helicopter on the White House lawn with Nancy and Nancy's dog straining on a leash–the dog not there by accident, so as to soften her brittle image.

It was a set-up, the White House knowing it as much as the furious Donaldson who therefore might as well take commercial advantage of it. The White House merchandisers knew what they had to merchandise: a good-hearted man, not deep, that Washington *éminence grise* Clark Clifford, adviser to five presidents, has told associates, in quiet resignation, is "an amiable dunce." They knew they dared not expose him to direct questioning from the White House press on complicated issues on Lebanon and Nicaragua and interest rates and Wall Street scandals and nuclear testing and so they pulled the helicopter dodge. Donaldson the heavy, the vulgar man in the trenchcoat *yells* blunt questions at the head of state, an obviously nice man who, cupping his hand to his ear, can't quite make them out. No doubt he would love to answer them if he could actually hear the queries over the whirr of the copter blades. Of course.

Michael Dukakis, narrowly behind George Bush in the 1988

presidential race, lost any chance of gaining the White House with one incredibly wooden response to an opening question in a televised debate. When the CNN's Bernard Shaw asked the crude question about how the Democratic candidate would respond if his wife were raped and murdered, Dukakis-instead of balling up the papers before him and throwing them in the face of the questioner, or shouting at him, or showing his disgust at the question-replied as if he had been asked the time of day. Showing no emotion whatsoever, he droned on about criminal rates and society and the environment.

All over America, viewers who are voters decided at that moment that, whatever Bush's other shortcomings, they wanted someone in the White House who at least had a personality. Dukakis sank out of sight after that one revealing moment.

One cannot quite imagine Churchill in the same position. Or John Kennedy, not to mention Charles de Gaulle. Not Maggie Thatcher. Not even Joe Clark. But on an afternoon just months before the election of 1988 that would give history's decision on whether his life had been a success or a failure, John Turner-watched by "Dr. Death"-was lying on the floor of his office learning how to breathe properly.

It was demeaning, it was humiliating, for a man who was such a matinee idol most of his life. He badly needed a media shrink if he was going to cope with modern communications. The leader of Her Majesty's Loyal Opposition, grown rusty after nine years on Bay Street, was so dreadful in the 1984 campaign as prime minister, with his staccato speech and nervous throat-clearings that, at age fifty-nine, he now had to be taught how to breathe.

The man supervising the strange office ritual-drapes drawn, Turner with tie and trousers loosened-was Dr. Henry Comor, a former actor who had earned the Dr. Death tag at Global television where as a medical reporter he often reported on fatal diseases. Although the Liberals didn't much like publicizing it, he was brought in as a media coach in hopes of preventing the political death of handsome John Napier Turner.

Brian Mulroney cinched his 1984 election with his rapier-thrust "you had an option" blow to a defensive and flustered John Turner. It was so effective that Turner, approaching the 1988 debates, made sure it would not happen again. Learning from the American presidential debating techniques, he employed stand-ins to pose as Mulroney and Ed Broadbent and to pepper him with every conceivable form of attack. He spent three pre-debate days doing nothing else.

An over-confident Mulroney failed to do the same and of course was bested by Turner in the celebrated passionate and finger-stabbing exchange on free trade that made a temporary hero out of Turner, for a few astonishing weeks revived his political fortunes, and almost saved his entire political career. The extended moments were so riveting that all three U.S. networks showed them over and over again as an example of what real debate could be like, as compared to the sanitized and frozen American presidential variety. (It was such a talking point in Canada that polling firms found more people claimed to have watched the exchange than had actually tuned in to the debate the night it took place.)

Dr. Death was largely responsible.

Henry Comor, a medical doctor turned actor turned media guru, was brought in by Liberal party strategists who knew that Turner's microphone mannerisms had become the staple of stand-up comedians and journalists' one-liners. They knew neither they nor Turner could endure another campaign with his harrumphing into the television sets of the nation and his frantic lip-moistening.

Dr. Death studied, over and over again, videotapes of Turner speeches and television appearances. What hit him, after much watching, was that Turner's eyes would bulge and he would waggle his arms as he tried to make a point. He looked awkward and ludicrous–something not lost on a television generation that assessed its political choices on the tube.

Comor's conclusion was that Turner was not breathing. He was concentrating so hard on making a point that he was forgetting to inhale. Dr. Death, in studying the videotapes over and over, could see Turner's eyes start to protrude. His voice increasingly would come in short bursts ("the only politician to speak in telegrams") as he fought to get the words out before he ran out of breath. Subsequently, though he wouldn't know why he was doing it, he would raise his arms so his lungs could expand.

The doctor's diagnosis? Turner had to do breathing exercises, lying on the floor in his darkened office with loosened clothing so he could relax. Viewed seriously, it was right out of a John Cleese Monty Python political sketch, but that's the way things are done these days in the age of telepolitics. Proud John Turner, a deeply religious man, stretched out on the office carpet for the greater good of the Liberal party, while the secretaries no doubt sniggered outside.

Comor took his medical degree in England but never practised, deciding to pursue his first love, the theater. He was an actor and director in London's West End, before coming to Canada in 1956 to act in and direct radio documentaries. He became president of ACTRA-the Alliance of Canadian Television and Radio Artists-hosted a radio show, worked as a Broadway writer, director and producer and taught a broadcast course at the CBC. As hobbies, he became a part-time antique dealer and a champion bridge player.

One of the things Comor taught Turner (celebrated for the intense eyeball-to-eyeball contact he inflicts on admirers, some of them female) was that the conventional wisdom that the speaker must maintain eye contact with the listener is perhaps not wisdom. Comor believes it makes most people uncomfortable. (In the animal world, eye contact is a sign of aggression-an apt analogy for the super-intense Turner of the 1984 campaign who turned off viewers who just happened to be voters.)

Dr. Death, instead, had Turner pausing, looking away and appearing to reflect on what he was saying. In the 1988 campaign, a smoother Turner was swivelling his head from one side of the audience to the other while speaking in actual sentences, rather than machine-gun bursts.

Turner, naturally, doesn't like to acknowledge the existence of the media coach. He didn't need to be shy. Brian Mulroney has also utilized the same type of image shrink, who tried to convince him to modulate the bedroom-baritone that so turns off female voters. So did Pierre Trudeau, Ontario Premier David Peterson and Quebec Premier Robert Bourassa, not to mention George Bush, who was fashioned in 1988 from the nation's most famous wimp into a bully who destroyed the passionless Michael Dukakis.

In the delightful, desiccated words of Liberal campaign communications director Daniel Despins–only a campaign communications director could phrase it this way–Comor "coaches the leader on his delivery and everything that has to do with oratory skills and presence. Henry's job as media coach is to suggest changes to the speeches to better suit the leader."

Clearly, one major effect television has had on politics is the homogenization of personalities. There was created, in the Kennedy era, an ideal that sold well on the tube–and politics has been chasing that ideal ever since. Just as the death of Kennedy at Dallas changed politics forever, and television forever, and the printed press forever, the advent of Kennedy as president changed presidential rites and traditions and conduct.

Franklin Roosevelt was made for radio, with his fireside chats, Kennedy with his breezy manner and his wit and his fashion-plate wife was made for television. He wasn't quite as spontaneous as he came across, but his family wealth was able to hire the speech-writers and consultants and camera experts who knew how to exploit the new medium that his predecessor in the White House, Eisenhower, did not like and did not understand.

For one thing, Kennedy, at 42 the youngest president in history, immediately changed the rules of politics. The qualifications for leadership of a political party no longer were long service, loyalty to the party brass and wait-your-turn-in-line seniority. Because of television and its immediate reach on one night to more citizens than you could ever shake hands with in a lifetime, a compelling candidate such as Kennedy could bypass the party brahmins and vault over the system–appealing directly to the voters without party machinery in the way.

Television turned standard political practices upside down. With the breakthrough, with the backroom pols being replaced by the cathode ray, a new type of candidate was needed. A new generation of politicians emerged, more suited to the studio than the hustings and not ashamed–as with the new generation of hockey players–to be known to own a hair dryer.

The passing of the guard could be seen in Canada, as one example, at federal-provincial conferences in the late 1960s (post-Kennedy). There were the bookends of Confederation, Wacky Bennett of British Columbia, always looking the funeral director in his stiff suits and homburg and artificial smile, and Joey Smallwood of Newfoundland, craggy and crafty and appearing as if he had just smuggled a crate of Screech in from the dock past the customs agents.

But the blow-dry premiers were taking over, like Kennedy, well south of fifty: Lougheed of Alberta and Bourassa of Quebec and Davis of Ontario and Schreyer of Manitoba and the ever-youthful Hatfield of New Brunswick and Moores of New-foundland with his stunning wife.

The premiers, as we approach the 1990s, are now almost interchangeable. Peterson is about as tall as Getty. Who in the rest of Canada could tell a Devine from a Filmon if encountering them on the street? Ghiz is a darker version of McKenna, and Buchanan, when you think about it, could be confused with Wells. Only the goofball Vander Zalm stands apart.

In the United States, which one was the Gephardt and which one was the Gore? The ruggedly handsome Gary Hart even adopted such Kennedy mannerisms as tucking his left hand (his left, not his right) into his jacket pocket. Which of Reagan's close aides, being equally slippery, was Michael Deaver and which was Edwin Meese? Their slipperiness obscured their personas.

One could suggest that television, by putting all these chaps into a blender and coming out with a selection of Arrow collar ad candidates, has demeaned the process of politics. The process,

surely, was served better–not to mention made more interesting–when individuals of widely disparate backgrounds came
together and had to bury their differences to achieve decisions by
compromise.

The system at present would rule out the desk-thumping,
anecdote-strewn style of little Tommy Douglas, who would be
advised by the media doctors (the Ed Broadbent campaign team
of the 1988 election hired a U.S. firm to do its polling) to shuck
his bifocals for contacts and would have hairdressers working to
tame his pompadour. John Crosbie, the brightest man in the
Conservative cabinet, has been ruled out for the highest office in
the land because he has the unfortunate habit of telling the truth
in unabashed, boyish fashion, and has suffered for it.

The blow-dry syndrome, needless to say, would have deprived
us of the regional shrewdness of the elder Bennett and the
primitive passion of a Smallwood, an original as authentic as
Gordon Sinclair. Does one expect nationhood flowing from the
forehead of a Devine or a Filmon? The current fashion is to
dump all over Richard Hatfield, but New Brunswick voters
couldn't have been wrong for every one of the seventeen years
he was elected and he brought a flavor to the provincial
gatherings that was second only to the verve of René Lévesque,
who didn't have enough hair to blow-dry but had a brain that
challenged that of Trudeau and happened to have a heart as
well.

John Turner, when a young lad growing up in Ottawa's
Rockcliffe Park, used to be sent out to walk the dog on paths
where he sometimes encountered Mackenzie King. In 1988, it
would have been hard to imagine who would be more
surprised–Turner or King's ever-active ghost–to come to the
realization that the leader of the Liberal party of Canada, in an
attempt to win back the crown he had lost, was forced to lie
down on the floor of his office to have breathing lessons
administered by a speech therapist/media doctor. Somehow, one
cannot imagine Willy King in the same position, his tweeds
pressed against the rug while a media shrink endeavored to
improve his diction. The winners, these days, have to be

packaged for public consumption, just as Diet Coke is and Kellogg's Nuttin' Honey and L'Eggs pantyhose. Neither Tommy nor Crosbie nor Hatfield nor Joey nor Wacky could be packaged for sale.

The Great Wasteland of TV, desperate to find something to fill its empty hours, in the 1950s and early 1960s discovered a great free show in the Democratic and Republican conventions. They were dramatic, they were lively and colorful, with thousands of over-stuffed delegates in silly hats, and they were full of suspense in that the presidential and vice-presidential candidates were actually selected during the four-day circuses.

Televiewers were fascinated by the spectacle. Walter Cronkite became famous as "Old Iron Pants" for his gavel-to-gavel coverage. A brash young Texas reporter named Dan Rather first attracted the attention of the CBS nabobs when he was roughed up by delegates on the floor of the Richard Daley convention in Chicago. John Chancellor, hustled off the floor by Daley's security goons, ended his report to the booth with, "This is John Chancellor, somewhere in incarceration."

It was all great television, what with the intrigue and wheeling and dealing and hotel room cabals and log-rolling, but the networks are now sick of the conventions–which indicates where the power now lies. Instead of being a show that the networks eavesdrop on, the political conventions have become shows in the ratings game, which the networks control and set the schedule for.

The four-day extravaganzas that helped to establish television news a quarter century ago now have little news value because the nominees are almost always decided months before. George Bush and Michael Dukakis put the final seal on any possible suspense in 1988 by picking their vice-presidential mates before convention delegates even had a chance to have a look at them, let alone make an assessment.

The networks, noting the slipping ratings as the drama dies, want a little action–a fight over a controversial portion of the platform or a vice-presidential contest. The parties, having been spoiled by all the attention, want quite simply to use three evenings of free time as an error-free launch pad for the fall campaigns.

The networks already control the schedule of events, demanding–and getting–only well-known politicians speaking in prime time. They dictate the decoration of the convention arenas, down to the most telegenic colors, since the conventions today are in fact giant TV studios, with the delegates used only for backdrop. For 1992, the networks have already warned the Democrats and the Republicans that if they do not cut their shows to two or three nights, ABC, CBS and NBC will do it for them. Without cameras and without lights, deprived of the chance to wave at the relatives back home, the delegates would prefer being in the bars of New Orleans and Atlanta. Television no longer covers politics. Television controls politics.

In 1988, Michael Dukakis went into the convention months of July and August as a Democratic candidate a full seventeen points ahead of George Bush in the polls. When the summer was over, his huge lead had disappeared. The Democrats were dumbfounded, in a year they had assumed was a Democratic year, since George Bush was perceived as such a weak rival. The Republicans, naturally, were elated but were honestly just as puzzled by how rapidly the picture had changed in the dog days of summer.

Dukakis's blunders in the TV debates played a role, but the overall television coverage may have had a much deeper impact. William Safire had a theory, which I think was correct. The Safire theory was that Middle America, after watching the Democratic convention in New Orleans, with all the summer to ponder, began to wonder who was really the party's presidential candidate–Michael Dukakis or the Reverend Jesse Jackson.

Blacks make up just 12 per cent of the American population. The Democratic party has always been the party for the black voter, and a disproportionate percentage of blacks become delegates and alternate delegates and official observers at Democratic conventions. The cavernous Louisiana Superdome in New Orleans, big enough for football but too big for the cozy TV theater that the networks like to construct for these events, was curtained off to make a tight scene for camera angles.

The Dukakis forces were greatly embarrassed by the goof in which the proud Jackson heard first from reporters that Dukakis had picked Texas Senator Lloyd Bentsen as his vice-presidential running mate. They wished to heal the rift and to let Jackson, the most spell-binding orator in America, have his moment of glory at the convention. He took it and ran with it. Every one of the handsome and eloquent Jackson children gave a speech in tribute to father. Jackson gave a mesmerizing speech (the better to show up the stolid Dukakis) that went past midnight, and even the networks didn't dare pull the plug on it. At the end, the entire Jackson family was greeted on stage–as if they were the winners–by the rest of the party elite.

During Jackson's brilliant and emotional address, the network cameras roamed the audience to provide close-ups of weeping black delegates. One might have assumed, as a viewer in, say, Iowa, that the audience was 50 per cent black, if not more. It was astonishing to this reporter, repairing from the New Orleans heat to a hotel room to watch portions of the convention on television and to discover the view that the voters in Iowa were seeing. From the press box, one could see the sweep of the arena and pick out the black faces. On television, thanks to the producers' search for the dramatic and their efforts to highlight the tension between the Dukakis and the Jackson camps, one got the impression that blacks were a huge proportion of the delegates.

Safire was correct. As Kennedy long before intuitively sensed, the illusion of reality can be more effective than reality itself.

7

The Boys (and Girls) on the Bus

The press is a peculiar, disembodied
melancholy creature driven by strange hungers,
never happy with its triumphs, wanting always
to be loved and incessantly suspecting that it is
not. In this, of course, it closely resembles the
politician. There the resemblance ends. The
politician and his appointed assistants have an
obligation to be responsible. The press has
none. It prints what it is given.
–*Alexander Haig*

The press is the enemy.
–*Richard M. Nixon*

The first time the Democratic party met in convention in San
Francisco was 1920, and it was a memorable occasion. Prohibition had just come in five months earlier, and despondent
delegates arrived fearing the worst. As H.L. Mencken explained
in a celebrated essay, the wholesale booze sellers of the nation
usually used these events to ship in the dregs of their
cellars–"rye whisky in which rats have drowned, bourbon
contaminated with arsenic and ptomaines, corn fresh from the
still, gin that is three-fourths turpentine and rum rejected as too
corrosive by the West Indian embalmers."

Instead, they were stunned to find that San Francisco mayor
James Rolph, Jr., had laid in carloads of the finest aged bourbon
and provided it, gratis, to the delighted visitors. There followed,
in Mencken's words, "a series of days so sunshiny and caressing,
so cool and exhilarating, that living through them was like rolling
on meads of asphodel."

Reporters Ring Lardner and Irvin S. Cobb got so swacked on the ultra-brew that they nominated each other from the floor and actually got a few votes. When the band leader swung into "The Sidewalks of New York," someone in the gallery began to sing, and suddenly the whole audience was bellowing out the familiar words. The band leader switched to "Little Annie Rooney," and someone started to dance. For a solid hour the band waltzed through "The Bowery" and "A Bicycle Built for Two" and the rest while the entire convention waltzed in the aisles, halting all proceedings until a young man named Franklin Delano Roosevelt could nominate Al Smith.

What was apparent then is still apparent today. There are certain elements central to political life: a gathering of people, a shared preoccupation with politics–and plenty of good booze. Among the things fuelling the continuance of the Stockholm Syndrome are a fascination with politics, proximity, and alcohol. No soirées last longer than those in hotel rooms at political conventions.

The political parties several elections ago learned their own version of the game. It is that the press, far from being the hostile, wary beast that is assumed, in fact is a cuddly bear that, once embraced, can be disarmed.

The solution proved amazingly simple. Once an election date is declared, closet the elite of the Ottawa Press Gallery in a silver cigar that zooms endlessly across this vast frozen waste with one or the other of our supposed leaders. The handlers and manipulators who chart these campaigns figured out, not unnaturally, that if most of the supposedly alert reporters of the land were spending up to twelve and fourteen hours a day seven miles aloft, there would be little time (and no real opportunity) to report the news. Instead (since the insatiable maw of the News Machine requires Content) they perforce must depend on the "Gaines-burgers" dished out to them at hourly deadline time by the smooth-faced press secretaries on the campaign jet.

Both sides understand the game. The media prisoners of the silver cigar, harassed by their papers or stations who now are in constant contact via cellular phones, must supply grist; the

Mulroney or Turner or Broadbent factotums know that nature abhors a vacuum and the press releases and position papers and counter-charges to opposing charges are churned out on the Xerox and fax machines in the front of the planes and shoved (*i.e.*, inserted) into the waiting Tandy 200 lap-top computers of the yuppie-age journalists sipping their Blue in the back seats while passing over Gimli and hoping that the cargo door doesn't blow off.

The Stockholm Syndrome has its variations. But though the roles may be switched, the bond remains the same. In a telling reprise-with-a-twist of the Stockholm hostage-taking in a vault episode, there was the "celebrated" Mary Steinhauser incident at the British Columbia Penitentiary in New Westminster in 1975. Steinhauser, a social worker who dealt with violent prisoners, was under much suspicion from prison guards for the time she spent inside the walls with a highly dangerous prisoner, Andy Bruce, a drug addict who had viciously killed a woman in the presence of her small daughter.

When Bruce seized a number of hostages, including Steinhauser, and held them in a prison vault, the subsequent negotiations made it clear that Steinhauser, to soothe the wild prisoner who had been demanding and receiving drugs, had used sexual relations with him in an attempt to calm him.

When prison guards finally stormed the vault, they shot and killed Steinhauser–not the convict. The subsequent inquiry showed that the guards had purposely not signed for the guns they had checked out; therefore the fatal bullets that killed Steinhauser could not be traced to any one guard. The guards' wrath was directed not at the prisoner–but at a member of the public who had intruded into their world.

Journalists who venture outside the magic circle can also find themselves in the line of fire. The press, to its shame, seldom reports on the press. When it does, the results are usually hilarious–and very informative. Evelyn Waugh's classic satire of Fleet Street, *Scoop*, is as good today as when it was written to spear the fat press lords and the feckless wonders they despatched to cover African revolutions. Ben Hecht and Charles MacArthur in their Broadway hit *The Front Page* portrayed the cop-shop side of ambulance-chasing journalism in a celebrated script that has been translated through Hollywood and is still on stage today. After the 1972 presidential election, *Rolling Stone* writer Timothy Crouse–unknown outside that venturesome bible for the rock crowd–revealed in *The Boys on the Bus* what he had found while travelling as a little-known, ignored young reporter reporting on the reporters on the campaign trail.

What he found was that there were definite rules. Wheels up, rings off. Anything that happened west of the Alleghenies was never mentioned east of the Alleghenies. The tales were the stuff of legend. *New York Times* reporter Jim Naughton, on the 1972 campaign, locked a sheep in a rival reporter's hotel room. The famous Dr. Hunter S. Thompson, the drug-crazed *Rolling Stone* reporter who invented gonzo journalism and became the model for Uncle Duke in the Doonesbury cartoon strip, was so outraged at being denied an interview with Jimmy Carter that he set fire to the hotel-room door of Hamilton Jordan, Carter's aide. There was the young lady on the 1972 George McGovern tour who expertly removed the trousers of the plane's pilot and hid them, forcing him to race up and down the aisle in his smalls, as the English call them, looking for his pants.

Renegades like Crouse apart, most journalists abide by an unspoken rule against reporting behind-the-scenes antics like these. Why? Because doing so might let the public in on one of the real secrets–the degree to which the two parties are members of the same club.

An outstanding example of this covert clubbiness is the ritual known as the Ottawa Press Gallery Annual Parliamentary Dinner. It has a long and storied tradition, the once-a-year gathering at which the supposed foes, the press and the politicians, fall into the nosebag and cut up until outrageous hours, with many a minor reputation ruined by dawn's early light.

The formula is simple. Each card-carrying member of the Press Gallery is eligible to invite one (1) guest–said guest supposed to be either a Member of Parliament, a high swivel servant, perhaps a provincial premier, or some related player in the great game that is supposed to be so adversarial in the public mind.

In its salad days, the Gallery dinner was a much-sought-after cachet among the nation's shovers and makers. The big papers, the *Star* and the *Globe*, and the CBC, would have executives in Toronto slavering and ordering about their minions in the Ottawa bureaus to capture the most prestigious cabinet ministers, or Margaret Trudeau, or Mila Mulroney, or Iona Campagnolo, as prize guests for the pre-cocktail cocktail parties that were sprinkled around town in the bureau chiefs' homes before the serious drinking in the halls of Parliament, before the black-tie dinner, with its serious pecking-order seating plan, before the floor show, which was followed by more heavy tippling and arguing in the marble halls once again, before everyone adjourned across Wellington Street to the National Press Club and a few fist-fights and much hilarity, before the whole thing wound up with the club staff serving bacon and eggs for breakfast as the sun rose over the hangovers.

At Mackenzie King's last appearance at an Ottawa Parliamentary Press Gallery dinner, in 1948, he confided to the gathered reporters that it would be his last. After the dinner, he reported in his diary that *Globe and Mail* reporters had come up "apologizing for the way the paper had treated me." Another newspaper's reporter "apologized for having ever written a line against me" and others were "moved almost to the point of tears."

Even allowing for King's tendency to dramatize, it would seem a rather sycophantic scene. Fitting, however, in the strange tradition of the Gallery dinner, which has demonstrated over time the psychic linkage between reporters and politicians.

The press club wisdom that has run this event over the decades has had one rule that may once have made sense but makes no sense today. It is that all activities within the evening are off the record, cannot be retailed to the public that thinks these two warring forces actually dislike one another and have nothing in common. In fact, both sides would rather chum with each other than be caught with a member of the public. (As Dave

Barry, a syndicated columnist with *The Miami Herald*, has written, most newspapermen learn early in their career never to leave the office for fear of meeting members of the public, most of whom are either under indictment or carrying unusually large vegetables.)

The Ottawa excuse is that the prime minister, the leaders of the opposition and the third party and the governor-general would not be willing to make their off-the-record speeches if their daring and sometimes rude remarks found their way into the public domain.

The evening, in fact, is very political–as Dief knew, with his artful use of a rumor about his leaving (he didn't). Businessmen and publishers arrange invitations so as to assess how a Mulroney or a Turner or a Broadbent can perform before such a tough crowd. One can detect, in the speeches and in the satirical show, just whom the members of the Press Gallery like and respect and which cabinet ministers are held in low esteem. Stanfield always out-performed Trudeau, and a banker or editor from Toronto or Vancouver can sense and feel, for himself, Mulroney's unease with the mob of reporters, who generally dislike him.

It's all politics, and to pretend that it is all secret–the businessmen and editors fly back to their offices and give their colleagues their assessment and the best one-liners–is nonsense. The pretence is based on the premise that it is okay for several thousand insiders in the country to know who bombed that evening and who didn't–but it's not okay for the public at large to know. It's media-and-politics incest.

Years back, Southam's Charles Lynch, on hearing with his own ears at a special testimonial dinner, John Diefenbaker confess he was about to depart the field, filed a story to his papers to that effect–and was suspended by the Ottawa Press Gallery for his effrontery–i.e., reporting on what was news.

Washington has a similar institution, the Gridiron Club, composed of the senior journalists on Capitol Hill, which annually stages skits and mocking imitations of White House figures. Nancy Reagan, ridiculed in her early years in Washington as a clothes horse who was concerned only about the White

House "china crisis," rescued her reputation before Washington insiders by appearing on the Gridiron Club stage dressed as a bag-lady and doing a "Second Hand Clothes" song-and-dance number in imitation of Barbra Streisand's "Second Hand Rose" classic.

The Washington papers, dutifully interviewing all the usual suspects, report next day all the shafts and *bon mots* and insults that highlight the evening. The Ottawa convenors, stuck in another age, haven't thought things through. Don McGillivray, the Ottawa columnist for Southam News, feels the dinner is an intensely political event and that the media muzzle themselves with the off-the-record rule. (The politicians themselves are so intent on scoring a success that they enlist outside quipsters–Larry Zolf writes Mulroney's lines–to write their texts.) After the 1985 Press Gallery dinner–the highlights of which are biting, witty, inside-joke speeches of the prime minister, the governor-general, the leaders of the opposition and the NDP and the Press Gallery president–McGillivray, an anti-social animal who never attends trendy public events, simply interviewed those leaving the dinner and reported all in his column the next day.

This scribbler, who loves parties as much as McGillivray shies from them, reported the same. I then received a stern notice from the Press Gallery notifying that its executive, after an agonizing debate, had decided to ban me from the 1986 dinner. (They couldn't ban McGillivray, since he never attended, and had no interest in doing so.) The following year, when I repeated the shamed action, I was banned for two more years.

I have since, Sancho Panza to McGillivray's Don Quixote, grown bored with the whole mish-mash, having seen a far more important town, Washington, able to deal with the conflict in a more civilized way. McGillivray is right. The cosy Gallery dinner is great fun, but it's too much a night at the Elks Lodge, smug in the knowledge that the public is excluded. Birds of a feather.

As society changes, so do politicians and so do the press–often in lock-step. Take the health and fitness trend, take the new monogamy. Or, for that matter, take the latest in high tech.

Two of the brightest reporters in Washington are Alessandra Stanley of *Time* magazine, whose very perceptive piece on the "Ralph Laurenization of the White House" in *The New Republic* at the advent of the Bush family has proven entirely correct, and Maureen Dowd, who does shrewd dissections of the presidential mind for *The New York Times*.

Both are in their thirties and view with vast amusement the new-breed, high-tech campaign trail journalists that they call "the dweebs on the bus." There is David Hoffman of *The Washington Post*, thirty-five years old, who gets regular front-page bylines on his terribly important paper. On the campaign bus, he keeps in constant contact with the world through a cellular phone. The state-of-the-art model has automatic re-dial, so he can pester his sources. He has programmed the phone with three speed-dial numbers: one to his lawyer wife and two small sons in suburban Maryland, one to his *Post* office and one to Bush national headquarters.

He carries the phone in one case, the modem for his rapid-transmission lap-top computer in another. He also packs with him his own printer and has on his wrist a Casio watch that displays the time in two zones, has a wake-up alarm and stores twenty phone numbers. This is the new Bionic Man of journalism. His advice for others on the bus: "Carry more files." Asked how he unwinds on the road, he replies: "I don't unwind."

Warren Weaver of *The New York Times* has been covering presidential campaigns since 1952. He is sixty-five. He says, "The new breed of political reporters is a little like the new breed of candidates: young and very serious, tireless, smart, tough, but almost without joy, a little pale and bloodless. Stunts are out, drinks are out. Some of them don't even seem to eat regularly."

The campaign trail is now high-tech, a Silicon Valley on wheels. A few years ago, Dowd and Stanley recall, the only noise you could hear in the morning was the raspy sound of grown men hacking. Today, there is the soft tap-tap of several dozen lap-top computers. Reporters wearing Walkman earphones transcribe tapes into their notebooks. Some murmur into their cellular phones, talking to their editors. When I first covered campaigns, one of the joys was to be so far away from the office: today's reporter seems to want be in constant touch with the mothership. Others watch the morning news shows on Walkman TVs. The bus ride now, says the Boston *Globe's* Tom Oliphant, "is like half an hour in a secretarial pool."

The boys on the bus used to swap stories on which hotels had the best bars. Today it's which hotel has the biggest Nautilus machine. Instead of Bloody Marys in the morning on the press planes, it's fresh fruit and Perrier. Jesse Jackson, who is a teetotaller, for months kept all alcohol off his press plane. The reporters not only didn't complain, they established their own smoking ban. The new robo-reporters don't interview candidates over cocktails; they jog with them or carry hand weights while power-walking with the man they are covering. One veteran on the 1988 trail said, "This group has a nerve calling Dukakis dull. Hell, they're soul brothers."

The new mood and the new brood has even taken a toll on sex. There was the celebrated case, recorded in Crouse's book, of the lawsuit filed by a stewardess who sued her former jet-bound lover–after finding out on the final day of the campaign that he was married–for "illegal acts committed over the state of Iowa." One of the more entertaining aspects of a Joe Clark election campaign was watching the tearful farewells of one particular Quebec radio reporter and her man at the Ottawa airport before she dashed on board and fell into the arms of her campaign lover. Two different TV personalities, now familiar on the screen, were astounded to find they were not the exclusive choice of a certain fetching Trudeau aide.

During the Jimmy Carter campaign of 1979, after an exhausting few weeks, the press mob found itself with a night off in Chicago. Reporters, Carter aides, TV cameramen, photographers and the charter-jet crew all went to the hotel disco to unwind and unwind. In the middle of the night the Iran hostage crisis became acute and the entire gang had to fly back to Washington. "It was like the Keystone Kops," remembers a

Newsweek photographer, "with people dashing around the open Hyatt atrium without shirts or pants, trying to get back to their own rooms. They could barely get a crew together to fly the plane."

In the 1988 campaign, if a male and a female reporter disappeared, they were probably in a room transcribing tapes and pooling notes. The young reporters phone their wives at home twice a day. On the Bush bus, Dowd and Stanley discovered David Hoffman telling a group of single women about the problems of his infant's teething and lecturing another young father about the dangers of giving skim milk to children less than one year old.

Hoffman and all his young jogging equivalents found on Canadian election campaigns are the product of Richard Nixon. The Watergate scandal, in making romantic figures (and millionaires) of Carl Bernstein and Bob Woodward, glorified investigative reporting to a generation that had never heard of Lincoln Steffens or the term "muckraking" and zoomed the enrolments of the journalism schools. *All the President's Men*, the movie starring Dustin Hoffman and Robert Redford as Bernstein and Woodward, showed the two hottest stars in Hollywood playing not private detectives or cowboys or politicians or lawyers–but *two newspaper reporters*. The dweebs who previously would have gone into commerce or law school set out to become journalists, but a different breed of journalist.

The boys on the bus who used to kick-start their brains every morning with Bloody Marys and Screwdrivers have been replaced by well-behaved and faithful young husbands who live in the new information age of satellites, cellular phones, fax machines, Federal Express packets, cable TV and all the electronic aids supplied by Sony.

Another factor that is breaking up that old gang of mine is the march of the females into the newsroom. The scene is a pleasant summer afternoon in 1986 on the back lawn of Stornoway, the leader of the opposition's official residence in leafy Rockcliffe, the elephants' graveyard in Ottawa where swivel servants go to

die. It is the occasion of John Turner's official garden party for
the members of the Ottawa Press Gallery, much gin and hilarity
when both sides in the supposed adversarial battle are allowed to
let down their hair and everything is supposed to be off the
record. Pam Wallin, however, is having trouble with her high
heels, it having rained the day before.

Pamela Wallin, the pride of Wadena, Saskatchewan, like her
close friend Marjorie Nichols of Red Deer, Alberta, has never
met a man in a high or low position who has frightened her. She
reduces strong men to jello with one verbal thrust–though most
always with a twinkle. She laughs more in a day than Herb Gray
in a year. Make it two years.

After university, she put in time as a psychologist in a
penitentiary before deciding to pursue more mirthful ways
through life. She had never written a news story in her life when
she applied to *The Toronto Star* for a job and got it, probably
because city editor Lou Clancy was so charmed by the audacity of
it all. She took to the Ottawa scene so boldly and successfully,
with her trademark hat, that CTV's Bruce Phillips recognized
her potential quickly and moved her onto the screen in a
print-to-air transition hardly equalled in Canada.

But now, standing with drinks before John Turner and a
clutch of male reporters, Pam Wallin was having troubles with
her heels sinking into the rain-softened turf of the Stornoway
lawn. She remarked how stupid she had been to wear heels to a
garden party.

Turner, in that left-over jock 1950s manner that still infects
him and so rolls the eyes of his admirers, remarked, "I wouldn't
worry, Pam, those shoes have probably been under a lot of beds,"
in itself a tired old fraternity line that goes back to his days as a
track star at the University of British Columbia.

Pam Wallin wasn't really offended by the remark. She knew
John well and he knew that she knew his bantering style. Much
later, as a matter of fact, she explained that it was probably
Turner's ham-handed way of demonstrating that she was just
one of the boys and would admire being talked to that way. The
person in the group who was the most disturbed, it turned out,

was a male, Elly Alboim, the CBC bureau chief who railed that it offended his feminist sensibilities.

More than a year later, CTV fulfilled its annual practice of sitting the leader of the opposition down before its cameras for a full-length formal interview. "There have been suggestions," said Pam Wallin to John Turner, "that you have, or potentially have, a drinking problem, and people are saying, 'You now want to be the prime minister of Canada–you're making a bid for that–and that we should have the right to know and ask you that.' " It was rather like the when-did-you-stop-beating-your-wife classic. Whatever the answer, it planted a thought in the minds of Canadian voters that only party insiders and journalists had talked about before. It was a question that only a woman journalist would ask, since no male had dared to raise the subject in public. It's still a clubby world.

What the advent of women in significant numbers into journalism has done is to introduce to readers areas of reality previously ignored. Until females flooded the journalism schools (as they have flooded law schools and medical schools), there was only desultory coverage of such essential "female" concerns as abortion, birth control and sexual abuse.

Men, including male reporters, are still uncomfortable for some strange reason while seated in their living rooms watching television programs that feature commercials about "feminine hygiene products" and those fancy euphemisms about light days and heavy days. Men squirm at the references, just as male newspaper editors for years have avoided covering the subjects that concern 50 per cent of the population.

It's why, when you see an article on pre-menstrual tension, the odds are nine to one that it will bear a woman's byline. As with most articles on abortion and birth control and sexual abuse. Reporters–male and female–fight for the stories that interest and excite them. (And that they have some personal expertise in.)

If our society, in fact, was structured in such a way that males were being raped and assaulted in underground parking lots and on leafy trails while jogging you can rest assured there would be a predominance of male bylines on those stories. As Gloria

Steinem has pointed out, if in our male-ruled society it was the men who menstruated, the men would soon be boasting about who had the "biggest" or "longest" period and the one who lost the most blood would be acclaimed the hero in the locker room.

So female reporters both in the newsroom and the TV studio have not only forced their readers and audiences to face issues once ignored but have made the once-verboten subjects not only no longer taboo but also more understandable, less mystifying and more mainstream.

For all the progress, the American figures show that it's a slow crawl. The day of August 2, 1988, was supposedly a historic moment for the media business. Of the six front-row seats in the White House press room that are reserved for senior correspondents from the three major networks and the news services, five were occupied by women. This was the first time this had happened.

So? So what. The National Organization of Women, which tracks such esoteric but telling figures, found in 1985 that women had written 24 per cent of the signed articles on the front pages of eleven leading American newspapers. The much-criticized USA Today, the "McPaper" that is said to have won a prize for the best investigative paragraph, led the way with women's bylines on 45 per cent of its signed page-one pieces. The mighty New York Times, which reports the views of the established order written by established-order reporters, ranked last with 10 per cent.

By 1988, studies presented at a Washington conference on "Women, Men and Media" showed that the percentage of female bylines had zoomed all the way up to 27 per cent in the ten major papers surveyed. USA Today, still ahead of all competition in paying, employing and featuring women and minorities (its publisher is Kathleen Black), led the way. Dead last? Still The New York Times.

With all the glitzy publicity about the millionaire anchorwomen, Diane Sawyer and Connie Chung and the rest, just 16 per cent of network news stories were actually reported by women. Females outnumbered males–the only area–on the bottom rung, as beginning reporters and in advertising sales.

The American Society of Newspaper Editors in annual convention in 1988 found that some 85 per cent of United States newsroom executives are male. The figures would be higher in Canada. Of the society's 1,000 members–meaning the top editors of the nation's dailies–about 80 are women.

In a business dominated by men, within a society dominated by men, it is not surprising that just 11 per cent of people quoted in major newspapers were women. Only 24 per cent of the photographs included women, usually with their families. You ain't come a long way, baby.

The situation is actually more encouraging in Canada–indeed remarkable–and there is a reason for it. I suspect the major role women play in the Canadian media is in reaction to their low role in political life. Shut out of one arena, they have decided to dominate another. Older, supposedly more hidebound societies can trust their future to a woman–but not youthful, zesty Canada. Israeli voters handed their fate to Golda Meir long ago, just as Britain does to Margaret Thatcher today. Sri Lanka has been run by a woman. So has Iceland. Indira Gandhi ran India and now that Cher lookalike, Benazir Bhutto, is doing the same for Pakistan. In Canada, the parties seem unable even to contemplate the horrid prospect of a woman at the top, the NDP having been frightened to death at Rosemary Brown's surprisingly powerful run for the leadership at the 1975 convention that chose Ed Broadbent, and the Tories pulling in 1976 their now famous trick of having some 338 delegates enter the balloting booths bearing Flora MacDonald buttons and emerging at the other end, only 214 of them having voted for her.

So, you see, the females in this country get their revenge by taking over the media. In other jurisdictions (the United States is the most obvious example) a few women are allowed power at the top–Barbara Walters and Diane Sawyer–and there is the mandatory coiffed blonde as co-anchor on every local station, but this is all on television. In Canada, women have a strong presence right across the field–in radio and newspapering as well as TV.

It is not just Barbara Frum, who dominates "The Journal" as she once did "As It Happens." "The Journal" was undoubtedly the only major news show anywhere with *two* female hosts when producer Mark Starowicz originally set out with both Frum and Mary Lou Finlay (a strange decision that didn't work and seemed more to demonstrate Starowicz's feminist credentials than to make any broadcasting sense). Finlay, with that distinctive throaty growl, now is the voice of CBC's fine "Sunday Morning" three-hour radio show. One more female anchor.

Wallin–with CTV fighting off big money offers to her from Global–hosts "Question Period" and runs the Toronto office. The two rising stars of the CBC in the reportorial ranks (both involved romantically with high CBC types but with credentials that pass inspection) are Wendy Mesley and Sheila MacVicar. Helen Hutchinson was the star of "Canada AM," and now Deborah McGregor, a shrewd Ottawa columnist for the *Financial Times*, has stepped into the AM co-anchor slot.

Valerie Pringle is the friskiest thing seen on daytime TV interview shows. Betty Kennedy reigned for decades on Toronto's CFRB alongside Gordon Sinclair. Adrienne Clarkson preceded the flood of female voices and faces, first on afternoon TV, then at "the fifth estate"–and is now back hosting a CBC arts series. Vicki Gabereau is the most entertaining thing on national radio.

In print, Marjorie Nichols is by far the toughest columnist operating out of Ottawa. Carol Goar is *The Toronto Star*'s Ottawa columnist. The *Star* bureau chief there is Rosemary Speirs. Barbara Amiel, the Black Queen, still infuriates readers with her columns in *The Toronto Sun* and *Maclean's*.

Most of what Canadians read (and see) about the United States is filtered through female eyes. The bureau chief of *Maclean's* in Washington is Marci McDonald, who is assisted by Hilary Mackenzie. The Washington bureau chief of *The Globe and Mail* is Jennifer Lewington. The Washington bureau chief of Canadian Press, Norma Greenaway has just moved to the

Southam news office there. The Radio-Canada correspondent in Washington has been Francine Bastien; her producer has been Katie Rydell. "The Journal" producer in Washington is Ellen Mason-Persina; her deputy is Pat Ellis.

Linda Hughes, who is all of thirty-seven, is not only the editor of *The Edmonton Journal*, she is the only editor on the Southam newspaper group's committee of publishers who oversee the Southam news service.

In 1988, for the first time in a federal campaign, two of the three CBC television reporters on the planes of Brian Mulroney, John Turner and Ed Broadbent were women. Wendy Mesley, now Mrs. Peter Mansbridge, was on the Mulroney plane. Anna Maria Tremonti travelled with the NDP leader's plane. Also for the first time, two of the three CBC producers on those planes were women.

At CTV, Fiona Conway coordinated the election coverage from the network's headquarters while Pam Wallin, the CTV senior correspondent, roamed the country in search of the major election stories.

At CBC Radio, Jeannette Mathey was the reporter covering the prime minister. For Southam News, Joan Bryden travelled with the Turner troupe. *Le Devoir*, not surprisingly, sent a female to cover Turner.

Publishers pepper politicians from afar with nicely timed books, but journalists do it every day. There's a constant tug-of-war over information and confidences, but the ties that bind the two groups together still seem stronger–especially on the campaign trail. It is hard to describe the atmosphere on board a leader's campaign jet after several weeks aloft. Each party charters a commodious jet from one of the carriers, Air Canada or Canadian International or whatever, and so normal in-flight regulations do not apply.

The airlines assign to these floating zoos the most attractive and adaptable and amiable and bilingual hostesses and stewards they can select, since different crews (aside from not believing what they were seeing) would upset the "family" feeling of the expedition. The bar is always open at the back of the plane, everyone is on a first-name basis and as the silver cigar seven miles high speeds back and forth across the nation for two months, a special feeling develops.

Ever since the classic *The Boys on the Bus* nearly two decades ago, the media gang, it seems to these eyes, has tried to emulate the antics in this book. The plane is plastered with photographs, cartoons, goofy headlines, clippings, paraphernalia. Because some of the reporters and cameramen are on the plane for weeks at a time, they guard their own turf carefully, making their specific seating arrangements rather as their own little cave, surrounded by their favorite things. It is, after all, their "home" for the duration of the campaign, that seat in 17B where they will spend more of their time than in a hotel bed or covering a speech.

There may have been great times back when Diefenbaker campaigned by train, with the boys late at night drinking and playing poker in the parlor car, but covering an election really became *fun* for the first time with Pierre Trudeau in 1968. It wasn't drudgery; though exhausting it was exhilarating as Trudeaumania unfolded. As with John Kennedy in 1960 (Trudeau could not have existed if Kennedy had not existed first), reporters were caught up in the enthusiasm for a politician who didn't act like a politician. His handlers, who first detected the unusual qualities in this unlikely candidate, soon capitalized on the press ardor and gave the cameramen every trampoline flip and kissable teenager they could handle.

By the time of the Ronald Reagan campaigns in the 1980s, the handlers were completely in charge. The press were helpless. One former White House aide confessed: "He's an actor. He's used to being directed and produced. He stands where he is supposed to and delivers his lines, he reads beautifully, he knows how to wait for the applause line. You know how some guys are good salesmen but can't ask the customer to give them the order? This guy is good at asking for the order, and getting it."

Reagan's amiability and the skill of his manipulators had also lulled the press to sleep. In his 1982 trip to Europe, members of the travelling press corps watched him doze off so many times–during speeches by French President François Mitterrand and Italian President Alessandro Pertini, as well as during a personal audience with the Pope–that they privately dubbed the tour "The Big Sleep." Most reporters scarcely mentioned the incidents in their stories.

Reporters are sentimental beasts and get captured, never more so than on the John Turner jet in the 1988 election campaign.

The inmates roamed the aisles, shouting, singing and carrying on. At each takeoff, as the jet gained speed down the runway, cabin lights off, one of the "techies"–a TV soundman-editor with an Elvis hairdo–blasted from his boom-box Wagner's "Ride of the Valkyries," all the while sending flickering lights bouncing off the roof of the darkened jet. It was an eerie and rather appropriate send-off, since the Valkyries, in Norse mythology, were Odin's twelve handmaidens who selected those destined to be slain in battle. Whether the doomed John Turner appreciated the symbolism is not known, but he had no choice but to listen. The antics of the animals at the back of the jet controlled the atmosphere of the flight–and the campaign.

In the 1984 campaign, with a rusty Turner just back from Bay Street, the techies regularly filled the plane with offerings from their ghetto-blasters; edited pieces from Turner's speeches that consisted of nothing but his throat-clearings and coughs. On the Joe Clark planes, they used to sing cruel, satirical songs that echoed through the cabin as Clark sat at the front, trying to work on a speech, his ears burning while Maureen McTeer fumed in rage. This time, in 1988, the gang that had mocked Turner in 1984 admired his courageous, spirited fight and there were no tell-tale tapes or satirical verses.

Like most wives of political figures, Geills Turner thinks the press, and television, and radio are unfair, and biased, and inaccurate. She has a notoriously short fuse and can singe the hide of the most thick-skinned scribe who may have suggested defects in her husband, their marriage or herself.

During the 1988 election campaign, she travelled the route on the Turner campaign as protective support, a regular fixture at the front of the plane with her high energy and slim skirts. But she didn't stay fixed in the Liberal leader's section at the forward portion of the cabin–which was out of bounds to reporters.

Geills Turner, who was in the forefront of the computer industry as a stockbroker in New York when she met Turner, had taken a full photography degree from Toronto's Ryerson Institute when her husband gave up his first chase for the leadership of his party and fled Ottawa for the delights of Bay Street.

She has had published many of the sensitive photographs she has taken in the Canadian North on the yearly frontier trips by canoe in rugged bushland the Turners and their children have attempted. With Geills Turner, an expensive camera can become a weapon. And she decided to use it to get even with the national press that had, in her eyes, tormented her.

At night, when the last of the six or seven stops had been made, when the last copy was filed, when the last videotape was despatched, the boys (and the girls) would party. The beer would flow faster, the dancing in the aisles would begin and the ace photographer with the shapely calves would begin her travels.

There were plenty of jovial shots of the boys arm-in-arm, the boys with the leaders, the boys with daughter Elizabeth Turner, a law student, who had evolved from a 1984 hater of the press to a wary observer of the species. Geills' camera flattered the boys (and the girls) and her prints soon adorned what little uncovered paint remained on the aircraft's interior. She had set them up perfectly.

As night wore on and the partying continued, she achieved the perfect photographer's role: she became invisible. No one paid any attention to her. Now before her lens was the chap dead to the world, his mouth agape, an ideal fly-catcher. Those in goofy hats and strange garb were exposed to her film. Those leaden of eye and droopy of face, victim of the grape or politics or both, were helpless to her camera. Spotting her game one night, I said to her, "Mrs. Turner, you can never again complain to me in the future about the press invading your privacy."

She smiled. She knew what she was doing. She had waited a

long time for her revenge and now had her evidence. After the election was over, she had discussions with a magazine about her devastating portraits of the press with their hair down. The discussions ended when someone found out what was going on. The magazine suspects Mrs. Turner's husband killed the idea.

Mrs. Turner doesn't understand the seductive powers of the Stockholm Syndrome. On the last weekend of the exhausting campaign, in a final desperate plea for votes, Turner and his camp followers flew from Toronto to Trenton, Ontario, then west to Winnipeg for another speech and then on to Vancouver. After collecting cash from everyone interested, Turner wagonmaster Andy Shaw, the cheerful chap who was the media earth-mother, making sure no one missed the bus or the flight, skipped the Winnipeg speech and returned to *Liberair* bearing black cowboy hats for the scribes out of Chicoutimi and Windsor and Halifax who had never seen a cow and never would.

There were cap guns and bandannas. The election was now either won or lost, and the final leg of the flight was Animal House in Roy Rogers costumes. Sunday night, in a Hotel Vancouver banquet room, there was a lavish feast and skits mounted by inmates of the skybound zoo, the most hilarious (and accurate) of which was one put on by the crew and attendants of the chartered jet, imitating the unmanageable conduct of the passengers they had got to know so well in their enforced companionship. As Turner and wife and four children watched, his mannerisms were mocked, but *affectionately* mocked. This troupe had been seduced, won over, by the closeness, the tribal instincts of those in a lifeboat at sea.

Wagonmaster Shaw, who apprenticed for this role by handling the press on the European World Cup skiing circuit, handed out his own awards: to the funniest reporter, the most earnest reporter, the most promising rookie and so on, the feared press eagerly marching to the podium to receive the commendations. The whole thing had the air of holiday-end badges night at summer camp, an us-against-the-world ambience. *The Toronto Star* veteran cynic Val Sears, who achieved minor fame decades previous by announcing to his colleagues one morning during a

Diefenbaker campaign, "To work, gentlemen, we have a government to overthrow," sat there in great anticipation and subsequent disappointment that he was not called forward for some derisive reward.

After the election, each of the some ninety reporters and columnists and cameramen and assorted spear carriers received in the mail a large group portrait of the whole gang-crew and media and the Turner family and his aides-on the tarmac in front of *Liberair*. It was signed by John Turner, with thanks for "the tour that worked." It was followed later by a private barbeque at Stornoway for the same group of survivors.

It "worked" because he got the media onside.

8

The Good, the Bad and the Ugly

I keep six honest serving men
(They taught me all I knew);
Their names are What and Why and When
And How and Where and Who.
   -Rudyard Kipling

People just read headlines. The secret of
political success is getting the press-with or
against is immaterial as far as I'm concerned.
   -three-time Vancouver mayor
   Tom (Terrific) Campbell

One of the biggest secrets of our age is that George Orwell, his fame obscured by *Nineteen Eighty-Four* and *Animal Farm*, was a brilliant essayist. He never bothered going to university but went to Burma to become a policeman instead (if you want to learn how to be honest, read his piece on having to shoot a berserk elephant), which may have had something to do with his evolving into such a perceptive writer. If you want to write, become a cop.

Lucidity shines through everything Orwell wrote. One of the more brilliant things he did was a piece called "Politics and the English Language." It is contained in *In Front of Your Nose*, the fourth volume of his *Collected Essays, Journalism and Letters*. In it he gives about the best six rules ever devised for writing well:

1. Never use a metaphor, simile or other figure of speech which you are used to seeing in print.
2. Never use a long word where a short one will do.
3. If it is possible to cut a word out, always cut it out.
4. Never use the passive where you can use the active.

5. Never use a foreign phrase, a scientific word or a jargon word if you can think of an everyday English equivalent.

6. Break any of these rules sooner than say anything outright barbarous.

The fight against bad English, Orwell points out, is not the exclusive concern of writers. The decline of a language, he argues, must ultimately have political and economic causes. By getting rid of bad habits in written English one can think more clearly, and "to think clearly is a necessary first step toward political regeneration." Orwell's point is that politicians can't think clearly because they can't write clearly. Their soppy, unintelligible meanderings do not come because they are fuzzy in their minds; their minds are fuzzy because they do not know how to use the language.

Orwell says that "the great enemy of clear language is insincerity." Those of us who make our living from listening, day after deadly day, to spurious piffle from the tonsils of our elected heroes are authorities on that simple truth. Fred Allen once said you could take all the sincerity in Hollywood and fit it into a gnat's navel with enough room left over for an agent's heart. That would be a good description of the average speech handed to a cabinet minister by some underling who has graduate degrees in obfuscation, pettifoggery, obscurantism and bafflegab. Orwell tells us that in our age there is no such thing as "keeping out of politics. . . . All issues are political issues, and politics itself is a mass of lies, evasions, folly, hatred and schizophrenia."

The abuse of the word "fascism" is clear today, but even in 1947 Orwell was writing that the word "now has no meaning except insofar as it signifies 'something not desirable.'" It is hurled across the legislative floor at British Columbia's Social Credit government. A member of the NDP caucus says that what the government is doing to the opposition could be compared with what Hitler did to the Jews in Europe. Eugene Whelan in the House of Commons used to pontificate about "racism" when the word he was groping for was "sexism." President Ronald

Reagan moved right into Orwell's Newspeak when he announced that a new killer missile would be officially called Peacemaker. A former speaker in the B.C. legislature used to plead with members not to throw "epitaphs" at each other.

It is no surprise that Hollywood, that temple of artifice, could produce the famous film mogul Sam Goldwyn, who once described himself as being "on the edge of an abscess." The author of the instruction "include me out," Goldwyn accused fellow producer George Cukor of "biting the hand of the goose that laid the golden egg" and referred to the French Impressionist painter as "Toujours Lautrec." Goldwyn gave James Thurber the screenplay of "The Secret Life of Walter Mitty" and warned him not to read the last hundred pages because they were too "blood and thirsty." Thurber ignored the warning, pronouncing himself "horror and struck."

Orwell's concern is not for the literary use of language "but merely language as an instrument for expressing and not for concealing or preventing thought." He shows that political chaos (this was 1947, recall) is connected with the decay of language. He points out that if you simplify your English, when you make a stupid remark its stupidity will be obvious, "even to yourself."

All political language, from all parties, is designed "to make lies sound truthful and murder respectable, and to give an appearance of solidity to pure wind." Pierre Trudeau, with his brilliant mind and Jesuitical certainty used to be the class example of this in Question Period in Ottawa, making logic stand on its head and denying the most simple truth, all in aid of the debating school ploy that one must never concede anything. Allan MacEachen, his *apparatchik*, was the perfect example of Orwell's case that language is used as an instrument for concealing rather than expressing thought.

One reason why the Liberals were deposed from their hegemony in Ottawa is that they thought they had perfected this trick. It was to them a game, concealing their thoughts and intentions by a smokescreen of words even they did not believe. One denounces wage-and-price controls and then brings them in. One denounces eighteen-cent gas tax to defeat the feckless Joe Clark regime and then piles on triple that assessment at the pumps. One promises to retire–and then unretires.

The abuse of the language can go on for only so long, until the public eventually doesn't believe a single thing you say. The debasement of the language leads inevitably to the debasement of politics. Because governments (the Mulroney one is no exception) don't respect the former, they don't respect the latter either.

Churchill's great piece of luck was his dismal record at school–mainly because he was a disciplinary problem, rebelling against authority. The lowest-ranked scholar in the lower form at Harrow, he was ruled out for Oxford or Cambridge. As a consolation prize, he was sent to Sandhurst, Britain's military academy. Shipped to India by the age of twenty-one, he spent the long, sweltering siestas in Bangladore educating himself, reading Plato, Aristotle, Gibbon, Macaulay, Schopenhauer and going over thousands of pages of parliamentary debates. Developing a flair for the language, he found he could earn extra income by writing newspaper and magazine articles and books.

In the 1920s, £20,000 in royalties from his six-volume history of World War I enabled him to buy Chartwell, his country manor. In his long spell as a back-bencher out of favor during the 1930s, he was so pursued by creditors that at one point he put his house up for sale. He supported himself through his pen, and as a back-bencher wrote and published a million words. He learned how to use language–as the British people, and the world, and Hitler, found out in the 1940s.

Churchill had an extraordinary gift with words that was right for his extraordinary times. Politicians still need fine words, but fewer and fewer now supply their own. A speech-writer for a senior British cabinet minister said it all: "The truth is that politicians are, with few exceptions, not very good with words." Churchill may have been the last great one actually to have written his own speeches. John Kennedy, known for his stirring and inspiring quotations, was stuffed full of them by his White

House ghost, Ted Sorensen, some enemies have charged. There is some evidence that *Profiles in Courage*, for which he won a Pulitzer Prize, in fact was written by Sorensen, an accusation Sorensen has denied.

Fond Washington anecdotes are still told about Senator Joe Montoya of New Mexico, known as the stupidest member of the Watergate panel that brought down Richard Nixon. When on the speechifying circuit, he would get off the plane, be driven to the obligatory fund-raising banquet and, without even glancing at it beforehand, read verbatim the mind-glazer of a speech handed to him by a junior aide as he took the podium. On one memorable occasion, when a gum-fingered stenographer had accidentally stapled two identical pages together, he read–without noticing–the same page through a second time. To the bemusement of his audience, he even read out loud the "(pause for applause)" insertions that his ghost had added as a help in the delivery.

Ronald Reagan, who could read a script like no other politician while giving the impression that he actually meant it, was made into something of a sensitive poet by thirty-six-year-old Peggy Noonan, who had all America choking with emotion when, at the time of the *Challenger* disaster, she stole lines from the RCAF airman-poet John Gillespie Magee to describe how the astronauts had "slipped the surly bonds of earth and touched the face of God."

Peggy Noonan temporarily turned George Bush into a human figure during his acceptance speech at the Republican convention in New Orleans in August of 1988 when she had him talking about his vision of America as "an endless enduring dream and a thousand points of light." No one, let alone the fumble-tongued Mr. Bush, has ever been able to explain what "a thousand points of light" means. Just as there was puzzlement when Ms. Noonan's fetching words had Reagan in his valedictory farewell to the Republicans claim to have lit a prairie fire and to be a foot soldier waiting by his phone for a call. What a telephone was doing beside a prairie fire might mystify some, but the wonders spun by speech-writers should not be questioned.

Bush, as we know, faded into a mush of horseshoe pits and puppies once Noonan decided she wanted to return to her kitchen and her babies. Without Noonan's voice injected into his jerky delivery, he resorted to being, um, himself.

It is surely no surprise that Maggie Thatcher's speech-writer for fifteen years has been Sir Ronald Millar, a successful British playwright. At one of his recent productions, a London newspaper reported, a theater-goer was overheard gushing to her companion, "Oh, this will be good. It's by the man who writes Mrs. Thatcher's speeches."

(There has been more than a speech-writer added to improve the image as the 1980 photographs reveal–showing a more plump, more gray and matronly Thatcher with a prominent gap between her teeth. Along with the elocution teacher and the classics coach have come the tooth-capper, hair-dyer, eyelid-lifter and varicose-vein remover.)

Sir Ronald often uses theatrical allusions in putting eloquent words in the mouth of the grocer's daughter. When all the speculation was that her government's economic policies had to be reversed, he wrote: "You turn if you want to. The lady's not for turning." Mrs. Thatcher, not being as familiar with Christopher Fry as her ghost, muffed the line and delivered it as "The lady is not for turning"–but it made all the headlines nonetheless.

When former Labour prime minister James Callaghan unwisely compared himself to Moses, Sir Ronald put into her mouth the advice to "keep on taking the tablets!"

Sir Ronald understands modern politics more than most politicians. "In the early days," he confessed, "she would say, 'I'm not an actress, dear,' and I'd say, 'You have to be, you have to be.' I treat her exactly as I treated my leading ladies in the theatre. Give them stuff they will enjoy saying."

Exactly! On stage, she is an actress, just as Ronald Reagan was such a successful actor at the podium and Bush is such a dreadful one. (During the late forties and early fifties when Reagan was an actor in one part of Hollywood, Sir Ronald was a screen-writer in another.)

Chief speech-writer for Ed Broadbent has been thirty-three-year-old Hilarie McMurray, a graduate of Osgoode Hall Law School, who had to become accustomed to watching her boss, with scissors and paste, rejig her texts to his own liking. During the election campaign, John Turner used staff man Michael Lanjill, who used to answer letters in Pierre Trudeau's office and who keeps a copy of *Bartlett's Familiar Quotations* on his desk, and George Radwanski, a former editor-in-chief of *The Toronto Star*, who wrote a favorable book on Trudeau.

Brian Mulroney's chief speech-writer for his first term was long-time Montreal friend L. Ian MacDonald who wrote a careful biography of the Conservative leader, leaving out the juicy bits. He has since returned to journalism with the *Montreal Daily News*. The PM also uses Bill Neville, a veteran backroom figure and Ottawa consultant who represents the Canadian Tobacco Manufacturers Council. "All the good stuff is Brian Mulroney's," he says, as any faithful speech-writer would.

A politician who understands the power of words will also understand–and try to harness–the power of the purveyors of words: the press. Franklin Delano Roosevelt, the wealthy aristocrat with the cigarette holder that made him appear different and the little dog, Fala, who made him appear ordinary, was a master at controlling the press. He created a news explosion. As David Halberstam explained in *The Powers That Be*, before Roosevelt arrived in 1932, there were perhaps five or six reporters who mattered who covered national events out of Washington–all gentlemen, "the beau ideals of the time, very properly dressed, men who wore fedoras and carried walking sticks."

In contrast, when reporters first attended on President Herbert Hoover, they had to proffer their questions in writing. When he answered them it was, naturally, in writing. Before Hoover become president, reporters had made this very aloof and formal man his reputation, and he had reciprocated with leaks and was a ready source of news.

As the Depression closed in, Hoover closed up. He blamed the press for his problems and, as a nervous nation waited for assurance from their president, he became ever more inward and reclusive. In his first year in the White House, he had twenty-three press conferences and his office put out eight press releases. In his final year as president, he had just twelve press conferences and put out twenty-six press releases.

Where Hoover was a klutz in media manipulation, Roosevelt proved a genius. He recognized that advanced technology could accommodate–and demanded–more news, and he inundated the nation with it. He flattered the press beyond belief by giving them almost more than they could handle–ensuring, therefore, that it was printed and broadcast as he thrust it at them.

When he entered the White House, he told reporters he would hold two press conferences a week and kept his promise: 337 in his first term, 374 in his second term, 279 in his third term. United Press sent four times as much news from the capital in 1934 under Roosevelt as it did in 1930 while covering Hoover. Suddenly, one-quarter of all the Associated Press world news wire came from Washington. As Halberstam deduced, Roosevelt had earlier determined as governor of New York that "the very high public official who gives the greatest amount of information can dominate the story, often define the issue in question and thus dominate the government." FDR realized that if you can control information you can control power.

Heywood Broun, the renowned columnist of his time, called FDR, in resigned admiration, "the best newspaperman who has ever been President of the United States." Roosevelt was crippled, as a result of the polio contracted in the family summer island retreat of Campobello in New Brunswick, but the compliant White House reporters never wrote about it, and the White House photographers never pictured him in a wheel-chair or on crutches. There was a compact; the public was secondary.

More than fifty years later, a most unusual authority on the same essential problem gained notoriety. It was Michael Deaver, convicted liar before Washington courts, Reagan's sound-bite slickster, Canada's $500,000-a-year consultant on acid rain problems. Deaver said that the pack mentality of the White House press gang in fact played into his hands. "You know," he confessed, in a shrewd insight, "they'd be much better off if they were in offices scattered all over town. But they beat on each other, and if they don't have a story, sure, they're going to take ours. Whereas if they were out on their own, they'd be hustling and digging and getting their own stories."

Bang on. Deaver is not stupid, he's just a devious perjurer. But he's saying the same thing as the solid *Boston Globe* reporter Walter Robinson, who took over the beat in the president's house in 1985. "It's hard to avoid the analogy of the White House press corps," he says in Mark Hertsgaard's book *On Bended Knee*, "as a bunch of caged hamsters thoroughly dependent on their masters for their daily feeding."

Sam Donaldson and the other cynical White House press-room regulars feel the same, but Roosevelt invented it all, knowing that the maw of the new media machine required constant feeding, and the feeder was the master.

It's tempting to assume that any politician's success or failure depends on the kind of press he or she gets. But getting "a good press" depends less on the members of the press than it does on the politician's gift for an indefinable thing called "the craft of politics."

It's truly remarkable how few skillful politicians there are, considering how many aspire to the trade. Peter Lougheed was a very good politician, both on the home field and nationally. Don Getty is a spectacularly inept one. Dave Barrett was a very good leader of the opposition for the British Columbia NDP; once premier, he lasted only three years. Pierre Trudeau enjoyed being prime minister very much; once in opposition he was hopeless. Tommy Douglas was a natural politician, full of the joy of battle. Colin Thatcher was less successful.

It is hard to imagine a more inept politician than Frank Miller, he of the plaid jackets who, handed the power of Ontario's smug Conservatives, squandered it so quickly. Unless it was Gerald

Ford, who freed Poland and was beaten by Jimmy Carter who wasted his time supervising the scheduling on the White House tennis court.

You don't have to be at the top to be a good politician. Ged Baldwin, the Conservative who never made a cabinet, was a very good one, a credit to his craft. Gordon Fairweather, still serving the public, was a good one. No one ever worked harder than Stanley Knowles. Elmer MacKay was a better MP than he is a cabinet minister, an example of the Peter Principle in practice. Gary Hart, though he was out very much for Gary Hart, was an intelligent senator with innovative ideas. Teddy Kennedy, though he will never be president because of Chappaquiddick, remains the conscience of the Democratic party's left wing. During the 1988 presidential convention in Atlanta, Kennedy with his great oratorical gifts brought the delegates alive with his repeated mantra, on George Bush's supposed non-involvement in key meetings cooking up the Iran-contra caper, "Where was George?" The Democrats loved it, and "Where was George?" became their gleeful rallying cry for a few weeks—until an enraged Republican congressman told a party picnic, "Where was George? I'll tell you where George was. He was at home, dry, sober, with his own wife." Kennedy once more disappeared from view for the whole campaign.

The good don't necessarily rise to the top; the bad don't necessarily sink to the bottom. I was standing down on the Mississippi shore in decadent old New Orleans one morning in August of 1988, pressed in among thousands of fat Republicans in too-pastel, too-tight T-shirts, when an excited young man rushed up and knocked George Bush's glasses off. It turned out he was Dan Quayle, who had just learned he was within a heart-tick of the most important job in the world.

Bush, the soon-to-be-nominated Republican candidate, demonstrated in his manner of picking the little-known senator from Indiana why he has proven to be such a strange president—inarticulate and relaxed, well-meaning and with no discernible views on anything. He had cinched the nomination six months previously, knocking off Bob Dole and Jack Kemp and Pete DuPont and the rest in the primaries marathon. He had all the time in the world to contemplate vice-presidential choices.

Late in the process, as the New Orleans convention loomed, someone in his entourage leaked to the press the fact that their speculations might include one Dan Quayle, an otherwise undistinguished junior senator from Indiana who was known mainly for his teeth and his hair, both being of TV commercial quality.

Bush, accused all his Washington career of being a non-elected appointee to high positions who never took firm views, kept the vice-presidential pick to himself, not even consulting his closest aides. As he flew into New Orleans for his coronation, he phoned former presidents Gerald Ford and, of all people, Richard Nixon, to inform them of his choice. As he landed at the airport to be greeted by Ronald Reagan who was flying out after his triumphant farewell evening, Bush whispered to the departing president the secret name.

Quayle at this time was strolling with handsome wife, Marilyn, and their three model children through the Latin Quarter, the New Orleans tourist haunt, when his beeper went off, telling him to get back to his hotel room pronto. It was the Bush people, informing him he had better be down on the levee, waiting for the paddle wheeler *Mississippi Belle* that was to bring Bush across the river from the airport in a made-for-TV extravaganza.

Dark clouds loomed, warning of a downpour, as the *Mississippi Belle* circled and circled off the dock, rather like the holding pattern over Lester B. Pearson International Airport. Bush couldn't dock until they found Quayle, who at that moment, sweating and excited, was trying to push his way through the crowd beside the river. Once Quayle was located, Bush made the surprise announcement as to his vice-presidential nominee, and the over-eager young politician rushed over to embrace Bush with such vigor that he dislodged Bush's glasses.

Quayle is our era's perfect example of a crafted-for-TV candidate. No one could figure out why Bush would choose him, but Quayle was strongly pushed by Roger Ailes, the advertising consultant who turned Bush in the election campaign from a wimp into a bully. Ailes had helped Quayle win his Senate seat and he thought him the perfect solution to the Bush "gender gap." All the polls showed that American women didn't like George Bush because of the whiney voice and waffling air. Telegenic Danny would be the solution. (When he hit the campaign trail, feminists waved signs reading, "He's Pretty, But Can He Type?")

There hadn't been such a strange vice-presidential pick since Richard Nixon plucked Spiro Agnew from the kick-back swamp of Maryland state politics. Quayle had a bland record in Congress, where his fondness for golf had earned him the nickname "the third Senator from Florida."

The brains in the family were obviously in the custody of wife Marilyn, whom he had met in law school and had wed within months. When a lobbyist/good-time girl finished the career of one Republican politician by revealing what she had been doing with him on a Florida golfing weekend that included Quayle among the party, there was printed speculation that Danny Boy might have indulged in the fun. "That's ridiculous," Marilyn told a Washington reporter. "Anyone who knows Dan Quayle knows that he'd rather play golf than have sex any day."

A militant hawk in his Senate voting record, he immediately got into trouble with the revelations that he had used the influence of his millionaire newspaper family to get into the Indiana National Guard so as to avoid duty in Vietnam. (What's the difference between Dan Quayle and Jane Fonda? Jane Fonda went to Vietnam.) Bush, in a contorted defense of his boy, pointed out that he "hadn't burned his draft card" or "gone to Canada."

Sent abroad to beef up his image, he stopped in Pago Pago in the Pacific on the way to Australia. Calling it "Pogo Pogo" in confusion with the comic-strip figure, he told his welcoming hosts, "You look like happy campers to me and happy campers you will always be." The mordant Washington joke was that if George Bush was assassinated the Secret Service had standing orders to shoot Dan Quayle. Regular health bulletins on the president became essential reading.

Considering the assassination, health, malfeasance and incompetence factors in past American presidencies, the choice of Quayle was a monumentally irresponsible one. Ronald Reagan was the first president in a quarter century, since Eisenhower, to complete two full terms. The choosing of the man who can be within a heartbeat (or a bullet) of the White House is no longer just the concern of Americans alone. It is of deep concern to the whole Western alliance. And J. Danforth Quayle was plucked from obscurity by an advertising consultant who knows that teeth and hair play well on color television.

Ronald Reagan was a terrible politician, but a remarkable showman, the finest of his era. Everything he promised didn't happen. Government under him did not grow smaller, but increased in size. The deficit, under his insane belief that he could both increase defense spending and cut taxes with no ill effects, zoomed through the ozone as anyone with knowledge of basic arithmetic could have surmised. He paid no attention to the Republican party (save for approving the patronage appointments put before him), but was a remarkable president, since he had spent thirty years mastering the gift of knowing how to speak on television–the key being that if you're going to be a phony, be sincere about it.

It is hard to imagine a worse politician than Richard Milhous Nixon–unless it would be Bill Vander Zalm. Nixon was destined for his evil end from the very start because of the simple fact that he never trusted the voters. Which means he didn't respect them. There was always a con job in operation, a devious way to do things. The way to get results was never the direct way; there always had to be a slippery way. The contempt for the public led to the largest scandal in American political history, but the seeds of it were there from the start of his political career in California as a young lawyer.

Some surprising people were good politicians and some surprising people were bad politicians. Huey Long was a good politician, because he knew his territory and his constituents ("There may be smarter politicians than me," he once said, "but they don't live in Louisiana.") Pierre Trudeau was a successful personality, but not a successful politician. He wiped out western Canada for Liberal candidates for years to come, didn't give a damn about the party's structure or longevity and left it hopelessly in debt, while also out of pique refusing to be gracious about John Turner's election as his successor.

The early (*i.e.*, instant historian) assessment on Trudeau when he left office was that academics in their books in the future would decide that, though he had ruined the Liberal party, he had kept Quebec in Canada–a fair enough trade-off. Today? Quebec, with the death of Meech Lake, seems as likely to go as it did before Gunslinger Trudeau bested René Lévesque in the Referendum. (Robert Bourassa, a prevaricator as always, was not only close with the Lévesque group of potential separatists drummed out of the Quebec Liberal party convention in 1967; the final planning meeting was held in his basement. He changed his mind the next morning. He can change his mind tomorrow.)

When Trudeau wanted to turn it on, as happened the night at the Paul Sauvé Arena in east-end Montreal when he raged at René Lévesque for mocking the "Elliott" in his name as proof that he really wasn't a French Canadian, he could become a magical, overwhelming presence. But in between those memorable moments, he was a man of shifting attention spans–unlike a full-time politician such as a Mackenzie King, who never stopped scheming.

Trudeau was against wage-and-price controls, and then suddenly for them. He allowed the Americans to buy up the country, then–convinced by underlings that nationalism was sexy–introduced the National Energy Program to tell the Yanks they were welcome only at a price. He flirted with the European link, which didn't work, and then, in the end, flirted with world disarmament. He was a flirter, as much with disparate policies at the end of his tenure as he was with teen-agers at the start of it. There was no consistent theme, since he was a dilettante who had to be persuaded to come into politics, and his personality was such as to obscure his desultory interest in the nuts and bolts of politics.

W.A.C. Bennett, a man of far inferior intellect to Trudeau, was a very successful politician. He did not care much about, or understand much, the large issues of Canada. He became a bit of a joke at federal-provincial conferences, his interest in the Quebec problem minimal, speeding out of town and back over the mountains once his screed had been delivered and before the conferences had wound up.

Bennett, like Huey Long, knew his territory and that was his strength. He had the courage of his convictions, as crazy as they seemed when, as a Tory, he walked out in disgust from the Conservative-Liberal Coalition that had ruled British Columbia so as to keep the NDP out of power–to sit as an Independent.

He must have sensed something was in the wind–mainly the public disgust with the venality of the Coalition partners who ruled from the Vancouver Club–and found it when a rag-tag band of candidates under the strange Social Credit banner formed the government with Bennett at its head in 1952–to stay there under him for twenty years.

Because he was from the hinterland, Kelowna in B.C.'s Interior, he knew that the province that was bigger than the British Isles needed highways to open it up and, when the highways ran into the sea, a ferry system that became water-bound highways. Because he was not from Vancouver, he played off against the instant hostility of the Vancouver and Victoria press, explaining that, as a kite needs a wind to rise, a radical new party needed the hostility of the Establishment press to raise its profile. W.A.C. Bennett, for his constituency, was a more successful politician than Pierre Trudeau was for his.

Most journalists make lousy politicians. René Lévesque was one of the few–the only one I've ever met–who was a good one. *Le Monde* of Paris observed, "Only in Canada would a man this intelligent not be prime minister." He was a tiny man, perhaps five-foot-four, his nervous energy exuding enormous charm. The best description I ever heard was that he was "a radical gynophile." Perhaps the reason for his intense passion for Quebec was that he was born in Campbellton, New Brunswick, it having the nearest hospital to New Carlisle, the English-dominated town on the underside of the Gaspé Peninsula where Lévesque grew up. As a child he had been tethered by a rope to the back porch railing because of his wild ways. In his formative years he lived closer to Halifax than he did to Montreal.

It is to be noted that in the spring of 1960, Jean Lesage, soon to become premier, asked four men to meet in a Montreal hotel room to decide who among them would join him in bringing Quebec out of the Duplessis era into the twentieth century. They were union leader Jean Marchand, journalist Gérard Pelletier, lawyer Pierre Trudeau and Lévesque. All four had to decide about changing their professions for politics. It is interesting that it was Lévesque, the most unlikely of the candidates, who made the move first, choosing that night to go with Lesage, and Quebec. The other three waited three more years before deciding to go for Canada.

As minister of natural resources intent on nationalizing Quebec's hydro power, he revived the "maîtres chez nous" slogan of Errol Bouchette, a writer and civil servant who promoted the cause of economic autonomy for Quebec at the turn of the century. Bouchette was the first Québécois to suggest that the province's hydro-electric resources should be nationalized. Trudeau, a professor at the University of Montreal, said, "And think how much faster this revolution–for it is a revolution–would have gone if there were more people like Lévesque in power, if all the forces of democracy were represented in the government now."

Lévesque, much later, was to write: "As for Pierre Elliott Trudeau ... how can one define the undefinable? He was extremely cultivated, certainly, but almost exclusively only in matters of jurisprudence and politics. I had the impression that, except for show, the additional baggage he had accumulated from studies in the humanities left him supremely indifferent, like seed fallen on rock. Even in conversation his thought constantly took on a dialectical twist, and to have the last word he would stop at neither sarcasm nor the most specious argument."

One suspects the reason why Lévesque felt so confident in taking on Trudeau was that he–unlike the wealthy hitch-hiking world traveller–had really experienced the world. He had a very interesting war, going through the Blitz in London as an American war correspondent, crossing the Rhine with Patton, arriving in Milan just after Mussolini had been strung up by the heels, being in the first group into the Dachau death camp, interviewing Hermann Goering. He went to Moscow to cover Khrushchev's meeting with Lester Pearson and was the preeminent CBC commentator covering the Korean War. Claude Ryan, when he was editor of Le Devoir, once told me that he thought Lévesque (the man who wanted to break up the country) actually knew and understood Canada better than Trudeau (who was trying to hold it together).

It is hard to put a fix on Brian Mulroney as a politician, as yet, since it will take history, or at least more perspective, to render that judgment. However, it is known, even this early on, that he is not really a "politician," he is a "striver after success." He wants to achieve something in life, and his natural gifts as a consummately charming person in private gatherings (absolutely none of which comes across in public) and his professional training as a labor negotiator led him into politics, where the two talents meet.

Mulroney has no philosophy of politics; he has only a philosophy of life. That is: be loyal to those who are loyal to you, punish your enemies, reward your friends, put up a good front and always speak in sonorous tones of deep sincerity, even when you don't mean it. No one can take away from him the feat of two successive Conservative majority governments; no one can ever make the public like him personally. The major puzzlement is why he does not have the self-confidence to reveal to the public that in private life he has a tremendous sense of humor and laughs a lot. The answer, it seems, is that all his preparatory years before actually running for office were spent in backroom Quebec politics where the formal front was a stiff and pompous act to be given to the voters. He should unlax.

Intellectual brilliance has nothing to do with success in politics. Adlai Stevenson, the brainiest man never elected president, was once greeted at a rally by an effusive fan who gushed,

"Governor Stevenson, that was the greatest speech I've ever heard. You will get the vote of every thinking American." Stevenson replied, "That won't do any good, I'm afraid. I need a majority."

The patrician Stevenson, a disaster as a campaigner in 1952, even by the 1956 campaign still did not understand television or its impact. Assigned a bright young television producer by the Democrats in hopes he could present a better image on the tube, Stevenson during a Florida swing objected one night to doing a long-scheduled program at the local TV station and complained that he could be speaking to a downtown civic club. The producer asked how many people might attend. "One hundred and fifty," replied the Democratic candidate for president–still never seeing that he could cover the whole state on TV.

On July 10, 1920, Arthur Meighen became prime minister of Canada. He was just forty-six, which made him then the youngest of Canadian prime ministers and, in Bruce Hutchison's words, "perhaps the most brilliant in mind." He had graduated from the University of Toronto in 1896 with first-class honors in mathematics (an indication of his mind's real intentions) and had encountered a plump and flabby student named William Lyon Mackenzie King. A lean and poor farm boy, Meighen neither liked nor respected King from then on throughout their remarkable political rivalry. King disliked Meighen equally but had the smarts to respect him as a politician.

Laurier, on hearing Meighen's first speech in the House of Commons in 1908, predicted he would some day be prime minister. "While language," Meighen once said, "is the vehicle of thought, it is a great deal more. It is part of the texture. It is inseparable from thought itself." He had a remarkable mind. At the age of sixty-two he gave a speech to the Canadian Club in Toronto, the subject being "The Greatest Englishman of History–Shakespeare." The speech contained 150 lines of quotations from twelve different plays. Meighen delivered it without a note and without an error.

But the mind did not translate into practicality. His sarcasm and the deadly venom of his oratory played right into the hands of King, much the lesser intellect. "It is too good to be true," King wrote in his diary on learning that Meighen was prime minister. Meighen disappeared into history as a prime minister on two brief occasions.

Among the more unsuccessful politicians, those who might have been better off delving into nuclear physics, is the brainy Jack Davis, Rhodes Scholar out of downtown Kamloops, who surfaced as a Liberal MP from British Columbia in the Pearson years, a humorless chap quite enamored of his considerable intellectual gifts. Having served his early apprenticeship in the Grit back-benches, and well aware of the speculation-since he could read-in the press that Lester Pearson was remaking his cabinet, Davis asked for an appointment with the prime minister.

That granted, he marched into the office of the always diffident but never unobservant Pearson, thumped on his desk and made the passionate case that he had to be in the new cabinet, deserved it as the brainiest guy from non-brainy British Columbia and, by gum, poop would hit the fan if he didn't get it. Pearson listened politely, thanked Davis for his deposition and, as the Rhodes Scholar left the room, returned to the cabinet list before him which had Davis already on it-and pencilled out the name. It was years before Davis finally made it into cabinet.

Even more years later, having retreated to the Social Credit government in Victoria, he revealed his high-I.Q. obtuseness once again when an airlines clerk outraged by a government rollback of a pay raise, detected his common practice of turning in his cabinet minister's first-class seats for economy fare and pocketing the difference. When Premier Bill Bennett arranged for Davis to stand up in the Victoria Legislature and confess his error, Davis instead sat silent in his seat and Bennett, in a rage, immediately announced his resignation from cabinet and never forgave him.

John Crosbie is another entry in the argument that really intelligent people shouldn't go into politics. They only get into trouble. Educated at the best private schools, he was the gold medallist when he graduated from Queen's University. He was the gold medallist when he graduated from Dalhousie Law School and, being picked the most outstanding law graduate anywhere in Canada, went off to the London School of Economics, that famed home of radicals which did not, however, change either Crosbie or John Kennedy into a socialist.

When he was a city councillor and then deputy mayor in St. John's, his brilliance showed but his essential shyness made him a dreadful speaker, a boring reader of texts who put his audience to sleep quicker than Sominex. When he moved into the Newfoundland House of Assembly, quickly becoming a cabinet minister, it was clear he needed an injection of something if he was to succeed in his clear ambition to unseat his Liberal leader, Joey Smallwood.

John Crosbie, the double gold medallist, read the ads and went to the Dale Carnegie courses that teach confidence and competence in public speaking. And so emerged the John Crosbie we know and love, the man the after-dinner head tables adore, the slanging Newfie who has them rolling in the aisles from Dildo to Come-by-Chance.

The platform manner has changed, but the shyness remains intact. Reporters on first interviewing him in private, or editorial boards encountering him, are always amazed that he doesn't like eye contact, an introvert who gazes at the ceiling while rolling out his droll answers. A crowd to control and amuse from a rostrum is one thing; real live people in front of him still give Crosbie unease.

Shyness from the truth is not a problem for him–only for his political future. Once Crosbie learned to speak, and to his great surprise became a platform favorite, his intelligence and his new gift for the gab combined with a natural arrogance to produce a rather dangerous package. The Crosbie family, one of a handful who controlled The Rock's economy, passed on a certain sense of superiority and a disinclination to suffer fools. When John, blocked on his way to the top by the stubborn Joey, in a fury crossed the floor and became a Conservative, Smallwood remarked that his young challenger was "neither a Liberal nor a Conservative–all he is is a Crosbie, always was and always will be."

When the graduate of the Carnegie charm school ventured into Quebec in the final stages of the 1983 Conservative leadership race, the Québécois press were lying in wait for him, ready to badger him for his non-existent French. After several days and too many press conferences of being asked the same questions and having to have the questions translated to him, the Crosbie temper and intellectual arrogance finally burst forth with his classic response that he didn't speak Chinese or German either–thus reducing in Quebec eyes the stature of Canada's other official language to the level of a far-off tongue. Bingo. There went the leadership candidate. Most politicians are one quote away from oblivion and Crosbie proved it.

When, in the 1984 election campaign, Crosbie in response to a reporter said that his party wasn't going to reveal its real platform–"elect us and then you'll find out"–he was only expressing out loud what all political parties intend to do but won't admit. The problem is "out loud." Reporters love covering Crosbie, because they never know when (and always hope that) the candid and politically careless man will let loose a zinger. As he once admitted, his lip had been so tightly zipped by party strategists that he felt he had "been weaned on a pickle."

His way to the top stymied, where his brains should have led him, the final insult came when Mulroney lost in the 1988 election Justice Minister Ray Hnatyshyn to the wisdom of the Saskatoon voters and had to find an acting justice minister for a few months over the Christmas break before a cabinet shuffle could produce a new one. Instead of letting the underemployed Crosbie, who after all had been justice minister, handle it, the prime minister gave the temporary chore to Joe Clark, who had flunked out of two law schools. (Mulroney's final choice for justice, Doug Lewis, reeks insincerity like garlic, speaks like a Dead End Kid and is the thinnest reed in the cabinet.)

Gold medallist John Carnell Crosbie is akin to the Robert Stanfield that Dalton Camp encountered when he was first brought in to see if he could help turn the taciturn Standstill into a politician in Nova Scotia. After meeting him for the first time, Camp told a friend, "He'll be very hard to get elected premier, but once in it will be even harder to get him out." It proved impossible to get Crosbie elected prime minister, but once in, it would have been very hard to get him out. He would have been a good one.

Good or bad, most politicians enjoy publicity–it's one of the things they share with members of the press, one of the things that fuels the relationship, however combative. Without that zest for attention, the relationship–and often the politician's career–withers and dies.

Bob Skelly, a quiet, polite schoolteacher, succeeded the flamboyant Dave Barrett as leader of the British Columbia NDP. He was a surprise choice to most everyone at the leadership convention, walking up the middle to emerge on the last ballot (as Joe Clark had done). He was paid little attention by the media, the spotlight being on the daily antics of the colorful Bill Vander Zalm, until an election was called and Skelly stood before the television cameras for a formal press conference to announce the NDP platform.

Whether the mass press turnout unnerved him, or the occasion, Skelly sweated profusely, stammered, and completely lost it. In desperation, he asked the mob before him to shut off their cameras and tape-recorders so he could start over. What he could not grasp was that he was on live TV. The cameras ground on. He was actually hyperventilating as, his wife later confessed, he had done before. He was *nervous* before cameras. All of British Columbia watched a man committing public suicide on the first day of the election campaign–a politician who had spent his life planning to be leader but revealing at the top that he didn't like public occasions. Vander Zalm of course thrashed him and Skelly quickly resigned.

For Skelly's polar opposite, take John Diefenbaker. With Dief, that master of spurious outrage, there was always the imperious command to appear in his quarters after some column that detailed his sad performance in the Commons in his final years, his gleeful upstaging of Stanfield or Clark–or savage put-down in some sly aside. There would be the doleful recriminations-how could you *do* such a thing?-which always had to be outwaited before, eventually, there would be a segue into anecdotes and slightly salacious stories about the very men he had just denied ever denigrating.

Pierre Trudeau enjoyed the bantering with the press in the early days, because he did not regard them as important and had a general contempt for them-going back to youthful days when he saw the Duplessis government supply the press regulars with an envelope of cash at Christmas and other propitious moments. On leaving press conferences, he used to step on my foot or deliver a jab to the stomach with his elbow as he inched his way through a pack of reporters. On his final day in office, when he resurrected the long-dusty white Mercedes convertible for a dramatic sweep up the driveway at Rideau Hall to deliver his resignation, with scribes and photographers lining the entrance, he attempted to run over my foot as he pulled up. That's one form of a relationship with a prime minister-rather like, in its final stages, the White House relationship between ABC's shouting Sam Donaldson and Ronald Reagan, who regarded him as a recalcitrant child. At least, he was a foil and slightly more interesting than the rest of the pack.

With Robert Stanfield, there was always an air of polite puzzlement-the same attitude he applied to his entire stay in Ottawa as Conservative leader, somewhat like Dorothy saying to Toto that she didn't think they were in Kansas anymore-but he could never quite figure out where, or why. Such dry wit in private, over a drink, such painful uneasiness before more than six people in public.

Joe Clark seemed genuinely puzzled, as a product of High River, Alberta, how a columnist born in Hearne, Saskatchewan, could be so hostile to a fellow western Canadian. It wasn't, in fact, hostility at all but mere astonishment at the incompetence and stubborn naiveté-as a hiccup in history-of his briefly lived government. One day on an airplane he expressed his regret that I was wasting my time in this daily drudgery of journalism when what I should really be doing was writing something worthwhile in literature, such as the true story of western Canada and its travails and history and frustrations. It occurred to me, though I did not bother telling him so, that if I were indeed doing that worthy task I would not be covering day in and day out the gathering incompetence of his crew. I smiled and went back to my seat in steerage class.

One does not have to chew over again the fact that Clark might very well have succeeded as prime minister if there had not been this unfortunate thing called television. Speaking in the House (for he was a good, aggressive performer in the Commons), being reported in *Hansard*, going home to his riding to tend his flock. But television intruded and Clark, never comfortable with his own body, seemed such an awkward, ungraceful figure – after the graceful, stylish Trudeau – that televiewers became obsessed with the way he walked and his non-existent chin rather than with what he said or did. He was a TV victim (as Mackenzie King undoubtedly would have been).

John Turner, who made Joe Clark look like a genius with *his* tiny tenure in office, is another kettle of puzzling fish. For all their differences (Turner thinks Mulroney is a cad with no background; Mulroney thinks Turner is a stuffed teen-age version of Anthony Eden) both Turner and Mulroney very much want to be liked. Trudeau didn't give a damn, Dief wanted to be *adored*, Clark, like Rodney Dangerfield, just wanted some respect (still does) and Stanfield couldn't really be bothered because he could never figure out how he got talked into this business in the first place.

Turner learned his *modus operandi* with the press from old Wacky Bennett in Victoria, with whom he enjoyed a good feeling. It was, in essence, never answer back – you can never win, the press will always have the last word. It is a distillation of Disraeli's life creed, which served him rather well: "Never explain, never complain."

While unadventurous, this approach involves relatively few risks. It takes a crafty politician to succeed in the dangerous game of playing with the press. Gary Hart's dare to reporters to follow him because they would find it "very dull" first appeared in *The New York Times* Sunday magazine the very weekend he was caught in his Washington townhouse with Donna Rice. Friends of the complex man feel he unconsciously wanted to be caught all along (as his brazen behavior would indicate) so that he could go through the rest of his life reasoning that he "could" have been president if it hadn't been for. . . .

John Kennedy, while of another era, for all his charm and courage, loved a similar type of danger, as his phenomenal philandering while in the White House (taught to him by his father, Joe Kennedy, and continued on by brother Teddy) seems to have demonstrated. With the arrogance and tremendous self-confidence of a Kennedy born to wealth, he almost gave the impression, in retrospect, of flaunting this in the faces of the reporters on his beat that he so assiduously sought out and courted and became friends with.

Tom Wicker of The New York Times tells the story of the Sunday evening in 1963 when the White House press plane–chartered by the White House transportation office, paid for by the newspapers and television stations of the reporters aboard–was returning to Washington from a routine presidential weekend at Newport. To everyone's surprise, the plane landed in New York–following President Kennedy in Air Force One. The unhappy press corps, knowing the Sunday night wrath at home among their waiting families, were taken by bus into Manhattan where for hours they had to hang around the lobby of the Carlyle Hotel.

Kennedy maintained a suite there and, White House aides told the media mob, the president was using it that evening for an informal meeting with Adlai Stevenson, the U.S ambassador to the United Nations.

No meeting with Stevenson had been scheduled or announced, in the usually precise White House manner, before Air Force One and its trailing press plane had taken off from Newport. No one saw Stevenson arrive or leave the Carlyle. There was no later announcement from Kennedy's press secretaries about the discussions or the news value thereof. There was no discernible international or United Nations situation that would have moved Kennedy to interrupt a Sunday night flight to

Washington to meet with a man with little influence in his administration-a man, further, whom he did not particularly like.

It was past midnight when the weary reporters finally were herded back into a bus for the airport. The president of the United States, as it turned out, had decided on a New York detour because he felt the need of a little nooky.

Kennedy's penchant for danger, as with Hart, led to the most notorious incident with Judith Campbell Exner, the moll introduced to him by Frank Sinatra. A 1975 Senate committee's investigation of the CIA disclosed that the woman, while having an affair with Kennedy, including visits to the White House, was also involved with two Mafia leaders through whom the CIA had sought to arrange the assassination of Fidel Castro. J. Edgar Hoover put a stop to that liaison.

Pierre Trudeau, with his rather macabre sense of humor and liking for the dramatic, had a similar delicious delight in mocking the press that he never respected and found so tawdry. The whole elaborate game in meticulously planning the secret arrangements for his wedding to the beautiful twenty-two-year-old Margaret Sinclair-her cover name to the priest as to whom she was to marry, the elaborate secrecy involved that had to stretch from the wedding dress to the vow of her whisky-loving father to foreswear drink lest he let out the news-was a telling proof that the snooping press wasn't very good at snooping out the best scoop of his career so far.

Similarly (and he has got away with this one still) there was the celebrated "walk in the snow" on February 29, 1984, when Trudeau made his supposedly sudden decision to retire for good. It was a great story, the image of a man tortured by indecision wandering through the lovely streets of Rockcliffe as the flakes fluttered down on Leap Year Day. But party insiders knew he had just received a report from the Martin Goldfarb polling firm informing him there was no way he could win another election. He chose the irresistible February 29 date, a great Trudeau touch, and God supplied the snowflakes-all the magic of headlines. The Conservative party's private pollsters had told them the same thing, and Brian Mulroney, on Labour Day, proved the correctness of the Trudeau "whim."

If Trudeau's mischief was calculated, the suspicion is that Bill Vander Zalm is blissfully unaware of how outrageous he appears. When someone once said that Vander Zalm was all style and no substance, the premier of British Columbia replied, "Style *is* substance." It's hard to argue with a man who uses that type of logic.

The remarkable thing about The Zalm is the child-like certainty of his beliefs. They babble incessantly from his lips, guileless thoughts on all the matters of the realm.

On having been premier for a few days: "I am amazed at the ease at which it's coming to me–I'm not bragging, but it's coming naturally."

On the special qualities of successful leaders: "I'd be a great employer. My employees would love me. I could run a big company. I don't think I'd ever have a strike, because I would want to work and know all the employees. I think loyalty is a two-way street."

On forestry management: "Let's cut down the trees and create jobs."

On the causes of economic recession: "Economic recessions are a heaven-sent blessing for B.C. I think God sent it. It was necessary and it had to happen when it did."

On the special qualities of Oriental peoples: "I have to tell you I fell in love with our Chinese community–I think they're just the most wonderful people–and, as I fell in love with the Chinese, I began to realize that perhaps, though they looked alike, there was another wonderful group–the Koreans and the Vietnamese, and they were super, as well as the Filipinos. Just [a] fantastic lot of people."

On literacy (after being appointed education minister in the Bill Bennett government): "I think a person has to be able to write good, read, spell, arithmetic–those basics I think are very necessary for no matter what you do in life today."

It was Marjorie Nichols, the Ottawa columnist, who said that she was tired of people making fun of Bill Vander Zalm. Willie

Wooden Shoes, she explained, plays a very important role in nation-building. Informed sources had told her that at federal-provincial conferences on Meech Lake he explains the difficult parts to Don Getty.

The Zalm is hard to pin down because he darts and shifts philosophically like a water bug. A municipal politician who knows him well from Vander Zalm's early days as mayor of a Vancouver suburb, says, "I'd say his prejudices are sincere – at least that day. He's a political animal. He's not in it to improve humanity. He switched from the Liberals to the Socreds without hesitation when it suited him. If socialism became popular, he'd be a socialist tomorrow."

Born in Holland, son of a bulb salesman who stayed in Canada during the war and built up a prosperous nursery business, Vander Zalm left school after grade twelve. (Fellow students remember him as a "sweet talker" who was always "putting on the dog.") There has been a consistent pattern to his rise. In *Vander Zalm: From Immigrant to Premier*, author Alan Twigg says, "Rules have been bent and laws have been broken."

Even while he was a cabinet minister in the Social Credit government, he built an addition onto one of his gardening stores without a building permit. Warned by authorities that he was violating a municipal bylaw, he refused to comply. He received the minimum penalty. When his two brothers violated agricultural land-zoning laws, Vander Zalm – then municipal affairs minister – intervened on their behalf.

Three Vander Zalm brothers had to plead guilty after being charged with illegally dumping pollutants. When Bill was mayor of Surrey, his own council once voted to investigate him on conflict-of-interest charges. President of a widely active consortium of relatives, Vander Zalm somehow like Houdini escaped from various family municipal messes – identified as the Manning Kless Mess, the Missing Newton Dirty Sewer Link and the Hazelmere Smear. Two days before the then NDP government was to bring in a deadline on public disclosure legislation designed to protect the public from political conflicts of interest, the Ricardo Montalban of B.C. politics quit the Liberals and joined Social Credit.

Earlier in his career (running for Parliament in 1968 in hopes of cashing in on Trudeaumania, running for leadership of the B.C. Liberal party among other things) he lost three times in seven years. He lost again when he tried to become mayor of Vancouver even though he didn't live in the city. He simply came back smiling. He's a hard man to insult. He essentially doesn't have any beliefs. As such, he's insensitive. You can't insult a man who doesn't believe in much.

Wife Lillian, who knits her trademark headbands, dropped out of grade seven. Asked by a reporter the last book she had read, she said it had taken her three years to finish it but couldn't remember either the title or the author. Vander Zalm, whose smile is always getting in the way of his teeth, made a speech to the British Columbia wing of the U.S.-based Campus Crusade for Christ, had it videotaped and sent the tape to 1,300 churches in the provinces. In the speech, he said, "Christ didn't have an easy way. He came into the world poor. He was taunted and ridiculed. He never had a University of British Columbia education. He would have been low in the polls."

Asked by reporters if he intended voters to make a comparison between his situation and Christ's, Vander Zalm replied, "No, obviously not." Style *is* substance.

9

Gerda, Gary Hart and the MP in the Towel

When a reporter enters the room, your privacy
ends and his begins. – *Warren Beatty*

The term 'idle gossip' means exactly what it
says. If you work at gossip, it regrettably turns
into an ungentlemanly pastime called
investigative reporting. – *Diana McLellan*

We've all heard the tale of reporters, at the back of the 1968
campaign jet, watching the wine steward bring a bottle of fine
burgundy for the new prime minister's approval as Trudeau,
without glancing up from his briefing papers, merely raised his
palm to check the temperature of the proffered sample. We
know all about the playful reporters, close to the end of another
election campaign on yet another long flight, tossing up to the
front of the plane obscure quotations to see if they could blank
the great man who, in an equally playful mood for once, not only
zapped them every time but eventually threw quotations back in
Latin and Greek.

He knew what he was doing; he was bullying them in an area
where a Clark or a Diefenbaker or a Pearson or a Stanfield never
could. And so, intimidated, they backed off in other areas that
had nothing to do with governing. His private life. No tracking of
the ladies zipped up in the white Mercedes convertible to
Harrington Lake. No relaying to the public when his wife would
show up at the National Press Club bar and indulge in a few
substances with the younger reporters of her generation. The
Ottawa press today, in retrospect, is ashamed that it did not print

from the beginning the obvious signals of distress in the Trudeau marriage–government agents arriving in the Press Club late in the evening in attempts to persuade the exuberant lady to return home.

By the time of the famous weekend flight to Toronto with the Rolling Stones, it was the American and international papers that were carrying the ball. Trudeau's intellectual bullying had worked its magic on his home press right up until the end.

(Which is why, in its chagrin, it leaped with over-eager alacrity on every spurious rumor about Maureen McTeer and Joe Clark and their alleged marriage problems, Joe supposedly living in this hotel and then that.)

We have a playback here, on the memory bank, to 1937 in Britain when the royal set and all of Fleet Street knew of the approaching crisis of the weak King Edward VIII and "the woman I love," the much-divorced Wallis Simpson who was regarded as an experienced trollop by those in the know in press-tycoon circles.

Part of the pact, between the birds of a feather, is that certain things are not talked about. There is an understood agreement among Members of Parliament that personal peccadilloes are never mentioned, however passionate and heated becomes the debate across the floor. The heavy drinkers are well known, the word on the skirt-chasers travels swiftly, Parliament Hill being an incestuous and closed society.

But it's not to be mentioned. Which is why the fury and the turmoil when the beleaguered Lucien Cardin, Lester Pearson's justice minister, blurted out in the Commons the news of a mysterious "Monsignor" file. Those were the bitter, mud-slinging Diefenbaker-Pearson days of 1965 and Cardin, a weak minister who was uncomfortable in English, was under attack for his handling of the case of George Spencer, a pitiful and aging British Columbia post office worker who had gathered some information for a Soviet agent subsequently expelled from his country's embassy in Ottawa.

The startled press soon discovered that "Monsignor" was the fleshy German doxy Gerda Munsinger, who had been the mistress of the Diefenbaker associate national defence minister, the one-legged Pierre Sévigny when the Tories were in power. (The story is that the RCMP, tracking Munsinger who had East German connections, discovered the identity of her lover when they wired her room. Replaying and replaying their tapes, they heard this strange "thump" that followed the foreplay and preceded the horizontal delight. After weeks of puzzlement, they finally figured it out. It was a wooden leg falling to the carpet, and the trail led to Sévigny.) When the intrepid Larry Zolf, representing "This Hour Has Seven Days," knocked on the door of Sévigny's Montreal home with a television camera recording the encounter, Sévigny whacked him over the head with his cane. (Zolf refers to it as his "Citizen Cane" period.)

What so upset the MPs–and the Ottawa rules of conduct–was that the flustered Cardin had violated the unwritten rules that you didn't talk about the other chap's drinking or his women. Otherwise, where would it all end? Just as the American press did not talk about sex until Teddy Kennedy and Gary Hart and were mum about alcohol until John Tower.

It wasn't quite the same in the post-Christmas doldrums of 1982, with the celebrated case of the MP in the towel. For weeks it put the press in a tizzy and enlivened all the gatherings of bureaucrats, where previously the most lively conversation was the heated debate over indexed pensions, the subject that in Ottawa replaces AIDS as table talk. The identification of the MP in the towel was the only thing that mattered in Ottawa. The MP had appeared in his towel (government issue) in the corridors of our hallowed Parliament, where all the major decisions are decided. He had made the wrong decision.

The situation was that said MP, perhaps bored by the Christmas solstice, was engaged in a favorite indoor sport with a lady friend of his choice when a House of Commons employee stumbled into the MP's office and was chagrined to discover the distinguished tribune of the people *in flagrante delicto*. Being discreet as well as shocked, she immediately fled down the corridor.

Our less-than-dignified MP fled after her, clad only in the government-issue towel, to plead with her not to snitch.

His lady friend, appropriately enraged at his decision to interrupt the heated action in hopes of protecting his reputation, slammed the door of the office and locked it. Understandably. Our feckless MP was left panicked in the marbled hallway and was forced to slink – a wiser man and, one trusts, a better parliamentarian – through the hallowed corridors to find a security guard to supply him with a key and, one might add, restore his suddenly missing aplomb.

Needless to say, no one ever revealed to the public the identity of this fan of funch.

The private pact between the press and the politicians goes back a long way. Sir John A. Macdonald was, as we all know now, a drunk. There was the celebrated occasion, during a long speech in the House of Commons, when he signalled to a page for another glass of what would appear to the eye to be water. On receiving it, in mid-sentence, he paused to take a sip, turned to the lad, shook his head, and said, *sotto voce*, "Too weak."

The eye-witness stories on the father of our country, the history books at a safe distance now tell us, are graphic. Once, being driven some miles by buggy to an open-air election rally, Sir John A. fortified himself too enthusiastically on the journey. It was a hot day, and the jiggling buggy was no help. Arriving at his destination, he was mounting the steps to the rough stage when he suddenly chucked all his cookies in full view of the faithful Conservative audience. Wiping the vomit from his lips with his sleeve, he opened with, "And that, ladies and gentlemen, is what I think of my honorable opponent's platform." The scribes of the day knew of his habits; they did not write about them.

Only recently, thanks to the diligent academics and historians, do we have accounts of Mackenzie King, the supposed lonely bachelor, taking in young prostitutes from the streets of Ottawa so as to "rehabilitate" them. It wasn't until Peter Stursberg's two-volume oral history on John Diefenbaker, published in

1976, that there was provided clear evidence that the supposed and sanctimonious teetotaller liked a glass or two of whisky with trusted reporter friends in closed circumstances.

Those were different times, true, but that does not detract from the fact that the press long protected politicians from the consequences of their excesses–whether to comply with "community standards," from fear of publishers or whatever. As well as never telling the American public that Franklin Roosevelt was a cripple through polio, the White House press discreetly steered away from his long-standing affair with his social secretary and the fact that the idyllic marriage between the charming patrician and his strong-minded wife, Eleanor, who had her own agenda and seems to have had male friends of her own, was a bit of a farce.

Every time a president comes up with the problem of picking a vice-president, every serious magazine article quotes an FDR veep, John Nance Garner, with his celebrated confession that the position wasn't worth "a pitcher of warm spit." Tis true, but he didn't say that. He said it wasn't worth a pitcher of warm piss. Which is not only more colorful, but also more accurate. The White House press cleaned it up for him (i.e., made it inaccurate). Lyndon Johnson had the most foul mouth in Washington, as Brian Mulroney did when he first came to Ottawa. In his much-quoted description of Gerald Ford, LBJ did not say that the dull Michigan politician, long before he inherited the presidency from the fleeing Richard Nixon, "was so dumb that he couldn't walk and chew gum at the same time." He said Ford couldn't "fart and chew gum at the same time." Better description. More accurate.

All this bowdlerizing would have depressed Mark Twain, another scribbler of note, who was a great fan of profanity and grieved over the fact that society had deemed it not acceptable between the printed pages. One morning, while shaving, he cut himself and let loose a lengthy string of the inventive phrases he was so proud of. His wife, who deplored this habit, happened to be passing the bathroom and, in an attempt to shame him, repeated all the naughty words. "You have the words, my dear," said Twain, lowering his razor, "but you don't have the tune."

Robert Caro, a Texan who is a respected journalist and author, set out to do an authoritative biography of Johnson, a man he had admired from a distance. He expected to spend several years on the project. The more he searched, the more he researched, the more he delved into Johnson's past, from college days in Texas on and up to becoming the most powerful man in Congress before accidentally becoming president on John Kennedy's assassination, the more the trail led him to more unpleasant revelations. Johnson was, he discovered to his astonishment, a most nasty and devious man. Because of his unexpected findings, the biography that was going to be admiring turned instead into an exposé.

Johnson, besides being an exceedingly vulgar man, was a storied womanizer – if not with the same ability for frequency as Jack Kennedy at least with the same wandering eye. Caro tells of the leggy blonde secretary who was summoned to the LBJ ranch in Texas for urgent stenographic duties. After an exhausting day of taking non-stop dictation she fell into bed dead tired, only to awake with a start in the middle of the night to the realization that a man was in her room and a dark shadow was approaching her bed. She recognized the drawl immediately: "Move over, honey. This is yore president."

No one dared to delve into those things in those days, but Watergate and Chappaquiddick changed all that. Once it was revealed that the occupant of the highest office in the land was actually a crook and a cheat and a liar to boot, every elected official in the land was suddenly under suspicion, every recruit in a journalism school automatically having a Pulitzer Prize in his sights.

Righteous in its new post-Watergate ethical standards, the press that had discreetly ignored the well-known facts of Jack Kennedy's philandering landed on Gary Hart with the thump he asked for. Why so hard? Answer: it was as much the guilt of the media in its past blind-eye approach as it was Hart daring the press to follow him.

Question: But where is the limit? Where does one draw the

line? How much business does the press have in the bedrooms of the state?

Answer: When it impinges on the business of the state. Gary Hart, in the spring of 1987, after his remarkable run in 1984, seemed quite clearly the man most likely to win the Democratic nomination for the presidency in 1988 and, considering the mood of the nation at that time, a good bet to be the next resident of the White House after Ronald Reagan.

He was, in fact, a hypocrite and a skirt-chaser–something known to Washington insiders and the press, but not yet revealed to the public because there wasn't a peg to hang it on. He was driven from the presidential race not because of the monumentally stupid Donna Rice caper but because of being faced with worse things to come.

A former senator, tired of persistent Washington rumors that his wife was having an affair with the randy Hart, hired a private detective to tail the Colorado senator for evidence that could be used in their pending divorce case. The private eye did indeed find evidence that Hart was entering a certain lady's residence late at night and leaving before dawn. But it was not the estranged mate of the aggrieved veteran of the Senate. It was yet another paramour, who had been told by Hart that once elected president he would divorce his wife and move her into the White House.

The delighted former senator, supposedly no longer a cuckold, rushed to *The Washington Post* with the evidence that the busy Hart was involved with another woman. Only after the Donna Rice debacle, with Hart's idealistic young supporters across the country reeling, did a *Post* reporter phone Hart's campaign manager and ask for comment on the evidence the paper had about Madame X. Confronted with the truth, Hart surrendered, collected his long-suffering wife and flew home to Denver and oblivion.

Question: Was the press justified in driving this man from public life?

Answer: Not from public life, but from serious consideration for the presidency. Hart had major personality problems: the serene belief that he could live a lie in his private life while seeking the most important job in the world. No resident of the White House has ever been perfect, but a chap who flirts so openly with disaster while seriously pursuing the goal has to be a risky proposition.

Scandals can clean house but supposed scandals can kill innocent politicians who-though misguided or inept-are not crooked or deceitful. The fall-out of how Ottawa and the Ottawa Tories and the Ottawa press treated certain good men from Quebec a quarter century ago is still being felt in that province.

Lester Pearson as prime minister in 1963 was desperate to discover a lieutenant from Quebec who could solidify the Liberals' traditional base there and apprentice as an eventual successor at 24 Sussex Drive. He chose Guy Favreau, a terribly earnest and somewhat corpulent man, as his Quebec hope. Pearson immediately loaded him down with an impossible burden of three jobs: federal Liberal leader in Quebec, House leader in the Commons and also justice minister.

The red-neck Diefenbaker cowboys just driven from power, filled with bile and bitterness, zeroed in on the over-worked Favreau over a series of minor scandals, his case not helped because of the imprecision of his English in debates. By October 1964, Favreau had to resign as House leader.

As the Tories and the press yapped at his heels, sensing his failing confidence, he resigned in June 1965 as justice minister. That December, two other Quebec ministers, Maurice Lamontagne-a very good man-and René Tremblay, had to resign from cabinet over careless acceptance of some furniture, not a big deal but horrendous in the days of Diefenbaker revenge.

By January of 1967, Guy Favreau, broken in spirit and broken in heart, had resigned as the federal party leader in Quebec. In April he resigned from the cabinet. In June he was dead. There are still those in Quebec who feel Pearson failed to back up Favreau when he could have in order to save his own reputation. There is some feeling, as with this scribe, that the tragedy of valiant soldiers Favreau, Lamontagne and Tremblay sowed the seeds for separatism and René Lévesque, proof in that province-that sending good Quebecers to Ottawa would never work. It took more than twenty years, and Brian Mulroney, to convince Quebec voters to forget what the Conservative knife artists in the Commons abattoir had done to the three.

Sometimes politicians and the press, insiders both, affect the political process by exchanging and encouraging rumors that are never passed on directly to the public. A prime example was all the beer-parlor-caliber stories whispered about Pierre Trudeau's alleged sexual preferences, put about by too many John Turner intimates after super-macho John was defeated by Trudeau in the 1968 leadership race. It is the basis for the Trudeau hatred for Turner that lasts to this day.

Printed on the memory is the televised tableau from the Ottawa ice rink the day that Turner was elected leader in 1984. Party president Iona Campagnolo at the microphone paid tribute to the beloved retiring leader Trudeau, a signal for him to come forward and offer his congratulations and best wishes to his successor. Trudeau, standing at the far end of the stage from Turner, took one step forward, gave a diffident wave of the hand in the general direction of the man he has never forgiven and stepped back-a chilling insult apparent to a national television audience. Revenge, as the Italians say, is better eaten cold.

When there was all the excitement, in early 1968, to recruit bachelor Trudeau as the successor to Lester Pearson, it was left to Walter Gordon, the courtly and wealthy Pearson close friend, to bell the cat. Gordon, while all the others whispered, went to Trudeau for a private meeting and told him quite frankly, in case he didn't know, that there were rumors among insiders-especially in western Canada-that he was a homosexual.

Trudeau's eyes blazed in cold anger and he told Gordon that whoever said that about him should leave him alone in a room with his wife for several hours and see what happened.

Jack Kemp, the robust and happily married former quarter-back of the Buffalo Bills, was delayed for months from formally declaring his bid for the Republican presidential nomination in 1988 because of a persistent press rumor of a homosexual alliance. It turned out that as a young man he had once shared a ski cabin with an acquaintance, who, years later, was suspected of being gay. No one ever printed any accusations about Kemp, only vague hints pertaining to "an upcoming scandal" involving a presidential candidate–this coming after the Gary Hart press furor that destroyed him.

There is, in the relationship between press and politicians, a natural reflection of the society they inhabit. In the days of FDR and Harry Truman and John Diefenbaker and Lester Pearson, in Churchill's time, it was a formal relationship. There was respect–and a certain distance was established. It was like the conventional marriage of the day, few intimacies displayed in public, a certain hypocrisy in that specific irritations were not mentioned.

Today, sexual mores have changed. Kinsey and Hefner tell us so. The goofiness of the singles bars has, thankfully, passed but the evidence is all before us: nurses and housewives picking up useful clothing income by becoming call girls one evening a week, Randy Andy and Koo Stark in Buckingham Palace before he finally marries Fat Fergie who had been living openly for years with an older man; even, heaven forfend, a divorced movie star in the White House. (Pierre Trudeau, ahead in all the trends, beat him to it by becoming the world's most famous–and pitied–single father in 24 Sussex Drive.)

The changes in sexual habits and sexual tolerance have been accompanied by sexual "intolerance" also. Because nothing is now taboo in the eyes of the press. Gary Hart–a saint in comparison with John Kennedy–is denied the White House. So is Ted Kennedy, because the rise of feminism has led to the death of the double standard in public life. (It still flourishes in a million suburban split-levels.)

Feminism has resulted in the fact that females now fill half of all the newsrooms and the television anchor screens, and those female reporters are more militantly feminist and unwilling to overlook "indiscretions" among male politicians. It was a female reporter in a widely quoted magazine article on Teddy Kennedy who detailed his drinking and ankle-chasing and jolted her male colleagues into realizing why the perennial presidential candidate had to be viewed in a new light.

The press-politician conventional marriage of the 1940s and 1950s is now closer to an open marriage, with plenty of lovers' spats. There is the famous Ottawa story of 1986, when some of the homosexual activists of the nation led by Laurier LaPierre, the broadcaster and historian now living in Vancouver, tried to convince Svend Robinson, the NDP MP from Burnaby, that he should go public with his sexual preference.

By doing so, they argued, he would legitimize their cause – a very intelligent and hard-working and high-profile Member of Parliament proclaiming himself a champion of the gay minority. Just as Barney Frank, a well-liked member of the House of Representatives from tough Boston, did in 1987, and raised hardly an eyebrow. Frank, who happens to be the brother of Ann Lewis, former president of the Democratic Party and a close adviser to Jesse Jackson, arranged his coming-out-of-the-closet announcement through an interview with a Boston newspaper and was applauded for his honesty by his constituents.

With Frank as one model, Robinson according to the NDP story scheduled a press conference in the National Press Theatre to make his big announcement. Ed Broadbent, with the NDP riding high in mid-election polls that supposedly showed the party heading for the second slot in national preferences ahead of the Liberals, heard about the plans and summoned Robinson to his office. Robinson did not make his announcement in 1986.

Two years later the climate of opinion toward male lovers and their cause had changed to such an extent that Robinson became the first MP publicly to declare his status, and the voters in Burnaby, not caring a bit, reelected him in the November election.

A man of few demands, I ask only one thing of my colleagues in the realm of scandals, which I enjoy as much as the next voyeur. It has to do with the abuse of the English language, a delicate creature, though flexible. Since Watergate, legitimately named after the office-apartment complex on the Potomac where Nixon's thugs did the original break-in, every two-bit example of malfeasance or bungling is dubbed some silly derivative.

At the advent of the Iran-contra scandal that George Bush never knew about (ha!), a Washington magazine ran a contest to find the appropriate label for the unfolding mess. There was submitted Iranamuk. And Contra-diction. And Gippergate, and so on.

When the amazing revelations about Brian Mulroney's shoe closet came out, it was immediately Guccigate. Tunagate elevated that smelly incident to a status hardly deserved. Even David Peterson's troubles with pushy social climber Patricia Starr were dignified with Pattigate. O Lord, please spare us.

The British scandals that imperil the nation are essentially stories known only to the insiders who populate Fleet Street and Westminster. An early Hollywood matinée idol was involved in the sensational divorce case between the Duchess of Argyll and her blue-blood husband, who alleged 102 cases of adultery.

He brought the case to court after discovering, in her drawer, a number of incriminating photographs. One of them, from an unusual angle, depicted his wife performing an act, better imagined than described, on one of her lovers. The photograph was taken from above, the lover obviously the practitioner of the camera. In fact, it was the era when the Polaroid instant-development camera had reached Britain and was the new toy of the moneyed classes at play.

Since the lucky gentleman's head could not be revealed in the photograph, considering the angle, he immediately became known in political and press circles as "The Headless Man." London insiders and gossips were frantic in their pursuit of the identity of The Headless Man. For a time Minister of Defence Duncan Sandys was a prime suspect on the Mayfair gossip circuit. Sandys, among other things, was a Winston Churchill son-in-law. The talk got so bad that his boss, Prime Minister

Harold Macmillan, faced him with the accusations and demanded proof that he could not be the chap in the now-famous Polaroid.

Poor Sandys, charged with the defense of the Tight Little Island, was forced to repair to a Harley Street physician, those toffs who take care of the British aristocracy and arrange for debutante abortions, to carry back to Macmillan medical evidence that his member did not resemble the specimen detailed by Polaroid.

That lead exhausted, investigators went back to further study of the Polaroid, until it was noticed that the well-formed body in the color photo had one of those year-round tans, and it was finally determined that The Headless Man was none other than the swashbuckling matinée idol.

Scandals come and scandals go, but some scandals particularly show the human species' flair for denial. A well-made movie that fascinated Canadian and American audiences in the spring and summer of 1989 was *Scandal*, the story of London's 1963 sex-and-government-and-spies sensation that ruined the career of millionaire Tory cabinet minister John Profumo and eventually toppled the Conservative government. It was interesting enough that it took twenty-five years before the story actually reached the screen. Even then, the established order in Britain was still trying to block it.

In the summer of 1988, a Palace Pictures film crew shooting a scene in the east end of London was disturbed by a fuss from the local Anglican bishop, the Right Reverend Jim Thompson, who complained that they were preventing him from parking his car outside his house. Bishop Thompson had other reasons for his objections. A personal friend of Profumo, he tried to dissuade actor Ian McKellen from playing Profumo; and he wrote to the newspapers denouncing the film (which he had not seen) as "celluloid rubbish."

Phillip Knightley is one of the finest British journalists of his generation. Formerly of the London *Sunday Times*, he once wrote in a guide to students that the only qualifications for journalism were "rat-like cunning, a plausible manner and a rudimentary command of the English language." He is an authority on the Profumo Affair and has written an intriguing article for *Vanity Fair* on it.

The scandal, says Knightley, along with lords and young prostitutes and drugs and orgies and spies, touched on the royals, the prime minister, the American president, the Russian secret service, the FBI and the CIA and the U.S. armed services. What really shook the Establishment, however, was that it "finally ended the reign of the grandee Tories of the Conservative Party, and paved the way for the grocer's daughter, Margaret Hilda Thatcher."

At the center of the affair was the Missouri-trained osteopath Dr. Stephen Ward. Son of an English provincial vicar, he had an amazing clientele and list of social contacts. Dr. Ward also had a seamy side, being a well-known figure in the sleazy Soho clubs where he liked to befriend and transform young tarts, so as to amuse his society friends. His best friend was Lord Astor, who gave Ward the run of Cliveden, the magnificent family seat outside London where Ward introduced his latest protégé, Christine Keeler, to John Profumo (and where *The Toronto Sun* board of directors had a sparkling black-tie banquet in 1988, everyone fighting to get booked into the bedroom suite where Christine and John got it on).

It was Ward, that 1960s weekend, who suggested that one of his guests, Soviet assistant naval attaché Captain Yevgeny Ivanov, drive Keeler back to London. Knightley thinks they never did sleep together, but, once Christine was selling her story to an agog Fleet Street, it was useful to claim she did.

Once Profumo had resigned in disgrace, the first step in the eventual defeat of the Conservative government, the revelations came out. Mandy Rice-Davies, a plump little blonde bimbo who was Christine Keeler's accomplice in Swinging London, told the *Washington Star* about a Mayfair dinner party that was highlighted by a naked man, wearing a mask because he was so well known, who waited at table like a slave.

Knightley recounts the panic of the time–especially since Khrushchev and Kennedy had only months before taken the world to the brink of nuclear disaster. When FBI head J. Edgar Hoover found that the two tarts had spent a week in New York the previous summer, his over-active brain concluded that Christine and Mandy had been imported by Soviet intelligence agents to service United Nations delegates and that Keeler had probably slept with the randy President Kennedy.

FBI bosses had worried meetings with Defense Secretary Robert McNamara and the *Washington News* called for Kennedy to cancel his planned June 1963 visit to London. Ward's American friends, including Claus von Bülow, raised a defense fund, but Ward's London society friends fled in terror.

After Dr. Stephen Ward committed suicide of a Nembutal overdose the night before the end of his trial, only two wreaths arrived at his cremation. One of them, a hundred white carnations sent by Kenneth Tynan, John Osborne, Penelope Gilliatt and Joe Orton, was ordained with an epitaph: "To Stephen Ward-Victim of Hypocrisy."

The British Establishment left no untidy items unattended to. An owner of an art gallery had planned a touring exhibition of Ward's portraits of the royal family. A mysterious buyer purchased them all for cash and took them away. In 1987, more than twenty years later, the buyer was revealed as Sir Gordon Brunton, at the time of the scandal a director for the Canadian newspaper mogul Roy Thomson.

As Sir Gordon explained to Phillip Knightley: "The portraits had been commissioned by the *Illustrated London News*, then part of the Thomson group. A travelling exhibition would have been very embarrassing for those people who had agreed at I.L.N.'s request to sit for Ward. So I bought the lot, wrapped them up, and they went straight into the company vault."

Several months after the purchase, Roy Thomson was made Lord Thomson by the Conservative government.

Final Thoughts

> The Big Media are replacing Big Government
> as a metaphor for unresponsive self-interest,
> self-perpetuating and self-justifying. . . . The
> public no longer regards the press as its
> defender against the establishment but as the
> establishment—as big business less concerned
> with rights than with ratings.
> —*Daniel Schorr*

Readers are amused—and bemused—when they look at their newsstands some weeks and find that *Time* and *Newsweek* have identical cover subjects. In 1961, this happened four weeks out of fifty-two. In 1985, their covers were alike sixteen times—nearly once in every three issues. It's not because there is some conspiracy; the competing staffs try desperately to keep their cover topics secret. It's simply that the editors in charge of the two rivals share similar views of the world and what was important to discuss.

Similarly, there is little in news content that separates the evening news broadcasts on ABC, CBS and NBC, the only differences being the personalities of their millionaire celebrity anchormen, Peter Jennings, Dan Rather and Tom Brokaw. In both cases, print and television, the very nature of the journalistic elite means the values espoused will be those of their own salary bracket. Tom Yellin, one of the original producers on ABC's "Nightline," says, "The political sensibilities of people in network television are mainstream, traditional and conservative; neither far left nor far right. We share the same basic assumptions of bankers, lawyers and the rest of the establishment. You ain't going to see a bunch of radicals coming in here."

Dan Rather of CBS makes $2.3 million a year, Peter Jennings of ABC, $1.8 million and Tom Brokaw of NBC, $1.7 million. Nonetheless, they are projected as champions of the common man. Key Washington correspondents get by on a quarter as much. Executive producers of the evening newscasts make up to $250,000 a year. To keep him from defecting to New York, the CBC agreed to pay Peter Mansbridge more than it pays its president. As mentioned, major syndicated columnists on *The Washington Post* and *New York Times* can make $500,000 a year in speeches alone.

Viewers of the CBS Evening News were treated to the spectacle one night of multimillionaire Rather asking Capitol Hill correspondent Phil Jones how proposed changes in a new tax law would "affect my pocketbook and the pocketbooks of other Americans." Beat reporters in Ottawa, during the "lock-up" in which the media is given time to peruse the finance minister's budget before official release time, always watch in sardonic glee as star columnists and famous TV faces immediately dive into the sections pertaining to expense accounts and free-lance income.

As even ABC's noisy Sam Donaldson, who sets himself up as Peck's Bad Boy, acknowledges in his autobiography, "The press, myself included, traditionally sides with authority and the establishment." The celebrated investigative reporter Seymour Hersh, who won a Pulitzer Prize for uncovering the My Lai massacre in Vietnam, in a 1987 seminar at the Institute for Policy Studies in Washington said, "It's a little harder for the boys in the White House to keep the troops in line than it is for the boys in the Kremlin, but it is true that *Pravda* and *The Washington Post* and *The New York Times* are alike in the sense that they don't report reality so much as what a small group of top leaders *tell* them is reality."

What is reality is that in addition to their upper-middle-class incomes, the media–especially in Canada and the United States–reflect the values of the established order. In racial identity–especially in Britain–they in no way represent the community they write for. Black correspondents at ABC (referred to in hallway gossip as "the watermelon caucus") made a presentation to ABC News president Roone Arledge about employment and assignment practices, telling him that "one of the problems was that 'This Week With David Brinkley' was more like 'This Week With Middle-Aged White Men.' "

Concentration of the established order grows. When Ronald Reagan came to power in 1981, fifty corporations owned or controlled the majority of media outlets in the United States – newspapers, television and radio stations, magazines, books and movies. By 1987, mergers and acquisitions had reduced the fifty to twenty-nine. The parent corporations of nine of the most influential U.S. news organizations – *The New York Times*, *The Washington Post*, *The Wall Street Journal*, the *Los Angeles Times*, *Time*, *Newsweek*, ABC, CBS and NBC – are all ranked among the *Fortune* 500. In little Canada, there is even more concentration. The Southam group dominates the big cities, except for Toronto. The Thomson chain monopolizes the small towns. The only challenger is the *Toronto Sun* group, now in four cities along with the daily *Financial Post*.

The public senses that it is being shut out, in effect, by the collaboration implicit in the press-political process. It is shown, in one way, by the special interest groups that demand their own sphere of information. Last year almost 500 magazines were launched in the United States, twice the number started up in 1986. In Canada last year, 77 magazines joined the Canadian Periodical Publishers' Association. In both countries, the new magazines ranged from fly-fishing tips to esoteric new guides to knitting by computer. The audience is fragmented, as witness the explosion of channels available on cable TV: 36 on most Canadian cable systems, which will rise to more than 50 by 1993 and an estimated 200 by the year 2000.

It all reflects the public's efforts to acquire – without filter if possible – the information it wants. It reflects a dissatisfaction with the information it now receives. The great unwashed have a sense that they are mere passengers in the great (and lucrative) information game. The solution to the filter? More and more sources of information. Newspaper readership may remain constant and may be going down, but there are more magazines, more pamphlets, more seminars, more night schools, more TV channels, more speciality radio stations, more advocacy groups, more protest demonstrations. It is all the result of a frustration with the monopoly information dished up in the past. There is a sense in the public mind that there must be a better way.

Information is power. It is now the biggest and fastest-growing industry in the world–as witness the titanic struggle over the *Time* magazine empire, the winner creating the largest media conglomerate in the world, surpassing Bertelsmann of West Germany and Hachette of France. It's why infotainment stars are now paid as much as movie stars. Dan Rather has more power than Clark Gable ever did. All politics is now telepolitics.

The pols and the press are in an industry together. They live off one another. They war, but in the great scheme of things it is a pretend war. They need each other. Birds of a feather.

Bibliography

Cockerell, Michael, Hennessey, Peter, and Walker, David. *Sources Close to the Prime Minister: Inside the Hidden World of the News Manipulators*. London: Macmillan, 1984.

Cocking, Clive. *Following the Leaders: A Media Watcher's Diary of Campaign '79*. Toronto: Doubleday Canada Ltd., 1980.

Comber, Mary Anne, and Mayne, Robert S. The *Newsmongers: How the Media Distort the Political News*. Toronto: McClelland & Stewart, 1986.

Cudlipp, Hugh. *Publish and be Damned!: The Astonishing Story of the Daily Mirror*. London: Andrew Dakers Ltd., 1953.

Downie, Leonard, Jr. *The New Muckrakers: An Inside Look at America's Investigative Reporters*. Washington, D.C.: New Republic Book Co., Inc., 1976.

Ericson, Richard V., Baranek, Patricia, and Chan, Janet B.L. *Negotiating Control: A Study of News Sources*. Toronto: University of Toronto Press, 1988.

Goulden, Joseph C. *Fit to Print: A.M. Rosenthal and His Times*. Secaucus, N.J.: Lyle Stuart Inc., 1988.

Halberstam, David. *The Powers That Be*. New York: Alfred A. Knopf, 1979.

Hertsgaard, Mark. *On Bended Knee: The Press and the Reagan Presidency*. New York: Farrar Straus Giroux, 1988.

Hutchison, Bruce. *Mr. Prime Minister, 1867-1964*. Don Mills, Ont.: Longmans Canada Ltd., 1964.

_____. *The Far Side of the Street*. Toronto: Macmillan of Canada, 1976.

Keate, Stuart. *Paper Boy: The Memoirs of Stuart Keate*. Toronto: Clarke, Irwin and Co., 1980.

Knightley, Phillip. "The Tarts Who Toppled the Tories." *Vanity Fair*, March 1989.

Lapham, Lewis. *Money and Class in America: Notes and Observations on Our Civil Religion*. New York: Weidenfeld and Nicolson, 1988.

Lévesque, René. *René Lévesque: Memoirs*. Translated by Philip Stratford. Toronto: McClelland & Stewart, 1986.

Manchester, William. *The Last Lion: Winston Spencer Churchill Alone 1932-1940*. Toronto: Little, Brown and Co., 1988.

Matusow, Barbara. *The Evening Stars: The Making of the Network News Anchor.* Boston: Houghton Mifflin, 1983.

McCall-Newman, Christina. *Grits: An Intimate Portrait of the Liberal Party.* Toronto: Macmillan of Canada, 1982.

Meyers, William H. "Murdoch's Global Power Play," *New York Times,* June 12, 1988, sec. I, p. 35.

Olson, Sigurd F. "A Certain Kind Of Man." *The Beaver* (Autumn 1968).

Orwell, Sonia, and Angus, Ian., gen. ed. *The Collected Essays, Journalism and Letters of George Orwell.* 4 vols. Middlesex, England: Penguin Books Ltd., 1970. Vol. 3: *As I Please.*

_____. *The Collected Essays, Journalism and Letters of George Orwell.* 4 vols. Middlesex, England: Penguin Books, 1970. Vol. 4: *In Front of Your Nose.*

Osborne, Stephen, and Schendlinger, Mary. *Quotations from Chairman Zalm.* Vancouver: Pulp Press, 1988.

Postman, Neil. *Conscientious Objections: Stirring Up Trouble About Language, Technology, and Education.* New York: Alfred A. Knopf, 1988.

Provencher, Jean. *René Lévesque: Portrait of a Québécois.* Translated by David Ellis. Toronto: Gage Publishing Ltd., 1975.

Reedy, George E. *The Twilight of the Presidency: From Johnson to Reagan.* 1st ed., rev. New York: New American Library, 1987.

Report of the Special Senate Committee on Mass Media: The Uncertain Mirror. Keith Davey, chairman. Ottawa: Queen's Printer, 1970. Vol. 1.

Sampson, Anthony. *The New Anatomy of Britain.* Toronto: Hodder and Stoughton, 1971.

Schickel, Richard. *Intimate Strangers: The Culture of Celebrity.* New York: Doubleday and Co., 1985.

Smith, Hedrick. *The Power Game: How Washington Works.* New York: Random House, 1988.

Steel, Ronald. *Walter Lippmann and the American Century.* Toronto: Little, Brown and Co., 1980.

Tynan, Kathleen. *The Life of Kenneth Tynan.* New York: William Morrow and Co., Inc., 1987.

Wicker, Tom. *The Press.* New York: Berkley Publishing Corp., 1975.

Woodward, Bob. *Veil: The Secret Wars of the CIA 1981-1987.* Toronto: Simon and Schuster, 1987.

Index